Ken Webster was born in
of UCW Aberystwyth in 1!
His main interests are cont
Parapsychology was not of

*for H*

Ken Webster

# THE VERTICAL PLANE

Iris Publishing

Copyright ©Ken Webster 2021

The Vertical Plane

Published by: Iris Publishing

Second Edition 2021 (First published 1989 by Grafton - a division of Collins Publishing Group)

Contact: info@thedodlestonmessages.com

ISBN: 978-0-9559831-5-3

Copy checked by Caroline Walker.

Layout, cover design and back cover image '"We are all but Shadows": Tomas': Debs Oakes.

Front Cover etching: 'Faust' (1652) by Rembrandt van Rijn (1606–1669). Originally titled 'A Scholar in His Study' https://www.metmuseum.org/art/collection/search/373045. (Colour overlay by D. Oakes).

350pp

Price: £17.99

Printed on demand by: IngramSpark 2021

Poem XXVI 'This is the first thing' from The North Ship by Philip Larkin reprinted by kind permission of Faber & Faber Ltd.

# *Preface to 2021 Edition*

Thirty six years is a very long time, half a lifetime for me. Give or take. And yet here we are with a new edition of the *Vertical Plane*\*\*. Before saying what's new and what's changed, I want to pay my respects to some of the key people in this book who have since passed away. Principal among them is Peter Trinder (died 2019) without whose encouragement, open mindedness, scholarship and persistence, the events of 1984-6 might have received less attention than they deserved. It was his thesis that many of the details in the language – including the apparent anomalies – would be the key to understanding what was going on.

All this in an era in which research meant many long hours in libraries making meticulous handwritten notes or asking improbable questions to librarians. Bravo Peter. I am also proud to acknowledge that Peter's son, Richard Trinder, will hopefully be publishing his father's work on the language, which is a vast project in itself, as there are several hundred messages. Richard was a teenager when these events took place but he has never forgotten the excitement and sense of adventure which these events brought – as well as the many frustrations. It reminds me that these events have indeed touched many people and they create a unique kind of bond.

A very dear friend, flâneur and agent provocateur, John Cummins passed away far too young (died 2015). His curiosity, his playful theorising and questioning always meant a lot, a kind of nourishment for the mind and the soul. We both miss him very much. Without his prompting, understanding these events or our reactions and engagement with them would have been very different.

\*\*There was a brief unauthorised reprint in 2017 by Thorsons Publishing (a division of HarperCollins)

A stalwart former colleague Frank Davies latterly based in the Isle of Man, was always a man to step in and babysit the cottage. He was rather fond of the input from '2109' – to the extent that he found a vehicle number plate for his car which included the number I'm told. Being connected to these events struck people in different ways. 2109 was nothing but an irritant to me, but recent discussion about AI and the future might yet change my mind on this.

Our thanks again to all those acknowledged in the First Edition of this book and also to many others, family and friends who were there and are sadly no longer.

This edition is a tidy up in many respects. Certain typographical errors had crept in when it was first published and we have tried to catch as many as possible. Additional images, or better quality images have been included and by way of follow up there is the short piece from the Fortean Times (Issue FT108 March 1998) at the back of this book, which sets the record straight on some comments made at a BBC filming (1991) and afterwards – at least from our side. Debbie has done a lot of work on this edition, using her many talents to create a much better cover***, reset the book and continued to keep tabs on the many online forums and threads on my behalf. I would also like to personally thank those who have already put much time and effort into researching the events further, particularly the historical aspects, which may help someone wanting to continue the research which I have been unable to do over the years. These initial research links are included in the back of the book.. Although I cannot give any personal claim or endorsement to the quality or usefulness of this research and links, they may prove of some help to other researchers. Thank you so much.

Lastly, I'd like to say that this edition is here as a way of defeating the speculators and the inflationary price put on my book of which I have had no control. It is a book I wrote about some experiences at the very beginning of the home computer age and it should be accessible at a mainstream price for as long as there is an interest.

**Ken Webster, Scotland 2021**

***Thanks to Dr Carl Williams for tracking down this excellent etching by Rembrandt)

# Acknowledgements

No book develops in a vacuum and this is no exception. Among those involved most intimately: my tolerant and artistic girlfriend Debbie, Peter Trinder, Frank Davies, Dave and Sian Lovell, Nicola Bagguley, and John Cummins. They all have their own important story to tell of these events, in particular Peter Trinder. He Put many vital questions and offered continual support and Scholarly commentary on all the communications. I was forced to leave out the bulk of the messages which dwell on language and history but I am pleased to say that Peter is Preparing a full set of annotated messages with accompanying glossary for the serious researcher. Thanks are also due to Deb's brother; Aunty 'M'; Carl Williams for introducing me to relevant literature; 'Haze' (Ian Hazeldine) for line drawings and sketches, Robin Peedell,* assistant librarian at Brasenose College, Oxford, for finding 'our man'; my mother Joyce and brother Brian for the love and money to keep me going. In Europe: Ernst Senkowski, Jules and Maggie Harsch-Fischbach and, for translation and liaison where necessary, Brigitte Meyer.

In preparing the typescript I had the benefit of the best secretarial team in the north west: Nicola Hamlett, who but for me would have made it perfect, and Penny Hevingham who worked long hours against the chaos of my writing. Thanks to Neil Bartlem and Rob Jones for reading the drafts and offering useful criticism, and to Jane Middleton at Grafton for copy editing.

---

* Sadly Robin Peedell died in late summer 1988 as this book entered the pre-publication stages.

# Author's Notes

This book is a record of a most unusual set of communications. They are described in the everyday context in which they occurred. It is therefore not a scientific document, but it does contain observations at first hand from a number of reliable persons. Despite the necessity of selecting from the communications I feel that this book is faithful to the events it portrays. I hope that the interest — and perhaps controversy — that this book will generate will not centre on the brief notes at the end of the book where I offer some personal thoughts on the genesis of the messages. These notes are simply to encourage discussion, for in all these matters I am acutely conscious of the inadequacy of my own knowledge. But I share the opinion and optimism of Sir William Crookes who, when asked to explain how the Psychic D. D. Home, managed his feats, retorted: *'I didn't say it was possible, I said it happened!'*

Chester, May 1988

# *Prologue*

*Most people do not take heed of the things they encounter nor do they grasp them even when they have learned about them, although they suppose they do.*

*Heraclitus (Fr 57)*

DODLESTON: four miles south-west of Chester in that anachronistic enclave of Cheshire on the Welsh side of the Dee.

Take the Kinnerton road from Chester – leave behind the suburbs of Westminster Park and Lache – turn left through the dark ribbon of Bretton Woods. Dodleston one mile.

Ahead flat Cheshire farmland runs carelessly towards the first Welsh hills, Hope Mountain and beyond that the high moors of Minera.

Along the lane appear the chicken wire and weather- boarding of the hunt kennels; the maize fields and ancient Greenwalls Farm are hidden by decaying orchards. The road is uneven, showing the effects of council neglect and the filth of tractors and animals by turns. A sharp right and left and there, tucked shyly into the verge, is the village sign.

Half the village is a dormer for the heavily mortgaged. The rest live on two roads. Church Road connects, at one end, the village school and a small council estate to the Red Lion, church and village hall at the other. Bisecting Church Road is Kinnerton Road, which contains two more pivots of village life. Firstly Mr Hughes's shop and post office, Chapel Stores, and, further along, the farm from which milk deliveries are organized early each morning.

The name Chapel Stores bears testimony to some of the dissonant influences acting upon this otherwise quite typical Cheshire village. Welsh non-conformism built the tiny chapel, flourished briefly then withdrew, leaving only the building. Facing it are the hard Ruabon brick houses, built by the Duke of Westminster, which represent the deeply conservative tenor of rural life. Each has a 'W' picked out in blue bricks across its upper storey as a permanent reminder of the all-pervading influence of the English aristocracy.

Many of the Duke's villages and hamlets find their names echoed in expensive areas of London: Belgravia, Eccleston Square, Eaton Square. But not Dodleston. For in truth Dodleston was never entirely beholden to the Grosvenors.

And there it rests between the Welsh border, a mile across the drained and empty lands of the Burton Meadows, and the Duke's estate at Eaton.

From the Welsh side, from Town Ditch and Golly, Dodleston can be seen clearly, straggling a low ridge above the Meadows. A castle mound and its trees form one landmark and the twin silage towers of Moat Farm another, but clumps of trees and then ones and twos break up the middle distance. This settlement, one thousand years old in 1982, settled for insignificance centuries ago. It is a place both confident and obscure.

Dodleston is not quite spoilt, and consequently the village is brimful of would-be squires, aspiring businessmen affecting concern and love for the slower more sentimental pace of rural life. So the Red Lion car park has its scattering of XJSs and Porsches but very few are in awe of this kind of ostentation. The landlord's coffers increase 'at the same rate as the girth of his sons', said someone unkindly, but equally Frank Cummins, a die-hard villager in a demob hat and coat, will be found fixing planks with secondhand nails. The village has no dominant group and although the ebb and flow of traffic along its roads points to many changes it is an even-tempered place. Sometimes the tempo changes at weekends, when the roar of motorcycles and modified Ford Escorts marks closing time or the sounds of a party drift across the houses. For the rest, the years bring noisy adolescents to the phone box at the junction to kick footballs, tin cans and occasionally each other, until they tire, grow older and gain entry to the pubs, falling in and out of love and the minicabs which ply to and from the city clubs.

Meadow Cottage stands between Chapel Stores and the phone box, the third in a row of four, tiny, 18th-century dwellings facing onto Kinnerton Road.

It is accessible at the front from Kinnerton Road and at the rear by Church Road. The village passes the door. Children throw wrappers and Coke cans into the small front gardens across the knee-high brick wall. In the sharp, raw mornings cars queuing alongside its gate, their engines ticking over excitedly, clog up the road by the shop. This is my house. It is late autumn 1984.

Meadow Cottage 1986

# 1

Nicola Bagguley stood with her luggage on the pavement outside the funeral director's in Delamere Street, Chester. I pulled across to her side of the road and parked on the double yellow lines. It was six o·clock in the evening and dark. The city was shutting down for the day and the traffic circulated slowly and painfully, all steamy exhausts and stoplights up and down the Ring Road. Despite this I was happy. Seeing Nic was always essentially soothing. She came perhaps in the hope that I knew something of the whereabouts of Rob Jones, a good friend, but the transatlantic wires were quiet and had been so for three months. Perhaps she also came for the company and to see how the renovation of the cottage was progressing. I had made much of the rigours of living without kitchen or bathroom all summer; of the money I'd spent and the frustrations of it all. Deep down I was pleased just to be able to sit on my own settee in front of my own fire without moving a bag of cement. Nic's being here was a statement of intent, signifying normality, simple pleasure and a better end to a shaky year.

Nic was broke, having come back from three months in East Africa. She had been living less than salubriously in hotels and trains which had insect infestation and bugs by the squadron. The better hotels, she said, had canisters of a spray called 'Doom' which, far from killing the roaches, served only to stimulate them. As Nic related her experiences it became clear that she had not escaped from her own recent past: teaching, unsatisfactory relationships, a sense of time slipping away. Life at the cottage, if not ideal, was a marginally better proposition for her. In return she was to help redecorate.

I was emerging from a long, terrible six months which had seen all the downstairs of the house gutted and then restored. There had been months of living in one room with only a kettle and dust for comfort. That and teaching. I was shattered. But for a holiday in Austria with the school last half term I'd have crumbled. Debbie, my girlfriend, stayed with me through the building work but our relationship suffered; it felt as if cement dust was eroding it. Now the work was all finished on the ground floor but it made the upstairs look shabby. Another season of work was inevitable but, please God, not until spring.

Some people love to tinker with their homes, but not me. I do what I have to do. This now meant decorating the finished part. Painting was on the agenda and alternating with bouts of eating wholemeal pizza, drinking wine and a few quarts of tea, some painting did get done.

'What's this?' asked Nic, pointing to some marks on the wall between the bathroom and kitchen. 'Has someone been putting their feet on here?'

I went over to her. 'They do look a bit "footprinty", don't they? You've got to be in the right place to see them. They've been there for ages.'

'Whose feet are they?'

'No one has owned up, too small for me or Deb. Deb says she can see six toes in the print.'

We laughed. All three of us began re-examining the dusty outlines for signs of an extra toe. Opinion was mixed. We then imagined how it was done, whether it was by standing on a chair or the table or both, for after seemingly emerging from the small, oblong electric wall heater they ambled diagonally upwards as far as the edge of the ceiling.

They had appeared in late August or September 1984. No one had much to say about them other than that they were size five. Quite obviously somebody was fooling around. By late autumn they were very faint indeed.

I remember those footprints disappearing and the kitchen area growing more homely as colour replaced concrete drab and grubby first coats.

At night Debbie and I slept in the front bedroom on an old creaking bed with a lumpy feather mattress. Nic got the back bedroom ('studio') with the four-track recording equipment, electric guitars and a single mattress on the floor.

The morning after the footprints were painted over I had been downstairs to the bathroom and passed through the kitchen perhaps twice before I looked closely at the wall (life's too interesting to spend time wondering about walls) but it stopped me in mid-stride when I did look. The footprints had returned. They were not exactly in their former position so it was not possible that they were the old ones come through. They were new, six-toed, composed once more of dust from the floor. I called the girls. Nic and Deb came down, they were more than just puzzled and Nic was, I'm certain, quite horrified. She had painted them out the day before. I thought she was just about ready to pack her belongings and go.

None of us had stirred that night, but we asked ourselves all the usual questions about whether the door had been closed and so on. We decided that one of us must have developed a strange form of sleepwalking. Nic soon recovered and was persuaded to stay, but equally none of us felt easy about it. The footprints were painted out once more. They did not reappear but, like children, all three of us avoided going downstairs in the night.

# 2

Some two days after the footprints had been painted out for good and the entire episode was beginning to seem hilarious we made a large-scale foray to Chester to stock up on food. On our return we left a raggy pile of about a dozen catfood tins on the floor and too many packets, tins, loaves and so forth tucked into too little cupboard space. Nothing was done about sorting all this before bedtime but by morning the catfood tins were neatly ordered in imitation of a human pyramid, striking out from the brick corner pillar towards the fridge like a peninsula on a rocky coast. On top of the pyramid were three further tins. I discovered this piece of silent housework at about 8.00 a.m. and stood there gazing at it, all the while trying to remember if I had heard anyone get up in the night. The girls regarded it with a mixture of interest and trepidation. There followed a breakfast time edition of 'Any Questions'.

The principal suspect was John, a lazy guitar player who, along with keyboard player Stennet, often used the little four-track in the back bedroom. They had pretty free access to the place. John in particular was keen on seeing Deb and had been whiling away a largely tuneless couple of hours here every few days. Nic was convinced he was a likely culprit as he had a very strange sense of humour. I was not so sure. The cottage was not particularly secure; almost anyone could get in with a little effort. Why bother with footprints and making mock-art structures out of catfood tins?

Next morning there was no disturbance but the following night another stacking occurred. This time we found a single column approximately four feet high composed of a couple

and Vauxhalls. Like many old people their cars wanted to be left in peace to die in dignity, instead they were mistreated in the name of life.

Weaving between these eternal actors are the toddlers and their dogs. Their purpose is to create havoc. The estate is not uniformly poor or even ravaged but Dave hates it because, or in spite of, the fact that he has lived there for ten years. His wife Sian stays slim on the nervous energy consumed in keeping a good house and despising every corner of it.

Nothing was complicated at Dave's. He boiled problems down. There were just two: not enough money or too much money. Depending on his mood he would elaborate upon one or the other. No pretentiousness here. Dave is a practical man – a builder, car mechanic, friend. Indeed there is a comfort in this sort of routine and besides he had some things that the cottage didn't have: a video and a television. On this occasion I think we spent about three hours setting the world back on its feet and drinking tea until restlessness took over again. Back, then, the six or seven miles to the cottage. The weekend was gone.

The computer was still on, nobody had remembered to see to it. The screen no longer showed the EDWORD menu but the basic screen message:

**BBC B 32K**

**Acorn DFS**

Nic must have pressed the BREAK key by mistake so I had to get back into EDWORD. I idly called up the index to see what she'd been doing. I had a mind to read one of her sketches. I also wanted to avoid making the coffee.

There appeared to be a new file named KDN. Nic's work was under single letter file names, e.g., D or O. The only other material on the disc was a colleague's timetabling outlines, as it was a borrowed disk. I called file KDN up, the disc drive hummed and clicked.

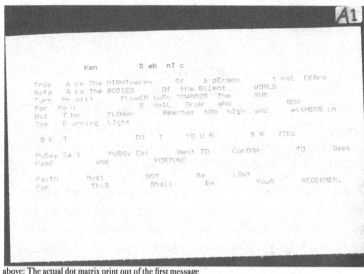

above: The actual dot matrix print out of the first message

>> Ken D eb nIc

True A re The NIGHTmares Of a pErson t hat FEArs

Safe A re the BODIES Of tHe Silent World

Turn Pr ettY FLowER tuRn TOWARDS The SUN

For Yo u S Hall Grow aNd SOW

But T he FLOWer Reaches tOo hIgh and witHERS in

The B urning Light


GE T OU T YO U R B R ICKs


PuSsy Cat PUSSy Cat Went TO LonDOn TO Seek

Fame aNd FORTUNE

Faith Must NOT Be LOst

For ThiS Shall Be youR REDEEMER. <<

I couldn't help it, the most disturbing and cliché-ridden feeling came over me. A shiver ran down my spine that threatened to shake my feet. I caught the first two lines and read and re-read them. The rest I didn't seem to see in those first seconds. It was obviously to us. It was appalling. I felt bad that I had called it into view. Deb started off the questions, and they got nowhere.

BBC Model B borrowed from Hawarden High School 1985

# 3

Hawarden School is a neat collection of brick buildings alongside the old A55 beyond Hawarden Village towards Ewloe. It used to be a grammar school and the ethos and prestige still linger. Most of the parents felt, and still feel, that this made Hawarden a 'good' school. I taught economics and worked most of the week in the school house: at one time the Headmaster's house, then a library but most recently the sixth-form area. The sixth, in their playfulness, had eaten away at the fabric and furnishings like adolescent mice, but the essential character of the building remained despite this. Solid, red brick, Edwardian aspects stretched upwards, encompassing metal-framed windows with leaded lights, and leading towards a red-tiled roof and two, now redundant, chimney stacks. The roof leaked and damp permeated the walls of the remedial department, housed in the attic.

On this Monday I parked at the other end of the school, as near as possible to the computer rooms. The 'poem' was stored on a three-and-a-half-inch diskette. It wasn't possible to print it up before lunch as bells were ringing for registration. Bells, bells, bells. As the diskette belonged to the maths department I had to leave it in a clanky metal cupboard with the others.

Tao-Tao-Bay-Beep . . . the computer club was . . . Beep Whee . . . little more than Space Invaders for kids deprived . . . Takka . . . of the arcade or practising for the evening. The room was divided into two . . . Beep . . . 'Yes! Darren!'. . . Beyond the partition was an oasis of comparative quiet as it was out of bounds. I found the diskette and printed the poem up. It looked quite impressive. Then again the printing up of any old rubbish improves its status immeasurably. The tabloid press is founded on this principle. I made a few copies all the same. It now seemed less resonant, less perturbing, to have it on paper.

Christmas drew nearer and the nights became unbelievably long. The end of term sagged like an overburdened washing line: carol services, cheap films and, as a backup to it all, fatigue. The last of my emotional energy had dissipated amongst the children weeks ago. I should have just walked out and gone home to bed. Most staff felt that way.

The cottage continued to brood. Nic decided to take Christmas with the folks, so she bussed down to deepest Basingstoke. The day before she left, a four-pack of lager was rearranged into an insecure tower. Parallel to it was a stack of four catfood tins. Once again the area within three feet of the exposed brick pillar in the kitchen was the focus of activity. Already the novelty of these things was wearing off but the discovery of blackened, drawn-out threads of plastic – all that remained of the ties around the lager pack – suggested that whoever was responsible was now playing with fire. I groaned inwardly. Neither Debbie nor I wanted this feeling of edginess to add more anxiety to our domestic arrangements, but it seemed beyond our control.

The stacking of objects continued every few days and on one occasion chalk marks were seen on the brick corner support. But it was the day before a party and we assumed it was part of the joke.

Next time I borrowed a computer was in early February. There were several reasons. Nic, by now returned to the cottage, wished to continue her sketches. She was certainly beginning to make contacts down south and talked of prospects on the alternative cabaret circuit. Deb and I wanted the distraction of a few computer games. Lastly I wanted to use the word processor to draw up an agreement between John, Stennet and myself. We were going to attempt to push a handful of songs towards a few music publishers. It was an act of faith, as there was no real unity of purpose between us. I suspected John of being behind any hoax and moreover of being as keen to see Debbie as to record a good song. Stennet was a really nice guy but a leaf in the wind.

Simple PG (poltergeist/RSPK) stacking?. March 1985

It was not a conscious decision to leave the computer in the kitchen, once more completely unattended, on another dull Sunday in winter, but there it sat, the power on, while we three rambled off in the rusty Volkswagen with its wheel bearing giving off the sound of a herd of buffalo.

Back at the cottage later that evening Nic said, rather camping it up, 'Shall we have a look at the computer, chaps? You never know, John might have been at it again.'

I fetched up the index.

'Not again!'

'Oh no!'

They weren't the most original reactions I've encountered. Once more there was an extra entry: this was called 'REATE'. Another click and burr and a short message unfolded.

>> I WRYTE ON BEHALTHE OF MANYE

WOT STRANGE WORDES THOU SPEKE, ALTHOUGH, I MUSTE CONFESS THAT I HATH ALSO BEENE ILL- SCHOOLED.SOMETYMES METHINKS ALTERACIONS ARE SOMEWOT BARFUL, FOR THEY BREAKE MANYE A SLEPES IN MYNE BED.

THOU ART GOODLY MAN WHO HATH FANCIFUL WOMAN WHO DWEL IN MYNE HOME, I HATH NO WANT TO AFFREY, FOR ONLIE SYTH MYNE HALF WYTED ANTIC HAS RIPPED ATTWAIN MYNE BOUND HATH I BEENE WRETHED A-NYTE.

I HATH SEENE MANYE ALTERACIONS (LASTLYCHARGE HOUSE AND THOU HOME), 'TIS A FITTING PLACE, WITH LYTES WHICHE DEVYLL MAKETH, AND COSTLY THYNGS, THAT ONLIE MYNE FRIEND, EDMUND GREY CAN AFFORE, OR THE KING HIMSELVE.

'TWAS A GREATE CRYME TO HATH BRIBED MYNE HOUSE

L W. <<

[ I write on behalf of many

What strange words you speak, although, I must confess that I too have been badly educated. Sometimes it seems changes are somewhat obstructive, for many a time they disturb me sleeping in my bed.

You are a worthy man who has a fanciful woman and you live in my house, I have no wish to alarm you, for it is only since the half-witted fool [trick?] ripped apart my confines have I been tormented at nights.

I have seen many changes (lastly the school house and your home). It is a fitting place, with lights which the devil makes, and costly things, which only my friend, Edmund Grey can afford, or the king himself.

It was a great crime to have stolen my house.

LW.]

All the time I was wondering, quite ridiculously, why the file was called 'REATE'. It came to me, the menu screen offers:

**CREATE**

**VIEW**

**REVISE**

**FORMAT**

**INDEX**

Someone wanting to 'CREATE' a file would press C and the computer would instantly offer up a clean file; the rest of the letters would then form the file name 'REATE'.

Another message; what a crazy business! No one had seriously expected anything. I had felt pretty uneasy after the last one but this was completely different. It was 'old' or 'quaint' in style. It was signed LW. Twelve lines of lousy spelling, disjointed sense and obscure reference. Whatever it meant, whatever Nic or Debbie felt about it, it sang to me. It wasn't a coldness or a dark apprehensiveness on this occasion. After the initial shock I became absorbed by it. We all were. The questions flew faster than storm-driven hailstones and vanished as quickly. A ghost? A spirit? A joke? A poltergeist? No clear answers, no answers of any kind. I scanned the disk index for other new entries. I found two more but both were blank.

When the fuss had subsided we looked at the content of the message from 'LW'. I was baffled by at least three words. They were 'wrethed', 'charge house' and 'bribed' (as used in this way). At face value we were in someone's house, someone who had felt the effects of the changes in the house. I was a 'goodly man' but I had committed a great crime. I had lights which the 'devyll maketh'. This prompted another round of discussion on ghosts and theories about them (which it was clear none of us had any grasp on). There was a feeling that we should try and link the disturbances, such as the stacking and the appearance of the chalk marks on the pillar, to this message. Perhaps we could tie in the 'poem'. That didn't take long: it was all some hoax. Look at the facts!

But it niggled me, those words of 'LW' spoke to me more than I could reason why. Nic was all for it being John. I scratched around for ideas, very few came. I'd show this message to a few of my colleagues, as I'd shown the poem weeks ago, to get some perspectives on it.

Dinner – only the staff and a few children called it lunch – was taken in a garish school hall on unsteady drop-leaf tables. These were trundled from a corner and returned there after every meal of every school day. The dinner queue, for a school, was tolerable but to minimize the amount of noise I took dinner as early as possible. Peter Trinder, Head of sixth form, had similar inclinations, I suspected. He was good, lively company; perhaps the one man in the school who would speak his mind to anyone on any subject whatever. He felt it the duty of an educated man. And, at times, almost everyone disagreed with him profoundly.

Long ago Peter had taught me English. Ignoring many of the technical details, what he really taught was the imperative that one should open up one's mind. Peter was a man of passionate conviction, which was more valuable, more provocative than anything most staff could offer. Education is about life not packaged mediocrity.

It was from him, then, one lunchtime before the milling of children and the noise began, that I detected some interest about those odd words on the computer.

The table was moderately busy and I sensed other ears picking out the crazy bits; some knew already, others would store up the snippets for future reference. Peter was alive to these words. 'Charge house' was an important one, 'wrethed' another, 'barful' yet another. I think he knew straight away that there was something most curious going on but I was surprised by his enthusiasm. The word 'wrethed' was completely unknown to him. At his request I supplied a copy of the whole message to him later in the day. He wrote a little note about it that afternoon and put it in my pigeon-hole in the staff room. It began, 'Utterly fascinating', and the rest was an analysis of the words with a little comment. It ended with the following '. . . if it's a hoax, what a romp!'

A day or two later Peter came to sit by me in the staff room. He then looked at me quite seriously and asked if it was a hoax, if I was stringing him along. I knew I wasn't making it up so I answered him quite sincerely. He asked if I would mind letting him have a copy of anything further I might receive. I readily agreed. From then on I knew that there was another person to whom I could turn for advice, someone outside the immediate experience who understood the position.

The following Saturday, 9 February, John Cummins, a good friend and part-time villager, as he now worked as a solicitor in London, sat briefly in front of the fire then stood up and resumed his exposition (it could be called nothing else) on the possible source of the message and the simple necessity, dammit courtesy, of a reply. He filled the air with his enthusiasm and pipe tobacco smoke as he moved from kitchen to fireside and back again. It began to seem quite natural that a reply could embarrass no one. John was discreet; after all, he was a solicitor. Debbie was already finding him pen and paper. Silence. What do we reply? Who were we talking to? John said, 'Of course the date, our date, must come first.' The pipe came out of his mouth and the perambulations continued. 'It seems that the message comes from someone using an older form of English so let's try the 17th century.' A disorderly run of questions followed, none of them carefully thought out.

We settled for the following imprecise jumble of questions. It was clumsy but on it went; it was little more than a joke after all. I typed it up on the computer.

*In the reign of Queen Elizabeth the Second.*

*Dear LW. Thank you for your message.*

*We are sorry for disturbing you. What would you like us to do? Did you live in a house on this land in about 1620? Do you want us to tell you more about our time? Why write a poem? Who is Edward Grey? Is he related to the Egerton family? Do you have a family? Is the King James or Charles Stuart? What is the charge house? Was this village called Dodleston in your life and how many families lived here? Thank you very much for your messages. Thank you for not making us afraid.*

*Ken, Debbie and John*

John stood beside me adapting and correcting as he thought fit, all the time enthusing in his charmingly tongue in-cheek manner. If he so much as laughed I was going to pack it all in. But he was restrained.

Later, feeling a little bemused, I sat by the front window and looked out on to Kinnerton Road trying to take in the course we had set out on. However, John's enthusiasm had taken root. I was already planning that we should leave the cottage that evening to give 'it' a chance to write back. As if!

Later the following afternoon John had returned to Islington and I was reading him the reply to our message down the telephone as Deb shouted it to me from the kitchen. It was tremendous! John was scribbling it down as he heard it. I hardly stopped to consider it as I spoke to him. John said he'd look up what he could and then ring back. Slowly, a degree of reflection and some analysis crept in.

'The Kyng, of cors, is Henry VIII who is six and fortie' was one confident line but the message was signed 'L W 28 March anno 1521(?)'. Not only was the date incongruous but the construction – especially the question marks within parentheses and the date – was a modern idiom. Deb joined me in the living room. I was now more sombre. I felt most strongly that we were being hoaxed and I wanted to have a good look at that message from LW. Debbie went to call it up again from the disc. No chance, it had gone completely. Things were getting worse. A dodgy message and a dodgy computer. John was the only one with a few notes about the message. I'd have to recover it as best I could. I was most unhappy about this. Poor Debbie got the blame but it was unfair of me. She said she hadn't touched anything. I rang John to ask him for his notes. We were all unhappy about the information the message contained.

Below is a transcript of the message, adapted from memory and from John's notes. Words which are in bold are as originally received.

(*)[?]

**'Twas an honeste farme of oke and stone**

It is helpful that you should **telle** me about thy time

**Dost thou hath** (?) **horse**

**Edmund Grey, brother of John Grey** lives at

**Kinertone Hall**(?)

**Thy Kyng, of cors, is Henry VIII who is six and fortie**

**I ne woot of Kyng James**

**Myne charge house is a place of loore** (schoolyng(?))

**LW 28 March anno 1521** (?)

King Henry, one of my favourite kings. He was the only one I found interesting. I knew something of him and it came clearly to mind that Henry VIII was not even close to forty-six in 1521.

He had been on the throne about twelve years and was still a young man. Even given that the 10 February message we had was secondhand via John's notes it stank of fraud.

It was some days later that Peter Trinder found out that Kinnerton Hall was built at the end of the 17th century and nowhere was there evidence of an Edmund Grey this side of Ruthin. This latter point didn't bother me as much as did the discrepancies over the date. John Cummins even doubted that the house would be built of 'oke and stone'. This seemed to leave the definition of 'charge house' as the only reliable item.

Above: Our good friend John Cummins, 1980's. Whose advice and guidance were so vital.

# 4

**16 February.**

A Saturday. The computer had been brought to the cottage once again but quite deliberately with the intention of obtaining, if possible, some more words from LW. I'd asked about his family and whether he went to Chester market and so on; I didn't want to challenge him, I'd let it ride, give him enough rope, etc. I was also keen to get down to Rick Steele's garage in Holt. I had bought an old XJ6 Coupe from Rick a little before Christmas. It was ready to be moved to another garage, in Ewloe, for some body work repairs. Being a Jaguar fanatic was a lovely diversion from teaching.

It was bitterly cold at Castle Garage and the car wouldn't start. They had to leave a fan heater on the engine for half an hour, and I wondered if it was an omen of things to come. But as I followed the Jaguar along the Chester southerly bypass it looked good and my spirits rose a little. Back to the cottage. A stack of three milk cartons on the kitchen floor. That was unexceptional but, by heavens, the monitor screen was full of text. More, two screens were full: evidently LW could cope with the scrolling action of the word processor. Gentlemen from other times can't do this!

But I thought it wonderful to see so much material. With this to work on we'd soon find out what was what. I saved the message to disk very carefully each time I looked at it. No mistakes.

›› MYNE GOODLY FREEND, I MUSTE NEEDS SAY, HOW COMETH THIS, THAT THER ARE MANYE THYNGS FOR WHICHE I HATH NO REKENYNG. ME THINKETH IT, THAT IF THOU CANNOT TELLE THEE FOR WHAT ART IN MYNE HOME, THEN I CAN NAMOOR HELPE YOW

THAN IF MYNE WITTS HAD GONE. I HATH NO KINFOLK TO FYND, MYNE WIF WAS WRECHED WITH THY PESTILENCE ANDMTHE LORD DIDST TAKE HER SOULE AND HER UNBORE SON (1517). MYNE FARME 'TIS HUMBLE BUT IT HATH A PRETTY PARCEL O LAND, IT HATH RED STOON FOOTYNGS AND CLEEN RUSHES ON MYNE BEETEN FLOOR. THIS SEASON I HATH MUCH TO DO, I HATH TO SOW MYNE BARLY FOR MYNE ALE, 'TIS THIS THAT IS MYNE CRAFT AND FOR WHICHE I AM BESTE ATTE I FANCY. ALSO I HATH TO GO TO NANTWHICHE TO MYNE COWTHE FREEND RICHARD WISHAL WHOIS FARME BE SO GREET AS TO TURN A FOUR YEER ROTA-CION O FALLOW. I DO SO ENVYE HIM HE HATH MUCHE THER, BUT NOUGHT THAT DELITS ME MOOR THAN HIS CHEESE IT CANNOT BE EQUALLED BY ANY OTHER FOR PLEASANTNESS OF TASTE ANS WHOLESOMNESS OF DIGESTION. I SHALL ALS CALLE ATTE NANTWYCHE MARKET 'TIS NOT SO GREET AS CESTRE MARKET BY THY CRIOS BUT 'TIS OF SOM DESPORT I SHAL NEED TO GO TO CESTRE THIS SEASON TO GET MYNE SOES MYNE GOODLY FREEND TOMAS ALDERSAY, A TAILOR BY CRAFT, MAKES THEM SOMETYMES, I ALS MAKETH SOES BUT NON OF MYNE SWYNE ARE REEDY 'TIS FAR TO COSTLY UNLEST I NEED KIL O.DO YOW KNOWETH THE COUNTRY OF CESTRE THE WATER GATE IS A PLAS THAT BRINGETH MANYE TRADERS 'TIS A SHAME THE PORT DOTH SHRYNK I CAN RECORD GREET SHIPPS NOW THEY GROW SMALL BY EACH TYDE, BUT CESTRE PORT IS STILL GREETER THAN THAT O LEVERPOOLE I AM OFT TO THE EAST WALL OF CESTRE, COW LANE, 'TIS NOT SO TYRSOME THER THAN BY THE CROIS THAT IS WHEN MYNE FOWL OR SWYNE DOTH NOT TRIP UP MYNE POORE BODY I HEAR TELLE THAT THOU ART A (TEACHE) IN HAWARDINE DOTH YOW MEENETH HAODINE (?) DOTH THOU STIL EARN THY GREETLY SUM OF TWENTY POUNDS PER YEER(?) I RECORDE MYNE

UNFAVOURABLE DEAN HENRY MANN, WHO IS LIKENED TO A FISSH 'IF ANY BOY SHAL APPEAR NATURALLY AVERS TO LEARNING AFT FAIR TRIAL HE SHALT BE EXPELED ELSE WHER LEST LIK A DRONE HE SHOULD DEVOUR THE BEES HONEY'.

NEY I CANNOT MAKE MERRY ON HOLY DAY FOR FEER OF MYNE LIF MYNE FREEND WAS ONCE A FLOYTINGE ON A HOLY DAY AND DID HATH HIS EARS PINNED TO THY WOOD BLOC METHINKS WHEN THOU SAYETH DODLESTON YOW MEENETH DUDLESTUN MYNE QUEEN IS OF COURCE KATHRINE PARR

LUKAS «

[My goodly friend, I must needs say, how is it that there are many things of which I have no knowledge. It seems to me that if you cannot say why you are in my house, then I can no more help you than if my wits had gone. I have no kinfolk I can tell you about, my wife was taken with the pestilence and the Lord did take her soul and her unborn son (1517). My farm it is humble but it has a pretty parcel of land, it has red-stone footings and clean rushes on the beaten floor. This season I have much to do, I have to sow my barley early for my ale, it is this that is my craft and which I am best at I fancy. Also I have to go to Nantwich to my known friend Richard Wishall whose farm is so great as to allow him a four-year rotation of fallow. I do so envy him, he has much there, but nothing that delights me more than his cheese it cannot be equalled by any other for pleasantness of taste and wholesomeness of digestion. I shall.also call at Nantwich market it is not so great as Chester market by the cross but it is of some interest. I shall need to go to Chester this season to get my shoes, my goodly friend Thomas Aldersay, a tailor by craft, makes them sometimes, I also make shoes but none of my swine are ready it is far too costly unless I need kill one. Do you know the country of Chester the Water Gate is a place that brings many traders it is a shame the port does shrink I can remember great ships now they get smaller by each tide, but Chester port is still greater than that of Liverpool. I am often to the east wall of Chester, Cow Lane, it is not so tiresome there than by the cross that is when my fowl or swine do not trip up my poor body I hear tell that you are a teacher in Hawarden do you mean Haordine(?) Do you still earn the great sum of twenty pounds per year(?) I remember my unpleasant dean Henry Mann, who is likened to a fish. 'If any boy shall appear naturally averse to learning after fair trial he shall be expelled elsewhere lest like a drone he should devour the bees' honey'. Nay I cannot make merry on holy day for fear of my life my friend was once a-fluting on a holy day and did have his ears pinned to the wood block I think when you say Dodleston you mean Dudleston. My queen of course is Catherine Parr.

Lukas]

It was the work of an intelligent man. His first name appeared in this message: 'Lukas'. Welcome to the puzzle.

The phrase 'red-stoon footyngs' caught my eye. We had red stone blocks, sandstone blocks, in a heap by the damson tree. They'd been dug up during the renovation work. Indeed, Dave Lovell recalled that several lay in a line parallel to the pillar and old outshut Wall. They were originally within three feet of the bathroom wall and the apparent centre of stacking and related activity alongside the pillar. They were certainly red sandstone. This meant nothing to the sceptic in me – well, it nagged perhaps. Anyone could see those stones whilst snooping around in the garden or house.

It seemed from that third line that we were in his home. He was quite indignant that we were actually asking him to identify what items he possessed. It should have been obvious but it wasn't. It was all quite confusing.

There were a whole lot of things wrong with the communication. Since we had not given a thought to Liverpool why mention it? Was 'Leverpoole' a natural choice for comparison with 'Cestre' in Tudor times?

The uncharitable found the line about his chickens and pigs tripping him up at every turn very twee. The punctuation still looked very modern, with its liberal use of full stops, commas, brackets and question marks. There were dozens of questions to be answered. For example, was it true that no one made merry on a holy day? I don't think I wanted it to be a hoax anymore, I was so intrigued by it, but a clever hoax was still the only likely answer. After all we were always out when a message appeared, and it was becoming predictable that I would bring a computer home at weekends. There was opportunity for 'Lukas' but still not motive, for if the idea was to scare me away or drive me mad it was failing. I was becoming excited by the puzzle, so were Debbie and Peter Trinder who, interestingly enough, had traced a number of Lukas's words and found them to be exactly right for the period, though naturally he was puzzled by the punctuation. As a result he was hooked on them.

I was still more interested in 4.2 litres of Jaguar engine and the prospect of driving away from Deeside in the summer with all the windows down. My Mills and Boon adventure I called it. But, of course, I couldn't resist the thought that what we were seeing might be from another time.

### Monday 18 February, half term

Unfortunately the exact questions we put to Lukas in reply to his message of the 16th are not recorded because I accidentally left the five-and-a-half-inch disk I was now using in a pile of papers the caretaker threw out (!) Principally I asked him how he could possibly use a computer if he was from the 16th century. Peter persuaded me to include a vague reference to Bristol, as the words he was using looked like a regional dialect form of the language of the time. How Peter found the time to discover this I have no idea but in the question went.

Since Lukas went to market occasionally in Nantwich I asked him if he used a bridge at Aldford. There is a private bridge these days, just for the Westminster estate, but I thought it reasonable to assume some crossing at the point, especially with a giveaway name like Aldford (old ford).

We left the message on the screen from around 9.30 A.M. on the 18th. Meanwhile an old friend, Peter Benbow, and I were making a dreadful row with drums and guitars in the living room. Nothing arrived while we were there. Debbie joined in on the saxophone. The neighbours were understandably pleased when we gave up about 4.00 P.M.

I took Peter back to Hawarden. Still nothing on the computer, so at about seven we locked up the house and went for a drive. We came back an hour later.

'Yes!' I said, calling up a file called KENI. 'This is getting good.'

I liked the way that if I put in a message on a file called LUKI he'd pick a file name that echoed it in some way, as above, 'KENI'.

>>MYNE GOODLY FREEND, MAYEST THOU TELLE THEE FOR WOTREA-SON ART THOU AXING MANYE QUESTIONS FOR WHICHE I NE CAN ATYNE I AM CONFUS MYNE SCRIT DEVISE IS A WONDEROUS THYNG SOMWOT UNKYNDE I FANCY UNNIST TO MYNE SELVE IT MAY BE BUT I HATH SEEN THEE MAKETH LEEMS ON THY BOYSTE AND ART SLYE. YEA I KNOWETH OF BRISTOW MYNE KINFOLK DIDST COME FROM BRIDEWALTER AND TANTUN BY THY RYVER TOON UNTIL THEY APASSED TO MAKE MERYE ME LIKS TO BE ATTE NALE YEA SOMTYMES I URES BRIDE ATTE ALDEFORD. YOW MERYE MAKYNG PLEASETH ME BUT TIS SOMWOT NOYSOM ATTE TYMES WILT THOU TELLE THOU WOMAN TO PLAYETH MOOR OF MYNE FLUTE THYN TIS A BLEELFUL SOOND METHYNKS, HOW DOTH THOU JOURNEY TO THY CHARGE HOUSE IN HAORDINE(?). I MUSTE MAKE HASTE MYNE LYME HOUNDS ART FREE A ART BEYNG TROUBLESOM TO MYNE FOWL.

LUKAS WAINMAN<<

[My good friend, can you tell me for what reason are you asking many questions which I cannot understand. I am confused. The writing machine is a wonderful thing; somewhat unnatural I fancy, unknown to myself it may be but I have seen you make lights on the box and am cunning. Yes I know of Bristol my kinfolk did come from Bridgewater and Taunton by the river Tone until they died. To make merry I like to be at the ale. Yes sometimes I use the bridge at Aldford. Your merry-making pleases me but it is rather noisy at times. Will you tell your woman to play more of the flute thing. 'Tis a pleasant sound I think. How do you travel to your school in Hawarden(?) I must hurry as my dogs are loose and are being troublesome to my fowl.

Lukas Wainman]

I'd hardly ever been inside Chester City Library but Debbie urged me to use it in search of some confirmation that 'Lukas' was talking history not bunk.

I looked in on the 1980s interior: all chrome, cloth and air conditioning through its Edwardian facade. Perhaps Lukas's messages were also a stylized pastiche. An inauthentic product of a clever little man with a few high-tech toys.

I hoped we'd find all the people Lukas had mentioned in the local history section upstairs. The librarian told us that someone else had been looking into the history of Dodleston only recently. This reinforced my doubts and as I followed our guide to the appropriate shelves of red hardback volumes it became quite clear that whoever or whatever we identified in these volumes from the 16th February message would ultimately prove nothing. If we found them all then surely it was a hoax – what were the chances of Lukas knowing people who were all significant enough in some way to survive the randomness of history over four centuries?

I became bored. The city people passed silently outside. How many of their lives will be recorded and endure four centuries? The hoaxer would have the same sources as ourselves and would, therefore, be revealed. If but a few turned up in obscure reference books it was no better. Anyone worth their salt would reach for, say, the references on 'declared wills' for the period, pick a few local surnames and invent the rest. One chap Lukas had mentioned, Aldersay, sprang to mind. The Aldersay Arms (now the Shropshire Arms) was next door but two to the library. A common name. It showed nothing but an ounce or two of scholarship.

Debbie took more interest than me. I began to feel uncomfortable, stifled by the heating system. She found Richard Wishall, I think, or maybe his father, but don't expect to find a reference about this. We weren't interested enough to keep proper files or folders on the affair. Bits of paper littered the bookcase or got chucked out or used for shopping lists. This was the fate of Wishall. Debbie still refused to be discouraged. She couldn't find Aldersay despite him being a skilled man and presumably, therefore, an important citizen; but there were a number of Aldersays to follow up. I was still looking out of the window at the people wrapped up against the cold. I wanted to go home, to read about something else.

Deb said, 'There has to be a way of proving it, doesn't there? We could wait up to catch the intruder or something, we could do lots of things . . .'

'Let's go home.'

Walking across the city up beyond the Northgate and the city walls I thought some more about John, the guitar player. He could break in quite easily . . . he wanted to upset me so that he could appear smooth and clear-headed to impress Deb out of my life and into his. I tried to dismiss such thoughts as nonsense.

# 5

**21 February**

John Cummins's flat is on the third floor of a large Victorian terraced house in Balfour Road, Islington. We had come to stay for a few days and I'd brought the messages with me in a red plastic folder.

John had bought Colin Wilson's *Poltergeist*. I realized then that I hadn't read anything at all on the subject before this moment and as I read I began to feel a little uncomfortable. Poltergeists, according to Mr Wilson's research, could remain for months and indeed could develop quite destructive tendencies. Some could even bite! I shuddered. This could be dangerous. A little later I read that this sort of behaviour is rare. Overall, their usual activities – stacking objects, rapping noises, etc. – are extremely well documented.

It was hard to obtain any clear understanding of what 'they' were. An adjunct of our own personalities? Unconscious activity on our part? Elemental or primitive bundles of some kind, 'entities' feeding upon the anxieties and emotional stresses of recent months in such a way as to preserve and reinforce these emotional states? Much poltergeist activity is fraudulent, an adolescent's prank, or perhaps due to someone slightly older looking for attention or developing an active fantasy world.

A little knowledge is often said to be a dangerous thing. Debbie was nineteen; had I been paying her enough attention? Before reading *Poltergeist* I had felt confident that she was uninvolved. Now I was less so. But it was only a popular book; perhaps I needed to look into the subject more deeply – make fewer excuses.

*Poltergeist* has very little to say on communication from such a source, which is rare and confined to the odd scribble on a wall. I was thinking of Matthew Manning's experiences at this point. Apparently, he had been the focus of a great deal of poltergeist activity and on at least one occasion the walls of a room were covered in signatures. He also seemed to be able to transmit the writing of others, supposedly famous or articulate people long dead. So-called 'automatic writing'. This train of thought led down the road marked mediums, seances, and spirits. It was very hard to take it seriously. It all looked exceptionally dodgy and a long way from economics, the social sciences and education.

But still John and Debbie pursued their ideas. The latest was ley lines, the old straight paths, the 'lines of force' supposedly crossing England – and elsewhere of course – which could be identified by lining up sites of antiquity. It was not a subject I should normally choose to discuss in company but since we had drifted as far as the 'biting poltergeist' and automatic writing, an excursion into ley lines seemed quite moderate and reasonable. On large-scale maps spread across the floor of the living room Dodleston was easily accommodated by two lines and John had once read of an association between ley lines and the frequency of 'parapsychological' events, especially poltergeists.

Our thinking led us to draw up this model: we had a rare type of poltergeist, a sophisticated entity, adept at word processing! Try again. We were experiencing activity commonly attributable to poltergeists about which, descriptively at least, quite a lot is known. The classes of activity commonly associated with this phenomenon were present: movement of objects, stacking of objects, noises and so forth. In addition the cottage may (or may not!) be close to a ley line, which supposedly increases the chances of this sort of occurrence. But we had no theory to offer about the genesis of the messages. This appeared to be unique – so it was just a big hoax!

A friend of John's , Rod Emberton, a gangling, intellectual, but talented architect, was the arch- sceptic. 'It's obviously a hoax. You're all being made fools of . . . Anyway I can prove it. There's never been a bridge at Aldford over the Dee. If there was a bridge a town would have grown up around it.' As an argument it sounded quite reasonable. Why mess around with pseudo-science when a little analysis, a little thought could bring you the answer?

In the gracious presence of Bartok. the huge, friendly, but somewhat incontinent Balfour Road cat, we considered the messages as a group. The first message, the 'Poem', didn't fit anywhere and was clearly unrelated, not only to the language but to the whole tenor of the later material. These later communications appeared to have one author, but the essentially modern punctuation cast a great deal of doubt on their authenticity. The message of 10 February was appallingly inaccurate chronologically, and contained the untraceable Edmund Gray at the then non-existent Kinnerton Hall.

16 February contained the needless comparison of 'Leverpoole' with 'Cestre', the spelling of 'cross' as 'crios' and the use of the well-recorded saying of Bishop Mann. Additionally the word 'rotacion' in an agricultural context was unrecorded at this period. This was a major concern of Peter Trinder as it was about 220 years out; hardly a mere detail. More subjectively there was the reference to Wishall's cheese: Cheshire cheese is famous and the stereotype of Cheshire country life was being, we sensed, unnecessarily reinforced. Similarly quaint or twee, to our sensibilities at least, was the reference in the 18 February message: 'Myne lyme hounds art free a art beyng troublesom to myne fowl.'

I could more readily understand this closing sequence from someone at the end of a telephone but it seemed to have been placed in this context to persuade us that Lukas Wainman was an approachable, gentle countryman with a needful eye on his livestock. So it was a big problem. Not as big as trying to explain the mechanism by which messages appeared. This alone would be enough to convince a thinking person that it was a set-up.

Nevertheless I wanted to find a copy of Wilson's book for myself so we took the Tube to Leicester Square and headed for Watkins Bookshop in Cecil Court. This is one of the major bookshops in London catering for the more obscure or esoteric topics, and it acts like a sensory waterbed for the insecure fan of parapsychology or the occult. Rows of books tell you that magic exists and you can learn it; books on astral travel, occult knowledge, poltergeists, ghosts, clairvoyance, philosophy, reincarnation, witchcraft. In such a place the curious messages thrust upon us could seem unremarkable or at least acceptable. My gaze wandered up and down the shelves. I don't belong here, I thought. I pulled Poltergeist off the shelf, hesitated, then decided against it and fled, confused, to a cafe in Charing Cross Road for a comforting cappuccino.

# 6

The poltergeist activity continued at the cottage; objects moved, sometimes in our presence, while our backs were turned. Debbie and I were quite edgy, but we attempted to diffuse our anxiety, to weave small threads of it into daily conventions and rituals so that nothing unmanageable remained.

The school in those early days acted as a kind of sounding board and moderator. In a sixth-form class I struggled with SJ 26 and 36 of the Ordnance Survey Pathfinder series and expounded on the suggested relationship between ley lines and the incidence of poltergeist activity. We should have been working on something like indifference curve analysis of consumer behaviour, but this was a sharp class. Any two points on the map would of course be connected by a straight line but what of others? The writers on leys insisted that it should be four.

I traced a line from Trueman's Hill, near Peter Trinder's house in Trueman's Way, Hawarden, through an earthwork at Broughton and on towards Dodleston. 'Isn't that interesting?'

They were more interested in my interest than the line or the map.

'The pencil line's a bit thick,' one said.

'Well, yes I suppose so.'

'Aren't they supposed to be precise?' said another.

'I don't know.'

'I bet you could just extend the line until you found something you wanted to include.'

'Yes, you probably could.'

This wasn't very useful and after a few more minutes I conceded that it was pretty vague theory. I put the maps away and returned to the safety of the syllabus.

The school knew about the 'poltergeist': that was almost acceptable. Indeed, in lower school a good ghost story is always welcome: "Ere, sir! Have you got a ghost that walks on walls?' I related something of the adventure: the stacking of objects, the footprints – always the footprints – the noises and the chalk marks on the wall. Sometimes I spoke about the messages but nothing much. This was a sensitive area. It was too close to the heart of the problem. I let slip a small item here and there, but for the rest I preferred to keep complete silence until I felt happier about the whole business.

27 February: a Wednesday afternoon. There had been no computer at the cottage for over a week. Debbie had started to rent a house in East Green, out of the way. I was in school. I took sixth form on the Wednesday, double upper sixth and double lower sixth and only one lesson of third year.

Period seven was the polite, middle-class Humanities group. Bright, well-mannered, dreadfully conservative: it wasn't their fault, but I was suffering: from utter tedium by period eight. I was still tired from London and helping Deb move house but mostly it was the time of year. Late February has almost become a traditional time of absence for many teachers; too many classes, dreadfully dull or cold weather and no sign of the Easter break. To sidestep this general malaise I was keeping a very low profile and imagined myself as a walking shadow, although a rather broad one, sliding along rooms and corridors.

I drove home at the earliest opportunity and I parked the wrong way against the pavement. Inside the cottage it was calm and quiet. The newspaper was in several parts on the floor. A mug, a woollen scarf and a tie were piled against the base of the kitchen door. The old brass pan had come off its hook on the purlin above the fireplace. From the windowsill had come the file containing the messages and the floppy disk, only the disk was not in the folder. Outside its paper cover it lay neatly face up on the kitchen table. It read Lukas W. That was what I had written on it but it said to my awakening mind quite clearly, 'Lukas W wants to communicate. He wants the computer back. If it doesn't come there could be a disturbance.'

Ah, the power of symbols: before me was such a disturbance. It seemed that from behind the kitchen a force strong enough to drag the plastic file eighteen feet to the door had caught other insecure objects in its field. I imagined the lightness of its touch but also its potential for violence, its determination. The cottage was calm and quiet. I fed the cats out in the yard, collected the mail, and left. I put nothing back, but slipped the disk into its paper cover for safety.

Walter the Cat surveys the handy work of the 'poltergeist'

# 7

East Green. In the loneliest, saddest corner of Deeside. Within earshot of the 'crack, crack' of the clay pigeon shoot, it is a late 1930s estate facing flat fields of arable or stubble. There is no sense of space, only dislocation. These same fields are confronted by a dual carriageway, shabby Garden City, the canalized River Dee and the dignified Queensferry swing bridge now painted blue – 'Clwyd Blue'. Clwyd has no identity. It is a makeshift county concocted out of the local authority reshuffles of the 1970s. The house on East Green was a makeshift house furnished from a skip, the whole thing a DIY nightmare: fake panelling, a plastic bath, the toilet at the wrong height for the bathroom floor. But it had a bed in which we could sleep at ease. Comfort and security. It was not home but a very welcome shelter against the rising swells and cross-currents of our anxieties. Or so I told myself.

In the cottage we could not sleep without the light on and yet the light kept us awake. We wondered if Lukas might appear by our bed (I should never have read about poltergeists). Would the light keep him away?

I don't believe we were being rational but there was still no way anyone was going to go downstairs in the cottage late at night. This was some poltergeist! Still, I borrowed a computer at the weekend and we left a message for him. It was a bit raggy because we were not sure what was going on, or what we should say and we were trying to make it sound reasonable even if someone owned up to a hoax. Lukas replied:

>> MYNE MOSTE NOBLE FREEND HATH I NAT BEENE ACCORDANT WITH THOU AND YET UNLESS ME FAYLE METHINKS THER IS NAT YNOGH AFFYE DESPITE THYS I HATH BEENE APERTFUL WITH YOW I KNOWEST NAT WER THOU CAME OR WITHER WIL YE GO NOR DO I HATH ACCOUNTYNG FOR WY YOW BEEST IN MYNE HOME BUT THOU ART A GOODLY VYSTER AND YOW MAY ABIDE AS LONG AS YOW LYK <<

[My most noble friend, have I not been friendly towards you and yet, unless I am mistaken, I think there is not enough trust. Despite this I have been open with you. I know not whence you came nor whither you will go, nor do I have an answer for why you are in my house but you are a goodly visitor and you may stay as long as you like.]

We were in his house! Later the same message:

>> MYNE GOODLY FOOL MYNE LINKMAN THINKETH THAT THOU ART BE AL IN MYNE PAN H'SAYETH THAT ME MAKETH LYK DIVINSTRE BUT I KNOW YOW LYVE NOWE HE ALS SAYETH THAT MYNE BLOOD BE POYSOND AN THAT IT BE MYNE WEEK HINGED FANCY BUT LUNE ME NAT METHENKE AN TOLDE HEM SO I ALS SEID 'TIS LYK FAIRYMGOLD AN THAT TO HOLD IT CLOSE TIL ME WRYTS BOOKE <<

[My pleasant fool, my servant, thinks that you are all in my head. He says I act like a seer but I know you live now. He also says that my blood is poisoned and that it is my weak-hinged imagination; but I am not mad, I think, and told him so. I also said it is like fairy gold [that he should] keep it secret until I write a book.]

What a prospect! Either he was dead and we were alive or he was alive and we were more than four hundred years from the dates of our conceptions. In fact we were alive and so was he. He thought it 'fairy gold', this communication. He was making notes of it for a book.

For such a book to refer to these events in recognizable detail – should this book still exist – would suggest the most overwhelming . . . er . . . 'coincidence'. This sort of coincidence would deafen one's thoughts, or prove us fools for even considering it.

Lukas was convinced that he wasn't mad and that we lived, as indeed he did, physically tied to a human body. Endless puzzles arranged themselves before us. The past is another country; a country without entry visas.

The last part of his message gave an answer to why he was here if he was born in Somerset.

>> I CAME TO CLIMATE HEER BCAUSE OF THY WORTHY FEEDYNG FOR WHICHE AT O-TYME I HATH TO PAY NO TAX UNLYK MYNE KINFOLK NOWE CHANGED HATH THYNGS FOR MYNE UNFAVORABLE KYNGS SHERYF DOTH PLAUGES ME SO METHINKS HE IS HEER FOR EVERY TURN OF MYNE GLAS I HATH HADDE SOM MISHAPPS WITH THY CONCEILD DEVYSE WHICHE MISFILLE MYNE WORDS BUT 'TIS NAMOOR UNDUN METHINKS IT IS TO FYTTING FOR MYNESELVE A-TYMES BUT IT DOTH REFRESH <<

[I came to settle here because of the excellent pasture for which at one time I had to pay no tax, unlike my relations. Now things have changed, for the unfavourable king's sheriff does plague me so it seems he is here every hour. I have had some mishaps with your hidden device which does not place my words but it is no more undone. I think it is too agreeable for me at times but it does amuse.]

The final section went like this:

>> I FISSH FOR HERYNGS AN SAMUN IN MYNE DEE AN SOMTYMES IN MYNE FLOOKERS BROOKE TELLE MYNE FREEND JON WHO YOW HATH DEELEN THAT I KNOWETH MUCHE OF MYNE FYSHYNG METHINKS THOU JEST WEN YOW SAYETH ABOUTE MYNE HORS-LESS CART TYGER 'TIS GOOD THAT WE CAN BE WANTON AND JAPE SO LUKAS <<

[I fish for herrings and salmon in the Dee and sometimes in Flookers Brook. Tell the friend John with whom you spoke that I know much about fishingI think you are jesting when you talk about the horseless cart tiger. It is good that we can be carefree and joke like this.

Lukas]

Why did he call it a 'conceild devyse' when it was plainly on show? It was a nuisance clogging up the kitchen table. He could have meant the disk drive or the disk. Or perhaps it was concealed in part of his house. I tried to be pragmatic. Although this was one of the most fascinating messages to date there were some very odd references, e.g. fishing for herrings on the west coast, that were obviously dodgy. Nothing as dodgy as a 16th-century gent using a computer though.

Another problem was Flookers Brook. It is a mere stream, mostly underground, running through Hoole. Rod Emberton saw this as more damning evidence. 'Impossible to fish there, its just a muddy ditch!!'

Every sizeable message to date had been like the fresh wholemeal loaf you discover next to the firelighters in your shopping basket. Probably delicious but smelling a little odd. So it had to be someone's joke, but every message came and went without anyone being seen or heard, without any let-up in the richness of the vocabulary. It was very disconcerting.

Lukas's line, "Tis good that we can be wanton and jape so', was quite apt, for this long message wasn't the only one that day. Under another file name we found a short item:

**>> MYNE MOST NOBLE FREEND HATH I NOT BEENE ACCORDANT NOR TREWFUL WITH THOU AND YET UNLEST ME FAYLE METHINKS THER IS NAT YNOUGH.......................... <<**

He was having 'difficulties' with the computer. It was, from its construction, an alternative start to the last message and looked like a telex that had gone astray or jammed in transmission. A nice touch if a hoax. If not, it wasn't the sort of problem that would arise from. difficulties in key boarding. He would merely have carried on. There would be no reason, no computer error that would give the line of dots for example.

Whatever the cause I had to laugh at this befuddlement. It was more 'real' to me than ever because it was so human.

Peter was doing a running analysis on the language, using the Oxford English Dictionary to date the forms of the words. This was proving positive with only the odd word needing further investigation or not recorded in the dictionary. The words used continued to be appropriate, and as far as Peter could tell they were used in a way which, in its entirety, was not only evocative of the period but was from the period. There was now no evidence of pastiche or parody, no howling errors. But the messages were infested with dialect and odd grammatical constructions associated only with certain regions. The language looked beyond good scholarship, it was top-drawer stuff. I didn't know enough about language to comment but I was impressed.

I replied to Lukas the same day with a few comments on cars and an invitation to talk more about fishing and his time at college. In addition to the message there was a photograph I had snipped out of a colour advertisement for a Jaguar XJ coupe. It was a different colour from mine but I thought it would do.

I was unprepared for Lukas's subtle treatment of the message and the photograph and I was even more unprepared for his reaction to what it represented.

>> MYNE GOODLY FREEND I HATH FOND THY CART PORTREYNG BUT 'TIS A CROOD THYNG FOR WITHOUT MYNE HORS IT SHAL NAT GOON FARR PREY WOT UNCOUTHE WOLD BE THYS 'TIS LYK SYLK THEROF I CAN NO SKIL <<

[My good friend, I have found your picture of the cart but it is a crude thing for without the horse it won't go far. Tell me what unknown wood this is. It is like silk, I cannot describe it better[?].]

Lukas considered the glossy magazine clipping to be a strange kind of wood. And the photograph was charred at the edges, in fact, showing signs of heat throughout. It was very brittle and almost crumbled in my hands. Deb said that he must have 'taken it with him'. She laughed. 'I bet that if he's the Devil it would burn at the edges.'

Burnt photograph of a Jaguar XJ coupe

I had opened my mind to the possibility of these communications being real. I didn't want to extend its range too far.

The message broke new ground in one other respect: Debbie was in the house, asleep upstairs, during the period when it 'arrived'. I was out with Dave Lovell. This was significant, for the Volkswagen was left outside the house and lights were on downstairs, so this meant that if there was an intruder s/he was taking a real risk of being discovered. There was no smell of smoke either (which one would expect if the intruder theory was reasonably extended to the charred photograph).

Leaving the issue of the photograph to one side we saw that Lukas had given some lively details in the remainder of the communication, which were, as requested, largely culled from his time at Oxford but included some domestic details.

›› MYNE PLAS OF LOORE BE ATTE MYNE JESUS COLAUGE OXFORD MYNE BESTE WAS LATAN AND GREKE I HAD TO DRESS WITH MYNE GOWNE AND QUIF JON COLET WAS MYNE BESTE SCHOLMASTER SOM OF MYNE BOOKES WERT EPISTOLAE OBSCURUM VIRARUM BY MUTIANUS RUFUSS PRAYSE OF FOLLY BY MYNE FREEND OF CORS DE ARTE POETICA BY MYNE MARCO GIROCAMO AND MYNE MOSTE

NOBLE JON SKETONS A GOODLY GARLAND AND COLYN CLOUTE
FOR WHICHE HE WERT IMPRISOUND BY MYNE UNFAVORABLE
WOLSY HE DID APPASS AT WESTMINSTER MYNE KYNGS SHERYF
BE TOM FOWLHURST HE WILL CALLE ON TWESDAYE MYNE MOSTE
WHOLESOM MEAL BEEST MYNE PUMPES WYTH PASTY AND PEESE
I KNOW NOT HOW TO PREPARE IT BUT MYNE GOODLY WOMANN
KATHRYN SHALT TELLE ME WOT TO SAY BOYL PORK TIL TENDRE
CHOPP SMALL AS YOW MAY TAKE CLOVES AND MACE AND CHOPP
RAYSINS OF COMTH TAKE IT AND ROLL IT AS ROOND AS YOW
MAYE AND PUT ON DYSH MAKE ALMUND MILK BLEND WITH FLOUR
O RICE POOR OVER MYNE PUMPES SET ON EECH A FLOWER AND
CHEESE I FOLLOW THYS WYTH MEAD 'TIS PLEASANT METHYNKS

LUKAS ««

[I studied at Jesus College Oxford. My best subject was Latin and
Greek. I had to dress with a gown and hat. John Colet was my
most important schoolmaster. Some of my books were Epistolae Obscurum Vivarum by Mutianus Rufus, Praise of Folly by
my friend of course, De Arte Poetica by Marco Giracamo and A
Goodly Garland and Colin Clout by John Sketons for which he
was imprisoned by the unlikeable Wolsey. He died at Westminster. The King's sheriff is Tom Fowlhurst. He will call on Tuesday.
My favourite meal is Pumpes with pastry and peas. I don't know
how to prepare it but my good woman Kathryn will tell what
to say, 'Boil pork until tender, chop into fine pieces, take cloves
and mace and chop raisins of Comth [Corinth?], take it and roll
it as round as you can and place on a dish. Mix almond milk and
blend with flour of rice, pour over the pumpes and set off each
with a flower and cheese.' I follow it with mead. It's good, don't
you think?

Lukas]

Peter caught my eye a day or so later as I passed the duty
noticeboards in the staffroom. 'It still has to be a hoax, Ken,' he
continued with only the slightest of pauses. 'The college, Jesus
College, is Elizabethan, founded 1571. It's too late for our man.'
He also said that there was an error in the Latin and that obviously John Skelton was the poet not Sketons.

Peter catalogued the results of his inquiries and added them to other apparent anomalies. I felt I had to try and find excuses since Peter had spent so much time with the dictionary and in and out of the reference libraries in recent weeks; I didn't want the blame for his wasted time so I said it was just a mistake or a name for some other college very early on. It was no good; I was fooling myself too. Big historical blunders confirmed equals big joke discovered.

The other personalities in this message were traceable but for one Mutianus Rufus. The 'friend' he mentioned was Erasmus, one of the most important writers in the pre Reformation era. The excitement that this latter information should have aroused was submerged: the whole twelve weeks since the first 'poltergeist' event was some one's joke.

The old brass pan balanced on top of the kitchen door.

## 8

The kitchen and bathroom area really is incredibly small but at the same time unoppressive, well-lit and quite airy. Rod Emberton's initial sketches had become a comfortable pair of rooms. It was so small that he called it a 'Bambi' extension after the Walt Disney cartoon character. We had to agree it was a small project for an architect. The original inverted 'L' shape of the extension had been preserved. It was and is a single-storey structure. A fine slate roof is supported on brick walls and a hip joint running across from the pillared internal corner of the 'L' to the wall of the main building. It is a very substantial roof set with 'Velux' skylights and the whole insulated with a layered styrofoam dry lining system. This helps reduce any outside noise.

The 'studio' bedroom overlooks the kitchen roof. There is no access to the roof from The Cottage (the house next door, towards the shop) unless the steep roof of the terrace is used. Corner cottage has a similar arrangement to Meadow Cottage in that there is a one-storey outshut but access is still difficult, if only because it means clamberingabout under the glare of the sodium lamps along the street at the busy junction of Church Road and Kinnerton Road.

This evening the Velux were closed. Above and behind the white wire chair at which I sat I could see the dark sky and the occasional star between the small knots of pale grey cloud just visible in the moonlight. The clouds looked awfully cold and lonely.

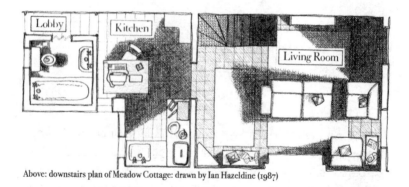

Above: downstairs plan of Meadow Cottage: drawn by Ian Hazeldine (1987)

Above: upstairs plan of Meadow Cottage showing position of the skylite over the kitchen and lobby: drawn by Ian Hazeldine (1987)

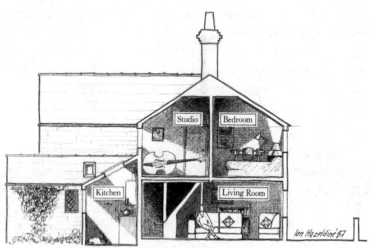

Above: elevation of Meadow Cottage: drawn by Ian Hazeldine (1987)

Above: sketch from the back of Meadow Cottage: drawn by Ian Hazeldine (1987)

I was at the computer looking back through a couple of files on the disk. Deb was half-watching me, but her attention and conversation were also on the goings-on in her new neighbourhood. All this gossip for such a small estate, but she was making friends. In an instant our conversation was shattered by the sound of footsteps, heavy, deliberate footsteps on the roof. I stood up and looked fleetingly at the Velux.

'That's it!'

I strode quickly out of the kitchen deliberately trying to control the weakness which threatened my knees. 'Come on!' I shouted to Debbie. She seemed very slow. Out of the living room, through the front door and onto the pavement, without turning. For the first time I was really scared. Scared of being scared.

'I don't need all this, do I?' I said nonsensically.

Deb was much more excited and then again composed. I felt small, for a big man. Shame brought resolve. 'I'm not going to give up this bloody house,' I whispered angrily in Deb's ear, and strode back in rather boldly. Perhaps rather too boldly in order to give myself the appearance of being in control. An image of Stan Laurel and Oliver Hardy, stuck in a haunted house, came floating into my mind. A couple of fools like me completely out of control. Too late, of course, we looked around outside the kitchen. If it had been our hoaxer we'd see some cracked slates in the morning so loud were those footsteps, but early next day we were London bound.

Nic Bagguley had invited us to see Elvis Costello in concert at Imperial College, London; she'd even bought the tickets in advance. In the daylight on the Inter City and flicking through a copy of Classic and Sports Car I could put the previous night's incident to one side. It belonged to another time. Gone.

To pass the time before the concert Deb went to the Westminster City Library. She wanted to find out more about Jesus College in the hope that Lukas could be justified or excused his comments. I thought it rather like hoping your summons for speeding would land on next door's parquet flooring unnoticed.

Later, we were sitting on a wall opposite a tarted-up South London terraced house, staring into the ground disconsolately. I'd forgotten the number of Nic's house. We were in the right street but that was proving to be of little or no consolation. No Nic, no Elvis Costello.

A late-night train home. We were so tired that come Chester General we chose to drive to the cottage. It was closer to the station by many miles than East Green. We didn't care any more about poltergeists or footsteps. It could stack a container lorry in the garden for all we cared. It was the custom for me to greet the new day first and – since I was up – make the coffee and breakfast, and, if it was a Sunday, take the car for the papers. It was just such a morning. I came back to the cottage perhaps half an hour later.

In a manner which seemed to mimic my more relaxed mood I found several tissues from a box I'd left on the kitchen table scattered over the computer and the disk drive. It appeared lightly done. Deb came down to inspect. We enjoyed this little display. Quite unexpectedly I felt encouraged to try and accept these events; to go along with them in an essentially practical sense. The six tissues, the soft morning sunlight and the fact that I had temporarily conquered my sense of fear encouraged me to plan new questions for Lukas.

Peter had said it would be unwise to correct Lukas on his errors about the college, etc. The idea was to make us seem still gullible. But on a day like this I looked forward wholeheartedly to the next communication. Last time it had come with Deb in the house so I went out in the car. Debbie sat in the living room very quietly with the door to the kitchen closed and everywhere locked up. A message was not long in coming. Debbie heard nothing and was surprised to open the kitchen door and see the following:

›› MYNE FREEND AGAYNE I MUSTE NEEDS SAYE I HAN NO WANT TO MAKE YE DISCONFORT I BEETH NAT ESEN MYNESELVE WEN I HATH ENTRECOMUNEYON WITH YOW BUT TIS SOE WE BOTHE ART FREENDLICH AND HATH INTELLECT YNOGH TO KNOWETH ANTICS OR DRONKES WE AR NOT AND TIS IF NOT TO YOURS MYNE COMMODITY FOR MYNE BOOKE METHINKS YOW NOT OF BEELEFUL FULL OF GOOD GOODLY UNLEST ME FAYLE MYNE COOKE SAITHE I SHALT REPENT FOR MYNE ADVENTURE AND THAT IT WIL COME TO FOUL ISSUE BUT METHINKS SHE BE YELOWE AN TOLDE HER SOE SHE DOTH NOT LYK ANOTHER SHE IN MYNE HOME AND NATO AS FAIR AS YOWR MAYDE ME FANCY MYNE REDE BOOKE BE STRANGE WOT SKIN BE IT AND MYNE KEY BE STRANGE ALS WHOS CHARACTER IT BE IN MYNE BOOKEPREY YOW HATH MANYE BOOKES BUT I FEER THEY ARN TO ILLSCRITIN TELLE ME WERE MYNE SCRIT DEVISE CAME FROM AND HOW DOTH IT MAKE MYNE LEEMS I HATH SOE MANYE AXYNGS TELLE MORE ABOOT MYNE WORLDE

LUKAS ‹‹

[My friend, again I must say I have no wish to cause you discomfort. I am not easy myself when I have communication with you but 'tis so that we both are friendly and have intelligence enough to recognize that fools or drunks we are not and 'tis, if not for yours, my material for my book I think. You [know] now of 'beeleful' – full of good, goodly, unless I mistake. My cook says I shall repent of my adventure and that it will come to a foul end. But I think she is jealous and told her so. She does not like another woman in my home and not one as fair as your maid, I fancy. The red book is strange. What material is it? And the key is strange also. Whose handwriting is it in the book, pray? You have many books but I fear they are too badly written. Tell me where the writing device came from and how it makes the lights. I have so many questions. Tell more about your world.

Lukas]

Initial reaction was mixed. Curiosity: that he had not himself discovered the error. Surprise: that a message could come while the house was occupied. Satisfaction: that he still spoke to me, not at me. I was, happy to see that he was able to joke about his cook's jealousy and to answer Deb's question about the word 'beeleful', except that Deb had asked this some two weeks previously. I took his comments about the red book and the key as referring to the plastic folder in which I kept the print-outs of the messages. The key was the slightly stiff key in the lock of the corner cupboard. Did he walk about my house? How far? Why mention only these items?

I concentrated my reply on his request to know more of our modern world. It was hard to know how to start or where. I later added a few lines about Peter, mentioning that he was an Oxford man:

IN YOUR TIME YOU USE THE STRENGTH OF HORSES TO TILL THE FIELDS, THE POWER OF THE WIND TO MOVE THE SAILS OF SHIPS AND THE MOVING WATER TO TURN THE MILL WHEEL WE HAVE MANY NEW POWERS NONE OF THEM MADE BY THE

*DEVIL ALL ARE MADE BY MAN. THE LIGHTS ARE WONDROUS BUT THE POWER IS NOT A FLAME BUT SOMETHING CALLED ELECTRICITY. IF YOU SEE STRANGE STRANDS JOINED TO THE SCRIT DEVICE THESE CARRY THE ELECTRICITY. THE ELECTRICITY IS MADE MANY MILES AWAY AND BROUGHT BY STRANDS OR WIRES CAREFULLY WRAPPED TO KEEP THE POWER SAFE FOR IT CAN KILL IF INTERFERED WITH BY FOOLS.*

Sunday 10 March, late evening: walking from the bathroom to the living room I heard the footsteps again in the same dreadful pattern, beginning by the wall of the house and moving across above my head. All resolve, all thoughts of acceptance and equanimity vanished. Fear resurrected itself. In a time-honoured way the hair bristled on my neck. Spooked. I was spooked. In another time, Lukas was also being spooked . . . by us.

›› MYNE FREEND PREY WOT STRANGE FURIE ART, THOU I AM CONFUS SOE. YE BE METHINKS GOODLY BUT YOWR LESINGES AGASTE ME MUCHE THOU SEYDE THOU LIV BUT THYS IS NOT SOE I HATH NO WANT TO AGILTEN THEE SELVE BUT YOW SEYDE ALS THAT THOUART A LEARNED MAN THAT AND YOW KNOWETH OF MYNE FREEND ERASMUS BUT YOW DOTH NOT MENCION MYNE ILL SCRIT WORDES IF YOW LIVD YOW WOLDE SAYE YOW KNOW NOT OF MYNE JESUS COLLEGE YOW ALS SEYDE ABOOT A POWER THAT I HATH NO REKENYNG FOR WER DOTH THIS POWER COME FROM AND WOT DIDST THOU STUDIETH IN THY PLAS OF LOORE WER IS IT FOR WY IF YOW N'OTE DEVYSE UNTO ME THEN I MUSTE MAKE ENDE TO MYNE WORDES WITH YOW THYS WOLDE CAUSE ME MUCHE DESPEIR 'TIS NOT I THAT MAKETH YOW AFFREY 'TIS YOW THAT MAKETH MYNESELVE AFFREY

LUKAS ‹‹

[My friend, pray what strange demon are you? I am so confused. You are goodly, I feel, but your lies frighten me much. You said you are alive but this is not so. I have no wish to accuse you but you said also that you arc an educated man and that you know of my friend Erasmus but you do not mention my misspelt words. If you were alive you would say you know not of Jesus College.

63

You also spoke of a power of which I have no knowledge. Where does this power come from and what did you study in your place of learning? Where is it? Because if you do not explain this to me then I must make an end to my words with you. This would cause me much despair. It is not I that make you afraid, it is you that makes me afraid.

Lukas]

A stiff wind cut across the field from the estuary towards East Green. Smoke blew from the chimneys every which way in the eddies and currents. I could see broken glass on the road, a child's tricycle, as I leant against the car. What a barren place! I was here not because I was poor, or out of work, unfortunate or derelict. I gazed across the fields, the street lights were very harsh. There was nowhere to look. I was here because my house was spooked and I was scared of a few noises, Oh, Lord! What a thought!

If Lukas was what he said he was, I should celebrate in some way. This gave no comfort. The wind sharpened yet more. It drove me indoors. Melancholy and self-pity were joined by confusion. They were 40-15 up against celebration. Eating away at me was the terrible thought that Lukas was going to reject us as 'devylls' no matter how encouraging or how sweet my message. I became unutterably depressed.

We had been arrogant and mindless in assuming that he couldn't possibly want to test us. To him, we were the devils. That electricity stuff and all the talk about power. I could see it now but . . . 'Sorry' wasn't worth saying. He was in the real world, we must be phantoms. I didn't laugh at the absurdity of it.

### 11 March

I wanted Lukas to write. I willed it of him, so I was very soothing, and a little awkward in my communication. I apologized for not noticing the errors and spelt them out for him.

The reply came next day. Debbie was smiling, simply grinning at the screen. She showed me the message proudly.

›› MYNE GOODLY FREEND WILT THOU MISPLAS MYNE MISDOUTES OF MYNE LAST MESSAGE I WERT SOMEWHAT CONFUS THOU FREEND FROM OXFORDE DOES MUCHE SCRIT IN MYNE REDD BOOKE PREY WOT DOES HE SAY 'TIS UNNIST TO MYNESEL VE BUT HE URSES SOM OF MYNE WORDES DOES HE COME FROM MY TYME 'TIS TREWE ABOUTE MYNE LYE 'TWAS JUSTE A JAPE MYNE LATIN BE NOT SOE BAD AS THAT AND I KNOWE MUCHE ABOUTE MYNE MOSTE WORTHY DESIDERIUS BOOKES HE WAS A MOSTE ARTFUL MAN WHO I HATH MUCHE LOVE OF AND HE DIDST HATH MUCHE WISDOME ON MYNE ILL FRIVOLUS AND MISGOVERN WAYS OF THY CHRITYAN DOCTRYNE METHINKS HE HAS OPEND MANYE EYES TO SUCHE SO-CALLED LEARNED MEN WEN HE WAS GIVEN HIS TITEL TO GREKE I BEGANE MYNE TYME AT BRASENOSE COLLAGE OXFORDE NOT JESUS COLLAGE AS I HATH SEID IN ALLE MANER THYNGS BY MYNE PAN HIS BESTE MUSTE BE COLLOQUIA THEROF I KNOWE NO BETTER MYNE COOKE KATHRYE ASKE WOT BE YOWR MOSTE WHOLESOM MEEL AND HOW DOTH YOW MAKE IT MYNE SOES BE MADE OF SWYNE. SKYN AND SHEPES COAT I HATH VIII SWYNE AND XVI FOWL ME TANNS SWYNE SKINN CUTS SKYN THEN SHAPES AND SEWS IT TOGIDER AND PUTS MYNE SHEPES COAT AND HERBES IN TO THEM TO KEEPE MYNE FEET HELEE ME WOLDE FORTH WOL YOW TELLE BUT MYNE GLAS MUSTE TURN QUID AGIS NOSCERE DE MEUS ADAGIA HABERE YE RECITARE HIC MEUS LATINNUS IS NON UT UTILIS

VALE LUKAS ‹‹

[My good friend, will you dispel my doubts in the last message? I was somewhat confused. Your friend from Oxford does much writing in the red book. Pray, what does he say? It is unknown to me but he uses some of my words. Does he come from my time? 'Tis true about my life. It was just a joke. My Latin is not so bad as that and I know much about my most worthy Desiderius's [Erasmus's] books. He was a most knowledgeable man for whom I had much love and he spoke much wisdom on the frivolous and misgoverned ways of the Christian doctrine. I think he has opened many eyes to such so-called learned men when he was given his appointment in Greek. I began my time at Brasenose College, Oxford, not Jesus College. As I said, in all manner of things, his [Erasmus's] best must be Colloquia than which I know no better. My cook Kathryn asks what is your most tasty meal and how you make it. My shoes are made of swine skin and sheep's coat. I have eight pigs and sixteen fowl. I tan the pigskin, cut the skin, then shape and sew it together and put the sheep's coat and herbs in to them to keep my feet healthy. I must go out, time is moving on. Quid agis noscere de meus Adagia habere ye recitare hic meus Latinnus is non ut utilis.

Farewell, Lukas]

✱ 'What do you have to know about my sayings? You read this my Latin that is not as useful'.

All was forgiven. Peter tried to make sense of the Latin phrase himself but eventually gave it to Valmai Bayliss, the only teacher in school competent in the language. She considered it rather careless 'dog Latin'. After all his efforts to convince us of his superior education he comes out with this.

I was taken by the question: 'Does he [Peter] come from my time?' Quite unselfconsciously Lukas was reinforcing the notion of two distinct physical worlds coexistent in some way but fluid enough to allow interpenetration. I think Lukas thought it rather more fluid than we did.

His talk was of the commonplace, of pigs and chickens, books, scholarship and scholars, friends and the lateness of the hour. I thought that this must be a starting point, for if this communication could be sustained I hoped that an investigation would uncover some of the mechanisms behind it. Some rather narrow-minded friends had said that since there was no explanation or even a hint of a mechanism to explain the messages then they should be dismissed out of hand. This I considered naive in the extreme and, as I said at the time, very much 'flat earth' logic. An investigation was needed and soon, but there were lessons to be learnt from this recent confusion.

Understanding must be allowed to develop, unforced and unhurried by our anxieties. We must think, as Lukas might, like a pre-scientific man – a farmer, a villager alone with his thoughts and us. An educated man amongst superstitious and ignorant people who would burn an old woman as a witch if their cattle died suddenly. The medieval was only receding slowly before the light of the Renaissance. Dodleston, clustered on its rise above the stinking marsh close to the 'heathen' Welsh, was a good place to be aware of superstition and fear.

For evidence we would gather his words, at least it made for a good start. If the apparent inconsistencies continued, and indeed grew in number they would soon reach a 'critical mass', an overwhelming case for fraud. On the other hand if the inconsistencies declined or the 'clear-up rate' improved as our researches delved deeper, then we could feel less wary. It would not add up to proof but it would add up to something. Most important, however, was time. Time to think, to investigate, to live this adventure.

### 13 March

Debbie and I travelled up to Hawarden to see Peter. It was the first meeting in which we planned to consider a framework for the coming weeks. Peter felt confident that I should continue to allow the communications and that something would indeed be gained, and he was keen to be involved. I in turn valued his encouragement and knowledge. The fact that we were planning future strategies demonstrated that this 'experience' was not being dismissed lightly. In a way it never had been. But a more coherent approach to the problem brought complications; for example it might increase suspicion that there was a conspiracy behind the whole thing.

Besides anything else, the words used in the messages were of utter fascination to Peter. He saw their value more clearly, more immediately than anyone. As I listened I realized that this strange affair was being placed at the heart of his life and people and events were beginning to gravitate around it. And as if in a mirror I saw how close it was to my own heart.

Debbie and I would continue as before: collecting messages, asking questions, establishing patterns of behaviour, talking with experts, reading up. We would try to be open and aware. Peter offered his continuing support, and for that we were grateful.

And if it was, after all, a hoax Peter said that he would shake the fellow's hand. Scholar meeting scholar. I could hardly agree less; I thought that a smack in the face with a baseball bat was a more appropriate response.

Three problems were identified. Firstly, someone needed to know where both Debbie and I were at the moment a message was received. Debbie volunteered to ask her mother and brother to sit with her. It wasn't exactly scientific but it was a positive start and would help allay fears that it was a result of Debbie's sleepwalking or having a crazy split personality. If Lukas wrote whilst members of her family were present – or even if a new file was created or a few pages scrolled up – I for one would feel relieved.

The second problem was clearly that of external validation. Peter was looking into the history, aims, and current organization of the Society for Psychical Research (SPR). He said we should contact them asking for advice and, if possible, investigators. I was suddenly not so keen, now that practical details were being discussed. After all, it would make for a cranky-looking letter. It was also my house that would be invaded, but I gave way eventually.

Thirdly, we'd have to try and improve security at the cottage. We were still planning on knocking bits of it about, and consequently I didn't hold out much hope, but I promised I would try.

# 9

Poltergeist activity continued at nuisance level. A milk carton returned time after time to the top of the coffee jar. It was amusing in a way. Perhaps because 'it' sensed we were tired of this game there was a change of direction. A sugar bowl and a coffee jar were found hiding rather shyly in the sink, like the children's story characters, Bill and Ben the Flowerpot Men, hiding from The Man Who Worked in the Garden who, in every episode, was thought to be coming back from his dinner.

Less funny was the colour of the XJ Coupe. It looked orangey when I saw it poking out of Jim Mackie's garage after its respray. Debbie laughed. Dark blue is my favourite colour so why had I picked coral red? The world was turning slightly unreal. A broad grin developed; I'd got myself an orange car, a poltergeist and a pen-friend from the 16th century. Lukas wrote while we were out, it was a long message.

›› MYNE FREEND WEN ME SAYETH DESIDERIUS MYNE GOODLY FREEND I MEENETH I HAN OONLY MET WITH HEM THRYES AT CAMBRIDGE I KNOWE MOORE OF HIS MOST FAVOURABLE BOKES BUT ME SHAL TELLE OF HIS DEVYSYNG HE WER A GOODLY MAN HE BIFEL TO MALADYE FASTE FOR HE WAS SOE SMALLE IN HYGHTE AN WAYKE IN BOUK BUT MUCHE STRENGTHE IN MINDE AN SOULE THAT I HATH NAT SEEN BIFORE HE HATH BLAKE HEER WITH SOM GRAY AN IN BROW HE HATH GRENE EYES STRONGE IN NOSE AND CHINN UPON HIS SCRIT HAND HE HATH II GOLDS AND IV ON THYNE OTHER LENE IN CHEKE AN BOON WHYTE IN SKYN AND DIDST ETE LITEL AND DIDST OONCE SWOWNE IN MYNE COMPANYE

FROM WOT ME RECORDE HE DIDST HAN A BARFUL YOUTHE THAT
MADETH HEM MOOR SOE DESPITIOUS TO WARDS THY CHRISTYAN
DOCTRYNE AND HADD NO FAVOUR FOR MYNE MONKS AT ALLE BUT
HE WERT SOE CRAFTY AND WERT NAT A MAN TO CONTEK WITH NOR
AT-REDE FOR HE WOLD WINNEN AN LEEVE YOWR WITTS AND FEY
TI FY HE HADDE GOODLY HUMOUR AN WOLD OFT BE PLEYFUL AN
SINGE TO HEMSELVE WEN HE WERT NAT SYK HE DIDST APASS
IN 1536 AT BALE

LUKAS «

[My friend, when I call Desiderius my good friend I mean I have
only met him three times at Cambridge. I know more about his
most excellent books but I will describe his appearance: he was
a handsome man. He easily became ill for he was so small in
height and weak in bulk but [had] so much strength in mind
and soul that I had not seen before. He had black hair with some
grey and in [his] brow. He has green eyes; strong in nose and
chin. Upon his writing hand he had two gold rings and four on
the other. Lean in cheek and bone, white in skin and he did eat
little and once swore in my company. From what I remember
he had a difficult youth that made him more contemptuous
towards Christian doctrine and had no liking for monks at all,
but he was so clever and was not a man to argue with nor to
contradict for he would win and exceed your wits. Dear me! He
had good humour and would often be merry and sing to himself
when he was not sick. He died in 1536 at Basle.

Lukas]

Peter wondered how Lukas had learned of Erasmus's death
in Switzerland. It did seem to be one of those awkward problems but, I reasoned, even in the 16th century news of such a
famous man would travel swiftly.

By the time he wrote this message, on 19 March, Lukas was
full of confidence. Confident enough to write to Debbie, chide
her for her lack of domesticity, compliment her on her good
looks and request the presence of Peter Trinder.

,, MYNE GOODLY WOMAN YOW ART WEL SCOOLED METHINKS FOR
A SHE BUT SOMWOT A TOMBOY IN SOM WA ME DOST NOT MEEN TO
IMPORT OFFENDYNG TO YOWRSELVE FOR YOW BEETH A MOST
PARFIT CONCUBIN THAT WOLD GIVE A MANN HIS FILLE BUT YOW
MUSTE KNOWE YOW PLAS AN SERVE MYNE FREEND WEL NEXT
YOW SHAL TELLE YOW HATH CART TYGRE OR THAT YOW CAN
JOURNEE ON SOME UNKYNDE BRID PLEASE AXE YOW MAN IF ME
CAN HATH WORDES WITH THY MAN YOW CALLE PETER FOR I MAY
SPEAK WITH HEM IN MYNE OWNE TONGUE 'TIS TYRSOM TO AREDE
VERBATIM OF YOWR SCRIPT THEN WE MAY HATH MOORE RECO-
NYNG FOR O ANOTHER AND OUR TYMES MYNE GOODLY FREEND
I HATH MANYE A TALE TO TELLE YE BUT THER IS NOUGHT
THAT METHENK WOLD PLEASEN YOW NATHELESS FERTH SHAL
ME TELLE 'TWAS IN TYME OF MYNE FERRE WHO WERT A MOSTE
NOBLE MAN AND DID TEACHE MYNESELVE BIFORE COLLAGE
HE DIDST SEND ME TO THY CITEE O BRIGHTSTOWE FOR SOME
BOKES AFT LONGE JOURNEE I GOOS TO MYNE FERRES FREEND
OF HE WAY GO THROUGH TEMPLE GATE INTO TEMPLE ST TURNE
LEFT INTO SAYNT THOMAS GO FERTH PAST SAINT THOMAS TO
SAYNT LEONARDS GATE AND TIS MID COTAGE ON MYNE RIGHT
I WERT AXE TO ENTREE AND REST MYNE TYRESOM BOUK AND
HENT SLEPE AFT TURN FOURE I WERT PULLED BY MYNE SLEEVE
HAND INTO A CEELAR AND TOLDE THAT A MAN OF THE CROWNE
WAS AXYNG FOR MYNE POORE SELVE FOR SOME REASON I NOTE
ATEYNE ME HERDS HEM MELLYNG WITH MYNE FREENS WIF AND
COLDE ENDURE NO MORE SOE ME TOLDE THY FUOLE CREATURE
TO LET THE SHE BE BUT NOLDE HE SOE ME SMOOT HEM HARD
AND HE DIDST FALLE FASTE THER WITH AL HE PUT ME IN CART
CAGE AN THEN INTO THY PIT SHORTLY THEM DIDST TAKE UPON
THEMSELVES TO PYNE MYNE POORE SELVE BIFORE THEM TOOK
ME TO MYNE JUDGE WHO ALLEDGGED THAT ME WERT A CAITIF
FOR I WERT A PYKEPURS AT THAT WINK MYNE FERRE CAME A
RIDYNG THROUGH ON HIS HORS AND DIDST QUOD HEER BE YOW
FOWEL AND DIDST PICCHEN A GOODLY POUND BRID AND PULLED
ME UPON MYNE HORS AND DIDST FLEEN METHINKS YOW BE TYREO
FROM MYNE LONG WORDES SO I SHALT GOO

LUKAS ,,

[My goodly woman, you are well schooled, I think, for a woman but rather a tomboy in some way. I do not wish to be offensive to yourself for you are a most perfect partner that would satisfy any man, but you must know your place and serve my friend well. Next you will say you have a cart tiger or can travel on some unnatural bird. Please ask your man if I can have words with the man you call Peter for I may speak with him in my own language. It is difficult to read the words you write. Then we can have more understanding of one another and our times. [To Ken] My goodly friend, I have many a good tale to tell you, but there is nothing that I think would interest you; nonetheless I will tell you. It was in the time of my friend who was a most noble man and who taught me before college. He sent me to the city of Bristol for some books. After a long journey I arrive at my friend's house the way goes through Temple Gate into Temple Street, turn left into Saint Thomas [sic], go past Saint Thomas, to Saint Leonard's Gate and it is middle cottage on the right. I was asked to enter and rest my tired body and take a nap. After about four hours I was pulled by my sleeve into a cellar and told that an official was asking for my poor self for some reason I did not understand. I then heard one of assaulting my friend's wife and could endure no more, so I told the foul creature to let the woman be, but he would not, so I hit him hard and he fell. Then they put me in a cage on a cart and then into the dungeon. They took it upon themselves to torture my poor self before they took me to the judge who alleged that I was a rogue for I was a pickpocket. At that moment my 'brother' came riding through on his horse, said 'Here is your fowl,' and did pitch in a good heavy bird and pulled me upon the horse and fled. I think you are tired from this long tale so I shall go.

Lukas]

The adventure he described was fascinating. Contemporary concepts of law and order and justice metamorphosed into prejudice, brutality and chance. It was action not words: 'due process' be hanged – or else you were. Lukas and his 'brother' appeared on the side of good. In the best tradition of storytelling: good triumphs, the maiden escapes (if slightly 'melled'). The prosecutor gets the bird for his troubles and the heroes escape in a cloud of dust. Bravo!

A detailed description of the location was an invitation to follow up; Bristol was the best place for that. Perhaps any decent reference library would have done but that was no adventure. We were on an adventure, I thought, so we might as well enter into it wholeheartedly. I would go in the summer.

Debbie was upset later that day. She was unwell and was trying to rest in front of the fire, her head on the arm of the couch. She heard noises from the kitchen. In the kitchen the white chair was poised, balanced on its rail. The coffee jar had moved to the centre of the floor, and it seemed to look up at her and whisper, 'Aren't I clever being here all alone?' To her right and on top of the fridge were two Schwartz herb containers, a salt cellar and a ketchup bottle in one stack. But there was worse to come as she recalls:

'There were many times when I was frightened, not by the communications on the computer so much but by the physical disturbances and the atmosphere it seemed to create. Ken referred to it as "polti-activity" in an attempt to make it seem quite normal. I called it many things.

On this night the disturbance manifested itself as small tapping noises on the door to the kitchen, which I kept bolted when I was alone. It made me edgy but I put some music on and they seemed to disappear. When all was quiet I took a look under the door into the kitchen to check if the coast was clear in the hope that I could go and make a coffee.

'Sure that all seemed clear I put the main light on, brazenly barged into the kitchen and made a drink. No problems.

'I came back into the lounge and sat down with the coffee. At that instant I felt a prickly coldness against the left side of my face and neck and something pulled at my hair. I thought it was my collar at first, until it persisted another four times then stopped, it happened so quickly I wasn't sure what to think until a few seconds later I felt a slight pressure bearing down on my left shoulder. I froze until the pressure gripping my shoulder was unbearable.

'I knew some one was to the left of me but could not see at the corner of my eye – I turned round and nothing was there. I ran outside the house and waited for Ken to return – the cold, damp rain didn't bother me as much as the house.'

Debbie said that if it happened again she'd leave and not come back.

# *10*

**21 March**

I was carrying out the daily routine of checking the notice-board and pigeon-holes at school when I was interrupted by another teacher, Reg Barratt. He had heard of Lukas and the connection with Erasmus, and he proffered a postcard-sized black and white picture of Erasmus that I could show to Lukas if I wished. It had been used in an essay of Reg's on education and I was to return it – if possible – as its absence made the essay look unfinished.

Various thoughts came alive: I'd leave this picture for Lukas. Perhaps it too would disappear . . . I could use the picture to impress Lukas . . . Lukas was very keen to hear from Peter and I had to let him know that Peter was coming down quite soon. Taking a message from Peter was easy enough but Lukas wanted Peter there. The main reasons for wanting Peter were, I suspected, the difficulties of understanding my messages and the fact that Peter was an Oxford man. Lukas probably saw me as uneducated, despite my earlier claims to a college background. Ironically it had been Peter's suggestion, nearly a month ago, that I write quite straightforwardly, i.e. avoiding pseudo-medieval construction, and the only outcome was that Lukas couldn't read my words. I was therefore cast as the ignorant peasant. Henceforth I tried to adjust my messages to suit the circumstances.

An unnecessary red-brick-university kind of inferiority complex arose in me when faced with these Oxford 'old boys'. Still, I had to remind Lukas who was in charge of this communication. I aggregated all sorts of imaginary affronts to my ego. I was like a selfish child with a new toy. I wrote to him that Peter would be coming down, left him the picture and questioned him further on the 'antic' mentioned in his first message. His reply:

›› MYNE GOODLY FREEND KEN WEBBSTER THYN CALLE SIGHT BE SOMWOT STRANGE YEA MYNE JAKES BE IN TA YARD BY MYNE SHEPNE BUT WY AXE THYS ME NOLDE ATEYNE FOR T'BE PLEYN DIDST YOW HATH MUCHE LAUNDE WHAN YOW LIVD THANK YE FOR THY PORTREYNG ME SHALT HATH IT PORTRAYD IN MYNE BOKE OF YOW TYME FORYEVE MYNE HASTEFUL LIPPES FROM LAKKE OF WITTS ME MEANST NAT TO CAUSE YOW JALOUSY BUT PETER METHENK WERT A MAN FOR MYNE RECONYG AN COULDST REME-DYE MYNE SORE EYEN A-NIGHT BY MYNE WASSAIL BUT YOW BE A PROFIT FOR MYNE WORDES I KNOWETH NOT OF A ANTIC UNLEST YOW MENT TA MAN WHO DIDST BETAKE THY COMUTER FOR YOWR TYME PREYE EXPOWN ME GOOS TO HAORDINE THRUGH MYNE KINARTON WODES THEN ONTO HE WAY I HATH BE BUT OONSE AND DIDST NAT FAVOUR THY WRETCCHED PLAS

**LUKAS ‹‹**

[My goodly friend Ken Webster. The sight of your name is somewhat strange. Yes, my lavatory [jakes] is in the yard by the cow shed, but why ask this? I cannot understand for it is plain to see. Did you have much land when you lived? Thank you for the picture. I shall have it put in my book about your time. Forgive my hasty words, it was thoughtless. I did not mean to cause you jealousy but Peter, I think, would be a man I could readily understand and be a remedy for my sore eyes at night. But you are profiting from my words. I do not know about an 'antic' unless you meant the man that introduced the 'comuter' into your time. Please explain. I go to Hawarden through Kinnerton woods then on to the high way. I have only been there once and didn't like the rotten place . . .

Lukas]

I felt rather deflated. He was answering a question left weeks and weeks ago. It was a suggestion of Peter's to probe his understanding of some particular words. 'Jakes' was one such word. It meant lavatory. Peter told me to write, 'Is the toilet in the yard?' No wonder Lukas thought me a peasant at times. The important point was the delay in answering it. Did this mean: a) a hoaxer had finally discovered the meaning of the word; b) Lukas had suddenly remembered the question; or c) the question had only just reached him?

This message was a real collection of current lines of questioning and areas left behind some time before. The picture did disappear and he claimed to have it. This was quite fascinating and ludicrous. I give him a picture today which turns up in his manuscript 400 years older tomorrow. I could never believe that. But I could see the funny side; it wasn't going to please Reg one bit.

Of some comfort was Lukas's interest in modern words. His word for computer was 'leems boyste' but he turned it into a Hounslow-to-Waterloo office worker – a 'comuter'. Peter wanted Lukas to stick to his own language and not to discolour it with modern terms. He thought it would help limit confusion if the words were at some time given to experts to analyse.

### 24 March

From the cottage the church clock is invisible but an ancient bell marks the half hour and the hour. On a drizzly, foggy morning or deep into a winter night the toll appears to sound across the years rather than across the gardens of Rose Cottages. The bell is inscribed 'Ava Maria', it is chipped and is possibly pre-Reformation. The parish church pamphlet tells me this. The bell joined the peal this Sunday morning, Passion Sunday, as it did every Sunday.

›› YOW BE GOOD OF MYNE SCRIT ME SHALT HATH WORDES WITH YOW AFT MYNE CHURCH ELS ME BE FINDE A SUM TO COSTLY FOR ME TO AFFORE

LUKAS ‹‹

[You are doing well with my words. I shall communicate with you after church or else I shall be fined more than I can afford [for non-attendance].

Lukas]

How eerie! It was Sunday for Lukas too. He could hear that damaged but resonant bell as we do now. Ha! The bell wasn't chipped in the 1540s. It was quite new!

Last night Debbie dreamt that she saw Lukas fleetingly, standing in the cottage kitchen. The image of him, of his expression as he saw her, was remarkably clear in her mind. It was then that she remembered something more of the circumstances. She had been quite soundly asleep in front of the fire and had woken only in order to visit the bathroom, or at least it felt as if she had awoken. As she opened the door to the kitchen there before her was Lukas. In a moment he was gone; incredibly she continued on her errand, returning cautiously through the kitchen and eventually back to the couch and to sleep. Her recollection of it is quite distinct. She felt perhaps that she was getting too tense, that she was hallucinating. It unsettled her greatly and we talked it through for hours. She said she'd keep a note of any similar dreams, but only for me to see. I told her that she wasn't crazy. She put her arms around me and asked if she was safe.

Two days later it was very different. We had one hell of a row. Deb and I build up really quickly. 'More like TNT than gunpowder,' someone once remarked. The sniping, the little digs are more a cue to mobilize the troops than a warning of trouble. Neither one of us wished to give way and so in patterns of movement and gesture which imitated or parodied the theatre of war, we set to.

Some other dreams had been broken by recent circum-stance: Deb's expectations in the antique business, where she worked for a time, had come suddenly to nothing. I was furious that she didn't want to tell me and she was furious that I want-ed to know. My role in the business, as wise counsel supporting and, in my mind's eye, directing part of it – my role as . . . well, who gave a damn? It was all as dust now.

'I do not need all this! Not only . . . but the damn poltergeist is back, writing on the walls again,' I said, pointing to some chalk marks on the pillar.

'What am I going to do about it?'

'This isn't my home anymore, it's a cross between a prison and an asylum.'

'What are you shouting for? My business is my business. I don't want to stay here either. What am I going to do? Do you think I'm writing it? Do you? Leave me alone . . .'

And so on. Familiar enough to any domestic scene, some would say, with the exception of chalk marks on the wall. It wasn't until the next day, a calmer quieter day, that I looked very closely.

Lukas had left his name.

And so we spent more and more time at East Green. We slept there every night. It was not so much that the poltergeist activity freaked us at the cottage but it was the sudden and quite dreadful 'atmosphere' that could descend. It almost froze our thoughts, it brought on tense, unforgiving headaches, angry exchanges or even tears. If ever one of those clouds settled it was best to leave.

# *11*

By 27 March and the Easter holidays I was absolutely shattered. The computer would be at the cottage continually for the
following two weeks. I must have been mad.

The first message was received that night while Debbie was
asleep downstairs. It appeared that we didn't have to go out at
all. Debbie was worried that if she didn't go out people would
think it was her. I told her not to be so childish, and another row
followed. To get out of the way I took the message to Peter for
his views on it. Peter was just so enthusiastic that at times it was
embarrassing.

Next day I did some recording on a borrowed eight-track
recorder. It came out badly, and I wrote in my diary: 'It is this
Lukas business and the plans for the next building work. I can't
concentrate. Maybe I'm bored with music. The New Musical Express still arrives at the shop every week but I only skip through
it. My life feels that it's off course. I should be whacking round
the country in a van with a band playing at village halls and the
pubs, not messing with houses and cars, a mortgage and some
poltergeist.'

Both Deb and I were tired all the time; just being in the cottage was tiring. Maybe it was because the house wasn't mine
with Lukas there. (Like having lodgers, you can never relax.)

I was so tired that evening that I had crashed out for a few
hours downstairs. Debbie had gone to East Green before I nod-
ded off, and Lukas wrote while I was asleep.

It was a reply to Peter's long piece about books and  words and Oxford colleges . . . oh well. In it was a great deal of reminiscing and this interesting section:

**›› PREYE YEVE ME SOM REMEMBAUNCE WOT WERT THY WORDES OF WYSDME ABOVEN MYNE FYR WHOIS POTREYING  BE ON THY WALLE . . . WE ARN ABOUTE THY SAME TYME O DAYE ARN WE NAT PREY . . .‹‹**

[Please give me an idea of what were the words of wisdom above the fire, whose picture is on the wall . . . we are the same age, aren't we?]

Lukas Wainman had evidently seen Peter at the cottage. Peter was about fifty years old, Lukas too, it would seem. There was one difference about this message compared with other recent ones: the file name was a little odd. I had used PTR as a name but it had been changed to TRP during my sleep. Funny I didn't hear anything. In moving from one file to another the disk drive makes a whirring noise: changing the file name would mean using the disk drive. And the computer makes a 'beep' noise if one makes a mistake in moving items about.

Peter decided to go to Oxford to read the inscription above the Brasenose College fireplace, as requested by Lukas. He would also try and trace the early members of the college, looking for Wainman.

Debbie and I were a lot more confident that we were not being hoaxed for the simple reason that we could be in the house or out of it, asleep or awake and we could leave the computer for very limited periods of time and still this stuff kept coming. The only thing we could not do was be in the kitchen. Watching the screen did no good, though we spent some hours in an attempt. I wrote in my diary, 'If this a hoax we are now the only suspects.'

Apparent historical anomalies in the messages had declined markedly, and as for the language, Peter maintained that he would not be able to produce such high quality work. He said he might get a simple piece done if given days to pore over it but, he reminded us, Lukas was writing at length and usually replied within a day or even a few hours to what we wrote; sometimes the question would only be there for him a half hour before he answered. Peter just could not see that anyone was capable of such scholarship, and certainly we weren't. I wrote in my diary, 'But then again it can't be us, not bright enough.'

These issues were coming more to the fore now that the Society for Psychical Research had no doubt received the letter I wrote to them on the 25 March. It had been a hard letter to write. I was so shy about it, that I gave my parents' address rather than my own.

There was something of a lull in communications between late Thursday and Sunday 31 March. We took a trip to Aberystwyth for a day and we were busy at East Green for a time. I didn't leave the computer at the cottage when we weren't there for more than half a day in case of theft. Even so Lukas had had opportunity to write but nothing came. I wrote another greeting and told him that Peter was going to Oxford. The computer was left in position late evening; Deb offered to wait in with it.

Debbie was still troubled about her future prospects, or rather the lack of them, so she was not in the most co- operative of moods. When I came back home after visiting Dave Lovell, Deb was rather troubled for a different reason; she'd had one of those 'funny dreams' about seeing Lukas. She was very worried that she might be subconsciously making up his character, that she was 'suggesting' him. The dream was very clear. She wrote it down.

'It's a bit like glancing into a magnesium flame. For a while just white light, then incandescent green turning to purple,eventually shadows form around shapes, still unrecognisable, then becoming darker and darker, bringing dimensions to the eye and clarity to the mind.

'I blinked and blinked again. There was something different, very different. Yes, I saw the room was unusual but that posed no problem as I was obviously dreaming; I bit on my bottom lip. There! There it was again, a feeling of being utterly insane, and how strange too that I should be questioning my own sanity, this I have never done whilst dreaming. And again, yet another question arose, even stranger than the last. Had I spoken aloud to myself or had I just thought "aloud"? I felt myself frowning; how very odd. Why was I standing in an overspread fireplace? Another intrusive idea squeezed itself into my confusion and took possession of my thoughts: a picture of Alice in Wonderland trying very hard to reach the bottle from a giant table way above her head.

'As I took a step forwards out of the fireplace a movement to the right of me caught my attention. It was a man. A poorly dressed man, whose presence was unpredicted. "How odd this dream!" I reproached myself for not being able to think of any words to describe my feelings other than "odd".

"'Tis strange indeed, maid."

'The man spoke with a thick accent and a look of complete surprise in his eyes. He placed some kind of hammer down on the large, primitive table then stood up in obvious bewilderment.

'Had he heard me think or did I speak? Why had I never had this problem in dreams before? I usually get a choice as to whether I'm heard or not. An unusual fear overcame me. I was not in control. Why was I so sure I was dreaming when I was dreaming?

'I knew that the man was trying desperately to hold a conversation. Was he listening to my thoughts again and responding? No, he seemed to be talking about Lukas, but why? What on earth did he have to do with the experiences at the cottage? Even for a dream this was an unlikely conversation to undertake with a stranger. I had realized that I was using the word "dream" every so many moments; why was this? Time appeared only to exist in my thinking of it. Why did I feel so insecure to the point of being suffocated by my own fear? What was this fear? Maybe, I thought, I'd died; it was a fear of no return. I withdrew into the fireplace in the hope that I could retrace my steps.

'The bright light returned and phased everything into the white. Then blackness hit me like an instant blindness. With a shaking hand I slid my index finger and thumb from the outer corners of my eyes inwards to meet on the middle of my nose. A feeling of relief flooded into me and out with a sigh – I had been asleep.'

Later that evening Lukas wrote:

» IT NERE NAT DAYE AND MYNE WASSAYL LYTE BE TO WANE

AND MYNE EYENS BE SOE WAYKE THAT THEM

WERE LOOTH TO KISSE THE MORWENYNG SONNE FOR WAN IT CAME

SOE ME DIDST PUT AWAYE MYNE CAS TO MAKE TO MYNE BEDDE
WHAN ME DIDST SEE A FAYR MAYDE WHO DIDST PASS IT DIDST
SOE AFEREN MYNESELVE TO SEE HER ANOON APPERE

SHE DIDST CACCHE MYNE SIGHT FOR A WYNK AND DIDST CASTE
AN EYE OF CARE WHAT BE YOWR WANT SHE DIDST QUOD BUT MYNE
LIPPES WER STILLE FOR HER FAIRNESS DIDST BETAKE MYNE
BREETH AND THEN SHE DIDST LEEVE MYNE PRESENCE

ALLONE IN THE DIM LYTE ME WILL NAT FORYETE HER SIGHT
AND ME DOST PREYE SHE BE KEEPES IT CLOSE AND TELLE
NONNAFROM THAT SHORTEST NIGHT

LUKAS «

We didn't understand it all, yet it needed no translation. A love poem to a beautiful girl, a girl who appeared suddenly to Lukas one fateful night. A night like the night of Debbie's dream, perhaps.

Peter had the misfortune to choose 1 April to open conversation with a stranger in Oxford about communications on a word processor from the 16th century. The stranger took it as an excellent wind-up. Fortunately Peter had a great deal more luck with the assistant librarian at Brasenose, Robin Peedell. Peter introduced himself with more circumspection this time.

There was certainly no Lukas Wainman or anything near in the records of Brasenose. This was not necessarily a problem as the records are incomplete. Even so Robin could find nothing similar until over a century later, and to make matters worse the inscription Lukas had mentioned was above the stairs rather than over the fireplace.

Peter was much taken with the poem Lukas had left. I did not mention Debbie's dream, which, she said, would only cause unnecessary problems. It was, she repeated, 'only a dream'.

# *12*

**4 April**

Lukas announced that he was to go to Stopford. This was, as we guessed at the time, Stockport. It seemed to us quite a journey.

He left a very long message to Peter the same day. It was in reply to Peter's discoveries at Oxford and his request to know more of the men at the college at around the time Lukas said he was there. Peter was trying to test Lukas's knowledge. He carefully pointed out the lack of an inscription above the fireplace in Brasenose but he did not disclose where in fact the inscription was nor what it said. I don't think he even told us. He hoped Lukas would offer the information. And he did:

›› ME MUSTE SAUF MYNE SHAME ME DIDST MAKE WRONGE THY WORDES PLACD ABOVEN FYR TIS POORE RECORD ON MYNE PAN THY WORDES BE ON THY FYRST STEEP ANNO CHRISTI SOM DAYE ET REGIS HENRICI OCTAVI PRIMO NOMINE DIVINO LINCOLN PRESUL QUOQUE SUTTON HANC POSU ERE PETRAM REGIS AD IMPERIUM PRIMO DIE LUNII . . .

DOST YOW KNOWE ANY OF THISE MEN ROLAND MESSENGIR A RICHARD SHERWOODE A JON SMYTH A JON FORNBY A MAFEW SMYTH A RALF BOSTOCK A ROBERT HOLMES A TOM WIGHT AND TOM TIPPYNG ‹‹

[I must cover my shame, I made a mistake about the words above the fireplace, it is my poor memory, the words are above the first stairs ANNO CHRISTI – some date – ET REGIS HENRICI OCTAVI PRIMO NOMINE DIVINO LINCOLN PRESUL QUOQUE SUTTON HANC POSU ERE PETRAM REGIS AD IMPERIUM PRIMO DEI LUNII . . .

Do you know any of these men: Roland Messengir, Richard Sherwoode, Jon Smyth, Jon Fornby, Mafew Smyth, Ralf Bostock, Robert Holmes, Tom Wight and Tom Tippyng?]

Lukas had coped very well with the inscription and in pulling out the right names for his fellow students. Peter was delighted.

Lukas was as good as his word about leaving for a time and despite the computer being available he only returned to it later in the week, on 10 April. We had a name now for this waiting around: 'ghostbusting'. It was jokey and deliberately so. 'Ghostbusting' was becoming the central evening activity, messages weren't 'discovered' anymore, they were allowed for, sometimes expected, so calling it 'ghostbusting' helped us keep the whole thing in perspective. I didn't believe in ghosts. If Lukas wasn't a sophisticated hoax then he was real, a man out of time.

Deb's Morris Minor bounced along the very uneven road between Pentre and Saltney Ferry. Alongside the airfield ran Manor Lane. On the corner loomed an emplacement, a pill box from the last war, which guarded the junction of Manor Lane and the straight upon which we found our selves. As the car turned up the lane I looked up and saw broken white clouds mottled with grey. I felt as if I hadn't seen the sky for days, so busy had we been. The light was penetrating, and a cold front had engulfed the west coast. Up on the wooded skyline the keep of Hawarden Castle showed clearly. There were no houses in view. The castle was on the ridge which carried the old road towards England. It was the 'way' Lukas would follow. We were in the marshland of Lukas's time. Deep drainage ditches run along Manor Lane at the Sandycroft end, deeper than any near Dodleston. If Lukas ever came to these places I wondered if the view included these woods and the round keep of the castle. Perhaps it was a little more intact in those days, before Cromwell's soldiers stole a stone or two. My thoughts drifted ahead to the cottage. I reread the print-out in my hand as best I could. It was slightly worrying.

›› GO ME DIDST SEE MYNE LEARNED FREEND ABOUTE YOWR TYME HE DIDST HATH MANYE A WORDE TO SEY AL BE IT HE THENKS ME BE SYK HE DIDST CONSELLE MYNESELVE WELL HE SEID THAT ME MUSTE NOT TELLE A CREETURE O THYS UNWIST WORLDE AN OF YOWR PEPLE ELLES TBE NON LESS THN CAPITAL BY MYNE CROWNE ANON ME AFFERME THAT YOW BE GOODLY BUT THAT IT SOMTYMES FORGES DREAD TO A WIGHT AS MYNE LINK MAN ALS HE AXE ME NAT TO WRYTE TIL HE DOST COME AND SEE MYNE COMUTER SOE ME SHAL SPEKE WITH YOW BY MYNE V DAYE

YOWR GOODLY FREEND LUKAS ‹‹

[I saw my learned friend concerning your time. He had many a word to say although he thinks that I am sick. He advised me well. He said that I must not tell a soul about this unknown world and about your people, else it is nothing less than a capital offence, according to the Crown. I immediately swore that you are honest but that it sometimes makes some people fearful, such as my servant. Also he asks me not to write until he comes and sees the computer, so I shall speak with you five days from now.

Your good friend Lukas]

Lukas needed reassurance. We had our friends with whom to chew over the latest turn of events. Lukas had not. Lukas had sought out an old friend in Stopford. Yet even he had counselled against Lukas writing more of this 'unwist world'. But this friend was to come to see for himself! Our fame was spreading. We should expect his friend around 14 April.

By 13 April work had been started on the cottage again. Outside the kitchen a whole lot of digging was in progress. A bulldozer, courtesy of a local farmer, a couple of very likely lads and a tractor and trailer had recently removed something in the order of forty tons of earth, broken bricks, tarmac and cobblestones. Mud was creeping in on boots and shoes, cement bags were piled up in a comer of the kitchen. The computer was switched on. It was often on despite the risk of dust damage. Inside the cottage it felt like a transport cafe, all teapots and plates and newspapers on the floor.

Debbie was looking at a cheap edition of a history of Chester. One incident caught her attention. This was a criminal case which was punished by 'pressing'. In a 'press' yard a prisoner would be made to lie down and a wide wooden plank or door placed over him. It would be slowly loaded with large stone weights until the victim expired. His only consolation was the right to pass on his land to an heir rather having it confiscated by the Crown. I had come across it before in school and was the only one in the cottage who knew its other name – 'peyne forte et dure'. Apart, that is, from Lukas. The door to the kitchen had been open throughout our conversation. The screen had been blank yet now it read:

**›› ME DIDST HEER YOW SPEKE OF MYNE UNFAVOURABLE PEYNE FORTE ET DURE WY BE THYS DOE YOW MEENST TO TELLE MYNE CROWNE ‹‹**

[I heard you speak of the awful 'peyne forte et dure'. Why is this? Do you mean to tell the Crown?]

Oh, Lukas! This was a strange lack of confidence on his part. He must have been fed a cautionary tale by the man from Stopford. This short message had two significant aspects. Deb offered the obvious: 'This means he can listen to our conversations.'

It seemed so. There had been no message from us to him, no hint or premonition of the events we were about to discuss. Secondly, Dave Lovell was with us both; none of us could have physically written that message unnoticed by the others. Deb also came up with the other idea: my/our thoughts had carried.

I left Lukas a message of reassurance. It was on the lines of, 'Please write to us, we can be trusted whatever happens'; and so on. Dave and I went back to work. Deb remained indoors but left the kitchen door slightly ajar.

Nearly an hour later I went in and glanced at the screen on my way to the sink for some water. There was a message, but because my clothes were dirty and dusty I kept my distance and didn't take it in. It was a poem. It was good to see but for now back to work.

Outside, Dave was driving the great hulk of the Jaguar backwards and forwards on the soil, trying it for size in the newly cleared area around the damson tree. He didn't stop the car but called out from under his moustache: 'Anything?'

'Yes, a poem . . . looks a goodie. Do you want to see it?' 'I'll look at it later.'

We were getting very matter of fact.

The noise and the practical implications of manoeuvring a large car in a small space prevented us from noticing the light in the kitchen go out and the music from the tape recorder in the studio stop abruptly.

There was nothing to see when we next went in. A power cut. The poem was gone, my message to Lukas with it. Work stopped. I tried to blame Debbie for not saving the information to disk and thereby protecting it from just such an interruption.

The power came back on at tea time and the music took up where it had left off. There was nothing there. If the information is not saved to disk then it can only live in the BBC computer memory while there is power to the machine.

Lukas didn't write again until his friend from Stopford arrived. Debbie asked him for the poem again but the first sign of his presence was this rather confused item:

» FGGRRRRPAIJBEP JJJJJJJJJJJJJJJGGGGGGGNZ CCCCCCCCCSSSSSSSSSDDDDDDDDDDFFNC

COMUTER THYS BE

HOWE 'T MAKES MYNE LEEMS   J O HN E4GZESSRTGR3JH-GMNMBNSDFDGDF «

Lukas then curtly introduced his friend, but giving no names. The 'freend' offered no names either.

›› MYNE FREEND ME SHALT YEVE YOW MYNE SAD SONGE TO MORROW FOR THYS DAYE MYNE FREEND HATH COM TO SPEKE WYTH YOW

MY GOODLY MAN    I HAVE HERD OF THY GRIPPES LEOUNS AND WONDAROUS POSSESSIOUNS AND YT IS TOO FANTASTYK   TO REKNE   AND THY PEPLE BE UNKIND THOUGH I HAVE NO

ABODMENTS THOU ARN A PHANTASIME OF GRETE POWERS   'TIS TO MY THEOREC THAT THOU BE TO COME SO THOU CANST TELLE FOR WHEN THE KYNG DOES END HYS REYNE  AND WHOIS TO TAKE THE CROWNE HOW DO THEE PHYSIC THY PEPLE OF THY TYME IS THE COMUTER THYNE PREYE   THE FASHYON OF OWRN TYME BE SO THAT I WILL NOT GIVE MYNE NOR LUCAS WEYNMANNS TREWE DEVYSYNG AND  NAYME

I BEGG YE FORGIVE ME: FOR MY DELAY FOR I WER UNCOLTED FROM STOPFORD IN PACE

A FREEND ‹‹

[My good man, I have heard of your griffons, lions and wondrous possessions and it is too fantastic to understand and your people are unnatural although I have no dread. You are a phantasm of great powers. It is my theory that you are in the future, so you can tell when the King ends his reign and who is to take the crown. How do you cure the people of your time? Is the computer yours, pray? The fashion of our time is such that I will not give my own name nor Lukas's true description and name. I beg you forgive me for my delay for I was uncolted [thrown from his horse?] from Stockport in my hurry.

A friend]

Lukas was not his real name. It was now impossible for us to pursue our historical enquiries. It was not good news. Perhaps they were criminals, or scared that we were devils who would take them if we had their names, but we guessed that Lukas's friend was called John from the 'practice' message (above). This 'freend' could evidently see the screen, he could read our message but he could not see us. Lukas, however, appeared to have quite a different access to our time: via the screen, certainly, but he had apparently demonstrated that he could eavesdrop on conversations, and see some items in the kitchen (although not beyond), and it was possible that he could write on the walls. Someone said that 'John' could be an invention, another of Lukas's tests. If indeed this was Lukas's friend then the puzzle deepened.

The man from Stopford wanted hard information, some of it political. To me it was schoolboy history but as far as he was concerned this knowledge might allow him to place his loyalties with due and careful regard. Mischievously I did not want to tell him of Elizabeth's accession after Edward VI and Mary. He might confidently turn Catholic in 1554 only to be hauled up before the courts a mere four years later!

It flattered me to think we were a 'phantasime of grete powers'. I thought that the one really useful narrative we could give would be on how to rid England of the plague.

How noble I felt as I looked through another schoolboy study. It's the rats, isn't it? That is the vague idea most people hold. Until one discovers that it might have been more than black rats, the rats needed a suitable environment in which to thrive. It might even have been a variety of plagues over the centuries. Even the Black Death in 1338-50 had three strands to it. It might . . . I couldn't see much progress if all we could say to one man was, 'Redesign your towns, burn your flea-infested clothes and get the cats to work.'

# 13

Later that week a Mr John Stiles rang me at home. He was, he said, the research liaison officer for the Society for Psychical Research. He had a very academic, very correct manner yet he seemed relaxed and at ease with himself. I was trying hard not to sound silly or a crackpot. It is difficult to talk to strangers. I filled him in on the back ground and he moved quickly on to three theories. Firstly, the hoax. The usual schedule of culprits emerged, Debbie and myself top of the list. Secondly, he thought that one of us might be causing it unconsciously. This was something which deserved serious consideration, although the apparent authenticity of Lukas's language militated against it somewhat. However, John Stiles didn't see much of interest in the language. This irked me but he had only a snippet or two to go on and it can seem quite inauthentic on casual inspection. Thirdly, he introduced the notion of mental 'interference' with computers, although this usually resulted in nonsense or merely screen failure or equipment failure. There was, he said, only indirect evidence for it, but he gave no further clues.

To interest SPR we would need to eliminate the first two possibilities. John Stiles suggested putting locks on all the relevant doors and windows and depositing the keys with a bank while the computer was left on and waiting. I didn't take up this suggestion; I'm afraid I simply could not afford to be without access to the kitchen during building work, nor did I want to risk not being able to respond to Lukas during this sealed period; he might think us gone and stop his communication. Far better, I thought to keep it all going and accumulate material. If there was a hoax it would show eventually.

However, there was much we could do to remove suspicion from ourselves. SPR was rather underfunded but John Stiles promised to put us in touch with a suitable investigator as soon as we had made some progress towards eliminating the obvious.

Debbie finally got round to inviting her mother and brother down which, although hardly scientific, would be a useful start. The conditions were to be as close to the usual successful pattern as possible. The computer sat on the table by the refrigerator in the kitchen. A short greeting or message from us would be put on the screen. Normally this was all there would be on the particular file we were using; the computer would be left alone. The door to the kitchen would be closed. If Deb was staying in the cottage she would sit in front of the fire very quietly. Perhaps she would fall asleep. Anything from half an hour to a couple of hours later she would open the door and check beneath the message by scrolling the screen with the cursor keys. If the computer then made an infuriating 'beep', the file was not open beyond the particular page and line indicated.

The next stage was to look for any new file names which might indicate a new communication. Lastly the existing files would have to be checked for additions. Lukas had been known to use existing files and tag something on further down or indeed wherever. On this particular occasion I left a message asking Lukas for some information on Thomas More then I went to Dave Lovell's house for the evening, deliberately keeping away. As I have said, the conditions weren't scientific but I should like to quote from some notes made by Debbie's mother.

'My son and I arrived at Meadow Cottage at approximately 7.45 P.M. on 15 April 1985. A few minutes later a friend of Mr Webster's called at the front door for something. After a few words were exchanged between my daughter and the caller he left and we three – my daughter Debbie, my son and myself – went into the kitchen.

'We checked the windows and doors in the kitchen and bathroom. The back door was locked with a chain on the inside. The windows were closed, including the sky lights though we did not have time to check if they were locked. We then gave our attention to the computer. All previous entries on the disc were inspected; Debbie typed a few lines on to the screen and as far as we knew there was nothing entered after that.

'At 8.03 P.M. we went into the living room, closing the door to the kitchen behind us. I noted that the light had been left on inside the kitchen. We settled down, quietly reading or writing or occasionally speaking- I was not listening intently for noises, this was unnecessary as we were very quiet ourselves, but I did hear one or two noises which appeared to come from the kitch-en: the sort of noise a mouse might make.

'I felt cold at times and at one stage was shivering, we all kept our coats on as there was no fire in the hearth . . .

'We went into the kitchen again at 9.00 P.M. Debbie left a weight on one of the keys [to scroll the screen] because she needed to go to the bathroom and there did not appear to be anything entered [in the file] since we left it last. After a min-ute we were startled by a high-pitched noise coming from the computer. This indicated to Debbie, I believe, that something had been entered [Note: it indicates that the cursor has reached the bottom of the file]. She swiftly came to the computer (or rather the monitor) and we all saw a new entry displayed, start-ing with a poem. We were short of time and I was unable to understand all that was entered at the time, but did manage to read and understand one or two lines. We then left the cottage.'

Here is the text of the message received that evening: it con-tains the poem lost on 14 April.

›› GOOD NYGHT   GOOD RESTE WO NIETHER BE MYNE SHARE

SHE BAYDE GOOD NYTE THAT KEPT MYNE RESTE AWAYE

AND DAFFED ME TO A CABYN HONGE WYTH CARE

TO DESCANT ON THY DOUTES OF MYNE DECAYE

FARWEL SHE QUOD AN COM AGAYNE TO MORROW

FARE WEL ME COLDST NAT FOR ME DIDST SUPPE

WYTH SORROW


YET ATTE PARTYNG SHE DID SWETELY SMYLE

IN SCORNE O FREENSHYPP NIL ME CONSTREWE

WHETHER

'T MAYE BE SHE DELYTE TO JESTE AT MYNE EXYLE

'T MAYE BE AGAYNE TO MAKES ME WANDER THITHER

WANDER A WORDE FOR SHADOWS LYK

MYNESELVE

AS TAKES THY PEYNE BUT CAN NAT PLUCK THY PELF


TOMAS MOORE WAS NAT UNLYK ERASMUS FOR HE WERT A MAN O
WYSDOME AND DIDST HATH BENEOLENENCE FOR ANY CREETURE
HE DIDST SHOWE MUCHE WORRY FOR MYNE CHIRCHE AND DIDST
NAT KEEPE HYS THINKYNGS TO HEMSELVE AND FOR THAT REA-
SONE WAS HONGE BY MYNE CROWNE FOR BEYNG A TRAITOR AND
NAT BIKNOWYNG THAT THY KYNG BE SUPREAME BIFORE THY
CHIRCHE HE WAS AN OXENFORDE MAN WHO DIDST TAKE GREKE
AND LATYN AND WAS CLOSE FREENDS WYTH MYNE ERASMUS
AND TOGIDER THEM DIDST LEARN WYTH MUCHE HASTE MANYE
THINGS FOR WHICHE I CAN NAT SPEKE OF 'T BE BESTE FOR YOWR
REKONYNG THAT YOW REDE HYS UTOPIA OR ERASMUSES PRAISE
O FOLIE FOR WHICHE MOORE DIDST HELPE HYM WRYTE WHYLE
DWELLYNG IN MOORS HOUSE WEN MOORE DIDST DYE ERASMUS
DID WEEP FOR HE KNEWE NO MAN AS TREWE

LUKAS ‹‹

[Good night. Good rest. Woe neither is my share.

She bade good night that kept my rest away

And sent me to a cabin hung with care

To descant on the doubts of my decay.

'Farewell,' she said, 'and come again tomorrow'

Farewell I could not for I did sup with sorrow.


Yet at parting she did sweetly smile

In scorn of friendship, will not tell me whether

It may be she delights to jest at my exile

It may be again to make me wander thither,

Wander the word for shadows like myself

Who take the pain but cannot pluck the pelf.


Thomas More was not unlike Erasmus for he was a man of wisdom and had benevolence for any creature. He showed much concern for the Church and did not keep his thoughts to himself, and for that reason was hanged [executed?] by the Crown for being a traitor and not acknowledging that the King is supreme over the Church. He was an Oxford man who taught Greek and Latin and was close friends with Erasmus, and together they learnt with much haste [enthusiasm?] many things which I cannot speak of. It would be best for your understanding that you read his Utopia or Erasmus's Praise of Folly which More helped him write while living in More's house. When More died Erasmus wept for he knew no man as true.

Lukas]

    'Debbie?' I said, after I came back to the cottage, 'it looks like Lukas is upset over some woman . . . '

'Nothing to do with me.'

'You mentioned a few days ago when the power went off that you had had a dream about Lukas.'

'It was nothing, just fantasy.'

'His words keep echoing your dreams, Deb. Won't you tell me?

'No, it's soft.'

It was a long time before she told me:

'Katherine was working on the small kneeling stool, she was oblivious to my presence entirely. Lukas strode into the room speaking words I could not understand, they were for Katherine's benefit. He stopped and saw me and greeted me. Katherine stood up, she looked very worried. Lukas turned to her and told her not to be afraid and that I was harmless. But she just looked blankly at him. Then Lukas stiffened and his mood changed. I saw he was angry. He shouted something at Katherine and she ran to him, she seemed to be very frightened of him. I asked Lukas what he was saying but he cut me short. He pushed me into the centre of the room and asked me to pick up a knife from the table. To Lukas's and my own astonishment my hand went straight through the whole table; other than a prickly feeling in my right arm I felt nothing!

'Lukas seemed to think it was a conspiracy and started losing his temper some more. He pushed Katherine into the centre of the room to face me, she was very upset and confused. He seemed to be repeatedly shouting at her to look at me. She started to cry, she was very young.

'"Lukas, what are you trying to do? Please do not shout at Katherine," I pleaded. There is nothing more uncomfortable than seeing someone cry.

'"Be still, why do you not show?" Lukas asked me crossly.

'By this time I was getting upset.

'Lukas shouted at Katherine once more and she ran out. I think I felt nothing but hatred – this ruined my image of Lukas as a kind and gentle man. He was a real bully.

'In my upset and temper I said something but I can't re-member what, perhaps I was too upset to hear myself. But it really upset Lukas. He turned away to face the shelves, his arms were crossed, he gave out a little whine and just closed his eyes; I could not tell whether he was crying. I went to move closer but without looking at me he pointed to the chimney – he wanted me to go. I was so mixed up and so confused but I still hated him. I walked to the chimney and found myself once again back half asleep near the cottage fire, waiting for messages or a dis-tant sound of thunder.'

The following morning in Peter's ill-lit study in the school house I handed him a print-out of Lukas's message about Thomas More and gave him the news that we had succeeded in obtaining Lukas's cooperation with a third party present. It was naive of me but I was grinning with pride and pleasure. This would surely go some way towards interesting SPR in an investigation! Peter shared my enthusiasm but his joy at seeing the message was probably greater. Once more I said nothing of Debbie's dreams.

# 14

The computer was returned to school. I was full of confidence so it was a happy, easy week. I turned my attentions to the Jaguar and prepared for the annual Jaguar Drivers Club meeting at Oulton Park, Cheshire.

Frank Davies was the motor mechanic teacher in Hawarden. He'd worked on Jags, and through this and his interest in tales from Lukas we became friendly enough for me to suggest that he come down to the cottage in order to repeat the 'tests' we had undertaken earlier in the week. I suggested 22 April at approximately 7.30 P.M., thus keeping to the same day of the week and to the same time. Although I could see no reason for such replication, it felt more 'scientific'. Frank readily agreed.

On Friday 19 April the ritual of collecting a computer (rarely the same one) took place once more. I was very keen to hear how the world looked to Lukas and his 'freend', so Debbie and I typed in a greeting on the screen, locked up the house and entered the maelstrom that appears to envelop Tesco on a Friday tea-time.

›› THOU BE A FOND RAG WHOE HAVE BROGHTE NON LESSE THN BLACK UPON MY WRETCH I HOPE HE COMYS NOT TO SCATHE FOR I WARRANT THY DEETHE BY MY OWEN HANDE SOM WAYES TWAS UNAVOIDED WYTH YOR CHARM OF LEEMS AND NOWE HE SITTE IN THE PITT OF SHAYME YT BEE THY RUINE YF BUTT YOUE HELPE LUCAS HE SHALL NOT DIE YF YE SHEW THY SELVEN AND THE CROWNE FOR WHAT YE BEE AND DISPLEY THY POWERS OF CACODEMON THEYN HYS LYFE BEE SPARED

LAYE OPENN THAT WICHE YS TROUE AND GIVE NO FALSE BODYNG AND WHAT NEED BE COMUTER

FRYENDE ‹‹

[You are a foolish scoundrel who has brought nothing less than evil upon the wretch. I hope he comes to no harm for I guarantee your death by my own hand some way. It was not to be avoided with your charm of lights, and now he sits in the shameful dungeon. It will be your own ruin, unless you help Lukas he will die. If you reveal yourselves to the Crown for what you are and display your devilish powers, then his life is saved. Reveal the truth and give no false threats and explain what is the need of the computer.

Friend.]

I guessed that 'scathe' means 'harm'. It sounded more like the action of a scythe. Cut down. Finished. What had happened? How on earth could we possibly show ourselves to the Crown and display our powers? What powers? I still held the shopping heaped up in Tesco's plastic carrier bags. Deb and I exchanged puzzled glances. We hadn't expected any problems. It was absurd: 'Man with shopping bag meets death threat from the past' . . .

I replied immediately, and took it at face value.

*DEAR FREEND*

*IF YOWR TYME BE TO COM THEN THAT WICH I HATH SPOKEN BE TREW. LET LUKAS WRYTE TO ME NOW SOE THAT I MIGHT KNOW WY HE DOST SUFFER YF I AM TO HELPE I MUSTE KNOWE HIS TREW CALLE*

*KEN*

If we had his real name at least we could trace him and check whether he did fall foul of the authorities.

No reply to this. I drove around the lanes. Deb sat in the cottage, willing him to write but it was hopeless. We tried again:

*YOW HAVE NOT WRITTEN. WY BEE THYS? I WOLD SPEKE WYTH THE CROWNE IF LUCAS BEE SPARED. WILL YOW BRING TOM FOWLEHURST I CANNOT SHEW MYNESELVE BUT CAN WRYTE*

*AS TO WHAT YOU WOLD NOWE. WHERE BE THIS PITT OF SHAYME IN WICH POOR LUCAS DOES STAY WHOIS WORDES SENT HIM THER YOW HAVE NOT TOLD ME LUCAS TREW CALLE I CAN HELP LITTLE IF I DO NAT KNOWE I AM NO CACODEMON I AM A MAN AS MORTAL AS THE NEXT BUT I AM IN TYME TO COM I CAN TELLE YOW MANYE THYNGS . . . I CAN TELLE HOW THE PESTILENCE COMES AND HOW IT CAN. BE SOMTYMES AVOIDED BUT NONE OF THYS IF LUCAS BEE NOT SPARED. I HAVE ALL THE CALLES OF YOUNG MEN AT BRASENOSE SOE I SHALL SEE THAT WICH IS UNTREW. TELLE ME HYS TREW CALLE*

*KEN.*

Such a jumble of thoughts. I was doing a very poor job of saving Lukas from the Crown. Thoughts of press yards, witches being burned, executions, crowded my mind at one moment, only to be replaced by a dull, empty feeling of helplessness. I wanted to help Lukas but was at a loss to know how it could be done. All I could think to do was to ask his real name over and over.

### Saturday 20 April

Jaguar Drivers Day. There was a shadow over the proceedings but the smell of the racing oil and the sound of the cars on the circuit put my thoughts into a better frame. I was away with friends and the Tudors were long gone. Lukas was dead, whatever was done or undone. I looked at the sky and imagined being out in space looking down at the earth; a lonely planet covered in swirling seas of clouds. There was comfort in imagining an impersonal universe where nothing you did ever mattered.

I concentrated hard on the events surrounding me. A yellow Aston Martin won the Challenge race, the food we ate was appalling, but we didn't complain. These are the humdrum events against which life, by and large, is set. These days are all we own.

On 21 April Lukas's friend 'John' made his move;

»» I HAVE SPOKEN WYTH THE SHERYFF WHO SAITH YOUE ASKE HYM
TO COM UPON SHORT WARNING BUTT HE SHALL COM TO MORROW
THOU HAVE GEVEN TO ASKE OF THE NAYME OF LUCAS WAYNMANN
FOR REASONES I KNOWE NOT HYS CALLE BE UNKNOWNE TO
ME I DIDST MAKE HASTE TO ASKE THYS OF HYM BUTT HE SEID
HE COLD NOT SAY UNLESSE YT BE TO YOR EER ALONE HE DID
SEY IF THIS BEE WHAT YT YS TO HELPE MY FRYENDE THEN
I WILL TAKE HASTE AND MAKE FORSE THIS MATTER TO HYM
THE SHERYFF DID TELLE ME THAT YF THOU CANST SHEW THY
SELVEN FOR WHAT THOU BEE THEN THOU MUSTE GYVE THE
MIGHTIE POWER TO HYM AND HE WILSTE PARDON FOR OWRER
FRYEND LUCAS AND HE SHALL BEGG THE KYNG HYM SELVE TO
SPEKE WYTH THOU AND THY KYNG THYS BE A THYNG THAT THE
SHERIFF HEMSELVE HATH NOT HADD PLEESUER OF ««

[I have spoken with the sheriff who says you ask him to come
at short notice but he will come tomorrow. You have asked the
name of Lukas Waynmann. For reasons I do not understand his
name is unknown to me. I hastened to ask him this but he said
he could not tell unless it be to your ear alone. He said if this is
what it is to help my friend then I will hasten to press the matter
to him. The sheriff told me that if you can show yourselves for
what you are then you must give the mighty power to him and
he will request pardon for our friend Lukas and he will beg the
King himself to speak with you and your King. This is a thing that
the sheriff himself has not had the pleasure of.]

I called the file I replied on 'HELP'

*FRYEND OF NO NAME*

*YOUE HAVE SEID LITTLE. I WOLD KNOWE THE CALLE OF LU-
CAS BUT I CAN HELP ONLIE THROUGH MY WORDES I CAN
TELLE OF MANY THYNGS THES WORDES SHALL GIVE POWER
TO THOSE THAT HAVE THEM*

*YOW MUSTE TELLE WHERE BEE THYS COMUTER ? YS YT IN
THY SOLAR ? CAN ALL WHO PASS SEE THYS DEVISE? --------
YOW SHALL TELLE-------*

*KEN.*

*I WILL HAVE WORDES ONE TURN OF MY GLASS BIFORE NIGHT
TOMORROW*

## Monday 22 April

Whatever problems Lukas might be facing we had to continue with our attempts to make sense of the entire business. Frank Davies takes up the story:

'I arrived at Meadow Cottage about 7.00 P.M. My first impression was one of disappointment. There was no heavy or "spooky" atmosphere – just a lived-in feeling which was in no way extraordinary – not at all what I had been expecting during my drive down from Mold.

'Debbie showed me a number of messages which she said had been received via the computer. My interest was drawn to the word construction which was unusual to say the least. Some of the words I could read without difficulty despite the obsolete spelling but other words such as "wights","leems" and "boyste" were quite unknown to me.

'We established a new file, checked that the room was secure and then withdrew into the living room.

'At 8.00 P.M. a noticeable drop in temperature occurred which lasted some two or three minutes. The coldness did not seem to be due to any air movement, though there must have been some as the fire was burning gently in the grate. After a few minutes the room temperature became comfortably normal again.' On returning to the kitchen we observed a new message on the computer. The message was from someone calling themselves John and it told us that the sheriff had put Lukas into prison, apparently for communicating with us. Debbie appeared to be genuinely concerned at this turn of events.'

Frank Davies.

» TIS NOT FIT YOUE KNOWE MY FRYENDS NAYME YF THOU CANST GYVE NO REASONE FOR WY THYS BEE YOR ASKYNG  HOWE CANST YT HELPE HYM PREYE THE SHERYFF DOES ASKE THAT THOU SPEKE TO HYM WYTH TH SELVEN SHEWN TO HYS EYE FOR THY PURPOSE RATHER THROUGH THE COMUTER   WHICHE HE HATH NO SIGHT FOR ELLES  THE COMUTER  MUSTE BEE TAKEN TO LUCAS IN BOWGHTONE  PRYSUN OR NANTWHICHE IF HE BEE THYR NOWE TO SHEW HE SPAKE TROUTHS  BUTT TIS  NOT ETHE TO MOOV THY  DEVICE FOR YT SEEMS TO MISAPERE WHEN ENY HAVE TRYD ONLIE WHEN LUCAS BEE HERE DOES YT SHYNE AS  SOLYD

I CRY THY TELLYNGS TO POST

JOHN «

[It is not right that you ask for my friend's name if you can give no reason for why you are asking. How can it help him? The sheriff does ask that you speak to him  in person rather than through the computer, which he can't see. Otherwise the computer must be taken to Lukas in Boughton prison or Nantwich, if he is there now, to show that he spoke the truth. But it is not easy to move the device as it seems to disappear when any have tried. Only when Lukas is here does it appear solid. I beg a quick reply so I may go to him.]

The response hedged around the obvious problems. I wanted to talk to the sheriff, and I left the following message:

MY GOODLY FREEND

THOU MUSTE LISTEN WELL THE DEVICE CANNOT BE MOOVED. I CANNOT TELLE FOR WY BUT I LOVE LUCAS AND WOLD NOT LIE TO THEE. YF MY SHERIFF CANNOT SEE THE COMUTER THEN BRING LUCAS TO THYS PLAS SOE THAT YT SHYNE AS SOLYD THEN THES THYNGS BEE SHOWN AS TROUTHS THER IS NOUGHT TO FEAR BUT MUCH TO GAIN YF THEE FOLLOW MYNE BIDDYNG. LUCAS IS A GOODLY MAN WHO DOST ROT IN THY PITT BUT GOOD FREENDS HYS CRIME YS UNKIND TO US WE CAN PASS THE DAYS IN IDLE TALK WITHOUT FEAR LUCAS CAME UPON A GREAT MYSTERY AS INNOCENT AS A CHILD. WE ARE OF TYME TO COM MEN AS YOURSELVES WE ARE NOT

*DEMONS OR GODS BUT MEN WHO ALSO SEE THYS MYSTERY
AND ARE CONFUS THYS IS NOT A THYNG TO PUT A GOODLY
MAN IN THY PITT FOR BRYNG HYM HERE AND BE NOT AFFREY
FOR THES WORDES ARN AL THAT I HAVE THE STRENGTH TO
BRYNG BEFORE YOW. ONLIE GOOD CAN COM TO ALL WHO
SPEKE IN WAYS OF RIGHTEOUSNESS TO MYNESELVE*

*KEN*

My reply was sharpened by my desire to help. We saw some hope if he could persuade the sheriff to bring Lukas back. Offer a man power and you offer him corruption – any damn thing to get Lukas back. I felt it most keenly as it was I who had caused these events by firstly allowing then encouraging the communication.

### 23 April, late evening.

Something had worked. The next message was from Lukas, he was back.

›› MYNE GOODLY FREEND I KNOWE NAT WER ME CANS START TO EXPOWNE MYNE MISHAPPS BUT TIS SOE GOODLY ME CAN HATH YOWR TREWE WORDES OONSE MOORE WHICH ME DIDST THYNK NAT TO HEERE AGAYNE  ME DIDST TTHENK MYCHE O WOT YOW HATH SAYD AND ABOUTE MYNE LEEMS BOYSTE FOR T'BE THIS VERYE MATEER THAT ME DOST FEER FOR MYNE LYF THY SHERYF HAN FORFEND MYNESELVE LEEVE OF MYNE HOUSE AN ME ART ACHO-KEND BY THY SHERYFS MEN WHO BE TO EECHE ENTREE BUT HEM DIDST APREVED THAT ME BE LEFf TO MYNE OWENSELVE  THER BE NE OUGHT YOW CAN DOE FOR WY  I HATH TAKEN SEAL TO YOWR TYME AND HATH REKENYNG METHINKS YOW ARN A HISTORIE BOKE THAT HATH ITS FRONTE AN .BAK SKYN JOYNANT WE ARN EECHE A SYDE IN IT THY BOYSTE COMES NAT FROM MYNE NOR YOWR TYME BUT FROM GOD AS BE A GYE FOR SOM PURPOSS WE BE OF GOD BOKE ME CAN SEE WOT IS TO COME AND WOT HATH BEENE YOW CAN SEE OONLY WOT HATH BEENE WEN THY BOYSTE DIDST COME THER WERT A  VERSE ON'T THAT SAYD ME WER NAT TO AXE OF YOWR UNKYND KNOWYNGS FOR THY LEEMS BOYSTE WILT BE NAMO TWAS O MYNE TUNGE MYNE FELAWE PETER COLD NAT HATH HAD MYNE SCRIT SOE TREWE AS BE THIS WER METHYNKS

THEROF YOW KNOWETH NAT PREY ME HATH TOLDE MYNE SHERYF THAT THOGH ME HATH SEENE YOW MANYE TYMES AND BE IT YOWR SWETE MAYDE YHOW CAN NAT AFFRONT SPEEKE WYTH HEM NOT MYNESELVE ALS AN NE HADDE EVER BUT ME SAYD YOW BE O STRANGE DEVYSYNG AN APARAUNCE THAT T'WOLD AGASTE ANY WIGHT TO SEE HENNE ME THENK   AN TOLDE HEM T'BE NON TO WYSE NAYTHERLESS ME STILLE TO APAYE HYS AXYNGS BEFORN MYNE SEVENTHE DAYS ME KNOWES NAT WHOM DIDST BIWREYE AND ACCUSE MYNESELVE BUT YOW   ME KNOWE BEEST MYNE TREWE FREENDS WHO ME DOST HATH  MUCHE  LOVE FOR

YOW WOLD NAT DOE THIS TO ME AN RYP ATTWAYN THY AFFYR WE HATH METHYNKS YOW KNOWE OF WOT MYNE FORTUNE BE BUT I KNOWETH NAT WOT YOW CAN DOE MYNE GOODLY FREEND THYR MUSTE BE SOME WAYS OF YOWR TIME THAT CAN HELPE ME FROM MYNE FATE FOR ME SEE OONLY THY INIQUITEE AN COLD TEMPER OF MYNE CROWNE ABOUTE MYNE NEKKE YOW ART NOWE MYNE TREWE FREENDS WHO BE MYNE HOPE YEA   ME BE ALDE BUT ME HAN SOE MANYE AXYNGS OF YOWRSELVE FOR MYNE BOKE WHICHE BE ALLE ME WANT BEFORE ME DOST GO TO MYNE GOD

PREY YOW LOOSE MYNE SCRIT FOR ME FEER MYNE SHERYF MAYE AXE FOR WOT ME HATH SAYD UNTO YOW

· YOWR HELPELISS FREEND LUKAS «

[My good friend, I know not where I can start to describe my misfortunes but it is so good that I can have your true words once more which I did not think to hear again. I have thought much of what you said and about the box of lights for it is this very matter I fear for my life. The sheriff has forbidden me to leave my house and I am guarded by the sheriff's men who are at each door but he agreed that I should be left to myself. There is nothing you can do because I have communicated with your time and here are the consequences. I think we are a history book that has its front and back pages joined together. We are each a side of it. The 'boyste' comes not from my time nor your time but from God, as it were a guide for some purpose. We are in God's book. I can see what is to come and what has been. You can see only what has been. When your box came there was a verse on it that said I was not to ask about your unnatural knowledge for the box of lights will be no more. It was in my language. My fellow Peter could not have done the writing so true as this was. I think you do not know about this? I have told the sheriff that though I have seen you and your sweet maid many times one cannot speak with them, nor can I either, and never had. But I said you are of strange description and appearance that it would frighten any man to see you, I told him it is not too wise. Nonetheless, I am still to satisfy his demands before the seventh day. I know not who betrayed me and accused me, but I know you are my true friends for whom I have much love. You would not do this to me and betray the trust we have. I think you know what my fortune is but I know not what you can do, my goodly friend. There must be some way of your time that can help me from my fate for I see only the iniquity and cold temper of the law around my neck. You are now my true friends who are my only hope.

Yes, I am old but I have so many questions to ask you for my book which is all I want before I go to my God. Pray you destroy my writing for fear the sheriff may ask what I have said to you.

Your helpless friend, Lukas]

Deb was alone when this message came. She felt upset and replied immediately with a few words of comfort, saying she'd fetch me as soon as possible.

Perhaps it was the feeling of responsibility I carried but this communication moved me almost to tears. These were the words of a man in fear for his life, a man brave enough to face the future and speak out. He would be a condemned man if we did nothing. More than anything, this message had a heart, a soul of its own. It was no scholarly joke.

# 15

**27 April**

Lukas was writing throughout the day and into the evening. He didn't seem to be holding up too well, the messages were becoming funereal. It was desperately exhausting for us too. One message said, in part:

›› MYNE FELAWE PETER . . . ALAS WOT CAN BE DOON I CAN NAT EVEN TAKE YOWR HOND BIFORNE MYNE SENTENSE O WANHOPE ME WOLD HEER YOWR WORDES BIFORNE ME BIDDS MYNE GOODLY PETER FARWEL LONGE LYV OWRN OXENFORDE

LUKAS

YOW SAYD YOWR TYME BE 1985 METHOUGHT YOW WERE ALS FROM 2109 LYK YOWR FREEND WHOM DIDST BRINGE LEEMS BOYSTE PREY ‹‹

[My fellow Peter . . . alas, what can be done? I cannot even take your hand before sentence of death. I must have your words before I bid farewell to good Peter. Long live our Oxford!

Lukas

You said your time is 1985. I thought you were also from 2109 like your friend who brought the box of lights, pray?]

I looked at this little communication with open mouth. Deb and I had to sit down and look at it over and over. He thought that we were from the year 2109? We'd written our date to him in February, I reminded myself, but had repeated it only a few days ago. Was he suddenly aware that he was getting not one but two futures? Who had he been talking to on the 'leems'? What was the verse he referred to in his message of 23 April?

We read it all again. Even if Lukas was sometimes hard to follow, this section was impossible to misinterpret. From 2109? No, he must be hallucinating.

But we pursued the impossible. Had he too received the poem, the first message, which had been forgotten in recent months? A similar one? We watched or rather waited for a message from '2109'. We weren't confident of a response, as there had been no hint of another communicant until now.

'Apart from the [first] poem!' said Deb.

'Well, that rubbish isn't much of a future,' I muttered. But I was intensely curious about it and, carried away by this feeling and suspending all critical faculties, I stepped into the confusion with a message of my own to '2109'. In case it was all part of the hoax I used what I thought was a very tongue-in-cheek greeting. It was a bit Star Trek:

*CALLING 2109-*

I wrote to Lukas at the same time, telling him about the poem and offering to type in what it said if he wanted. I wanted to see the poem he had received. And in my thoughts these preposterous communications were flung out into a vortex and the one spun upward and the other, more sure in its travel, spiralled into the past.

An hour later, each was answered according to its nature. On the screen from an unsigned source to Lukas:

›› FREEND

YOW MUSTE REKEN FOR THY VERS FOR THYS SHALT BE YOWR HELPE

I CAN SEYN NAMO‹‹

From this same source we too received a few words. Words that were far more unsettling than anything received so far because however we looked at it we decided we were being used.

›› KEN, DEB, PETER

WE ARE SORRY THAT WE CAN GIVE YOU ONLY TWO CHOISES

1) THAT YOU EITHER HAVE YOUR PREDICAMENT EXPLAINED IN SUCH A NON-RHYME WAY THAT YOU MAY HAVE INSTANT UNDERSTANDING BUT CAUSE WHAT SHOULD NOT BE TO HAPPEN, OR

2) TRY TO UNDERSTAND THAT YOU THREE HAVE A PURPOSE THAT SHALL IN YOUR LIFE TIME CHANGES THE FACE OF HISTORY, WE, 2109, MUST NOT AFFECT YOUR THOUGHTS DIRECTLY BUT GIVE YOU SOME SORT OF GUIDANCE THAT WILL ALLOW ROOM FOR YOUR OWN DESTINY. ALL WE CAN SAY IS THAT WE ARE ALL PART OF THE SAME GOD, WHAT EVER HE, IT (?), IS.

'It is a hoax. They can't even spell!!'

'But,' Deb kept saying, 'we aren't doing anything different from what we do for Lukas. I just sit quiet, or we go out for an hour.'

I didn't listen, I was incensed by just reading the nonsense in front of me. It had echoes of the poem in that it began with an address to three people (Nic Bagguley's name had been replaced by Peter's). Talk of Purpose and History; talk of Destiny! Bullshit! If my universe was anything it was random, meaningless, absurd even. I could not square with Destiny. Not any old destiny at that . . . 'a purpose that shall in your lifetime change the face of history'. Rubbish! Who was writing this? Not me. I was ashamed, so ashamed, even making a note of it. Immediately I wanted to hide this material, wipe it out, but without denying Lukas it was impossible. He mentioned them. I didn't need this sort of complication. Lukas in trouble and some wacko from nowhere going on about 'destiny'. I was getting a rotten headache just thinking about it. I had to get back to thinking about Lukas. We wanted the verse from him. The waiting went on and Lukas came up with it at about 10.00 P.M.

›› MYNE GOODLY FREEND HERE BE MYNE VERS BUT METHYNKS YOW WILT HATH NON SENSE OF THYS THYNG  ME DIDST WRYTE IT FOR RECORDE FONGE WOT BE TREWELY YOWRS THO BE IT YOWR CONFUCIOUN AFORNE T AFFECTS TO A WIGHT WHO MAYE BE O ADVERSITEE

MANYE A YERE AGON SYTH YOWR DAYE

THYS KNACK BE NAY SUGGESCIOUN BUT REVERS TO THAT AN
AUNGEL OF GOODLY VENTURE FOR THEYM  WHO SHAYNE

WHOSOE BE YOWR COLOR  AXYNGS OF GRETE KNOWYNGS AFROME
THY THREE THAT DOST SHYNE WHO ALBEIT YOW HATH EYD WILT
CAUSE THY LEEMS BOYSTE TO BE NAMO SIKE CONVEY BE YOWR
CORRECCIOUN

FOR A LYTE DEETH BE NIGH FOR A WITE O A FREENDE WHOTH
CHOYS THY FOULE MAN MUSTE SEE THY KYNG TO TELLE HEM
OF THEY CAT THAT DIDST AFRIGHT A MOUSE AND REMEDY YOWR
SYK ECH O YOW MEN THAT HATH REKENYNG ME BEEST OUT O
DOUTE THAT YOWR PREYRS SHALT BE ABYDED

SO THAT YOW MAYE TEACHE WYSDOME UNTO THY FOOLYSCH

BEWAREY MYNE FREEND FOR YOWR LUST  THY PUDDYNG MAYE
BURNE

ME WILT WRYTE AMOROWE ME BEEST NON TO WELL

LUKAS YOWR LOVYNG FREEND ‹‹

[My goodly friend, here is my verse but I think you will make no sense of this thing. I wrote it for a record.

'Take what is truly yours it be to your confusion before it affects a man who may be in trouble [or danger?].

'Many a year ago since your day. This knack [device?] is not incitement to evil but the opposite of that, an angel of good fortune for those who shine, whatever be your motive [?] questions about important matters from the three that shine who, nonetheless [?], you have seen, will cause the box of lights to be no more. Such conduct shall be[?] your correction.

'For an easy [?] death is near for a friend of a [wise man?] who chooses[?]. The foul man must see the King to tell him of the cat that frightened a mouse and cure your sickness.

'Each of you men that have understanding I do not doubt that your prayers shall be answered so that you may teach wisdom unto the foolish. Be wary, my friend, of your lust. The pudding may burn.'

I will write tomorrow. I am none too well.

Lukas, your loving friend]

It was a collection of fragments rather than a poem. The other communicant said that it was all the help he could give Lukas, that there was a clue in there that would save his life. I rang Peter and asked if we could come and see him that night. It was now after 11.00 P.M. but Peter agreed. Time was short. It couldn't wait.

Such a long night but Peter focused on the part of the 'verse' which dealt with telling the King about the cat as he saw that it had similarities with part of the poem we had received. What would the King like to know? Who could tell him? The sheriff was the man. And the only reason he'd get near to the King? Treason.

Peter remembered Bishop Mann who had been the subject of a comment in one of the early messages, the one about the dean Lukas knew who was 'likend to a fissh'. Peter had been reading about this character recently. Mann, it turned out, had once been in touch with a condemned enemy of Henry VIII's new church, the 'Maid of Kent'.

It was after 2.00 A.M. by the time this was sorted through. We hoped it would be information Lukas could trade. If Fowlshurst was a King's man he could report it to the King, it might bring reward. A dirty business. All we had was a little knowledge. As another revolutionary once said: 'Knowledge itself is power.' We'd try it.

As we cruised home in the car Debbie started laughing. I had a furrowed brow and was still thinking about Lukas. She spluttered and said: 'We're trying to save a man from the 16th century . . . Can I tell my friends? You know, when they ask what I've been doing. "Oh just trying to save a lovely chap who's been dead for four centuries from this thicko sheriff. We were up all night finding out how to do it too!" What'll they say?'

I couldn't see the funny side but I was glad someone could. Deb saw that I wasn't laughing and began to stare out of the side window in politeness. I could tell that she was holding back from being hysterical.

I left a message to Lukas when we got in:

*MYNE GOODLY FREEND*

*PETER HATH LOOKED LONG AND WYTH CARE AT YOWR VERS IT BEE NAT ETHE TO REKEN AFT MANYE HOURS WE DID THINK THAT THER BE A CHAUNCE FOR YOW TO GOE BACK TO YOWR FARME. THYS BEEST THY VERS OR A PART THEROF WICH WE THINK MIGHT HELPE THEE*

*'THY FOWLE MAN MUST SEE THY KYNG AND TELLE HEM OF THY CAT THAT DIDST AFRIGHT A MOUSE AND REMEDY YOWR SYK'*

*DO YOW THINK THAT THY SHERYFF WOLD GOE TO LONDON TO SEE THY KYNG IF HE DID HAVE SOM REKENYNG OF HOW HENRY MANN SOE LATELY RISEN IN IMPORTANCE DID ONCE WRYTE TO DOCTOR BOCKYNG CONFESSOR TO THY MAID OF KENT ELISABETH BARTON AND SAY     (1533)*

*'I BEG YOW TO ACCEPT ME AS YOWR SPIRITUAL SON AN ASK THE PRAYERS OF ELISABETH BARTON TO OBTAIN GRACE TO MORTIFY MYNESELF AND LYVE ONLIE FOR CHRIST'*

*THYS DOST HAVE THY TAINT OF ATTAINDER FOR BARTON AND BOCKYNG DID APASS AT THYBURN 1534*

*THUS MIGHT FOULESHURST AFRIGHT MANN AN GATHER MORE OF THE GRATITUDE OF MYNE CROWNE. 2109 SAYETH THAT THE VERS HOLD YOWR SALVATCION WE HATH SEEN NO OTHER PART THAT DOST HELPE BUT WE ARN NAT GODS AN TIS AL THAT WE CANST FYNDE YOW MAY HATH A BETTER REK-ENYNG THAN OWR WRETCHED SELVES.*

*KEN AND DEB.*

### 28 April

Lukas replied towards noon. Deb was in, leaving the computer for about an hour each time. The first attempts did not produce results. It was never a certain business. We had expected him to write by the time we got up in the morning. No matter: as long as the bloke was still with us!

›› MYNE FREENDS

ME DIDST KNOWE NAT OF THYS THYNG OF MANN NOR DO I KNOWE OF A WIGH THAT DOST FOR THYS BE WYTHSEYES HYS TROUTHE TO THY KYNG IF IT VERRAY BE THY CROWNE HE WILT BE A TRAITOUR BUT HE CAN NAT BE ATHRALD B'CAUSE IT WOLD HATH THY CROWNE ASHAYMD SOE WILT BE HEM TOLDE TO WRYE AWAYE FOR A TERME TIL IT BE YNOUGH WHYLE FOR NON TO HATH RECORDE OF SUCHE AN UNFAVOURABLE ACT FOR BE THYS REASONE METHYNKS FOULEHUSTS WOLD GLADEN TO KNOWE AN BE SURE TO STINTEN MYNE ROUTE THYS WOLD SEME A FYTTYNG ANSWER IT MAYE ALS BE MYNE RESCOUS ME SHALT MAKES HASTE AN TELLEN HEM

LUKAS ‹‹

[My friends,

I did not know of this thing about Mann nor do I know anyone that does, because of this, deny his loyalty to the King. If it is true, according to the law he will be a traitor but he cannot be arrested because it would cause the authorities embarrassment, so he will be told to go away for a while till it is enough time for none to have memory of such an unfavourable act. For by this reason Fowlshurst would rejoice to know and be sure to stop [reduce?] my punishment [?]. This would seem a fitting answer. It may also be my rescue.

I shall make haste to tell him.

Lukas]

### 29 April, 5.00 P.M.

The silence was unnerving, I had written on two occasions trying to prompt Lukas. Finally I had to get away from the cottage. It was too much. I needed some air. I drove just a few hundred yards west to the edge of the village. There I could see the sky, the clouds, the huge open countryside. If a damp south-west wind blows, then sometimes pearl-grey clouds at one altitude pass over the hills below slower-moving and darker clouds. It looks like the approach of an army: the dense ranks preceded by skirmish line, the clouds appearing to spread out towards and beyond you across the meadows.

It might have been raining in Hope or World's End. While we were listening for the end of Lukas's own world. I was watching clouds while he fought for his life. That such thoughts invaded this scene and that such events could be the result of our own tinkering, our own interference: I wished I could melt into those clouds.

The Jaguar bled streams of steamy exhaust into the darkness. The engine choked momentarily, cleared itself and the car flew down the lanes. I couldn't just wait around for news, I had to shake myself free from melancholy. As ever it was to Dave's in Penarlag that those four wheels took me. An hour later the phone in the hallway rang:

'Ken . . .' was all I said.

'Come back now, Ken, ok?'

'Why? Is it a sad message? Deb?'

'I think so . . . Better come back anyway.'

I rolled the car slowly out of the estate. I must have appeared rude leaving with hardly a goodbye but Dave and Sian knew something of the situation.

It was so dark. I was not hurrying but I was feeling extremely anxious. The wheels rolled faster as I made into the straight between Hawarden Castle and the airfield. The lanes beyond Broughton seemed endless.

The car bumped up across the pavement and onto the back garden, stopping with a wheeze from the airpump. Without a clear thought in my head I brushed past Debbie, who was standing in the lobby. The kitchen was lit only by the light coming in from the corridor.

›› MYNE TREWE FREEND KEN

NAY ME HATH NAT SPAKE WYTH MYNE SHERYF AMOROWE ME DOST
GO TO MYNE KYNGS COURTETIS THIR ME CANS NAT SCAPENE THY
PYT THEM WYL LYSTEN NAT TO MYNE TALE O MANN TIS OONLY
THY SHERYF THAT CANS HELPE BUT HYM CANS DOE NOUGHT
TO SAVE MYNESELVE WEN ME BE WYTH MYNE COURTE I BE SO
WEYKE THAT ME DOST FYND IT NONETHE TO THYNKS RIGHTLY
ME HEER KATHRYNE AWEEPYNG FOR MYNE WRETCHED SELVE IT
DOST CAUSE ME PEYNE SO SHE BE OONLY FOURE AN TENN TO
YONGE TO BE BY HYR SELVE WYTHOUT A MAN TO GYE HER ME
HOPES SHE BE NAT TAKEN AS A WITCHE LYK MYNESELVE FOR
THYS BE THY WAYE OF MYNE UNFAVOURABLE CROWNE ME HAN
THENKS MANYE DAYES WITH OUT MYNE SLEPES WOT COLDST
SAVE MYNE SOULE IN MYNE AN YOWR VERSE BUT ME CANS NAT
RECORDE ALLE O YOWR VERSE FOR ME BE ALOWED NON FLAT-
SKYN TO WRYTES UN ME BEGGS THAT YOW THYNKS WYTH ME FOR
ME AM SHORTE O TYME IF YOW DOST NAT SPEKE WYTH MYNE
SELVE AGEYNE THEN ME ALS BEGG THAT YOW WRITES MYNE
BOKE AN PLASE IT IT THYS

TO ALLE MEN O MYNE GOODLY FREENDS KEN PETER DEBBY

THOS ME BE APASSED IN YOWR TIME ME WOLD LYK YOW TO
THYNKS THAT MYNE FREENDS BE NAT FURIES NOR DEVYLLS BUT
GRETE MEN AND GOODLY WOMEN WHO WRYTE THYS BOKE NAT FOR
THEYMSELVEN BUT FOR YOWR REKENYNG THO MANYE FOOLYSH
MEN WILT TURNE AWAYE AFROME THYS NONKNOWEN THYNG THEM
THAT CANS BE LEARNED WILT FYND GRETE KNOWLEDGE IF YOW
DO NAT TURNE AWAYE TO WOT BEEST TREWE MYNE MEN O MYNE
TYME CANS NAT LEARN FOR WE ARN THREWN IN THY PYT FOR
REASONYNG THY NONEXPOWND THUS WE LEARN OONLY WOT THY
CROWNE WILT TECHE AN NAT WOT THIR IS TO BE LEARND ME
BE A MAN O GODS BOKE BUT ME WILT DYE FORN THYS VERRY
RESON I PREY YOW HATH REKONYNG FOR LYF BE TO SHORTE TO
GO TO GOD WYTH NON THYNG LERNT FARWEL MYNE TREWE AN
GOODLY FREENDS MAYE YOWR GOD HATH YOW ANDLONGE LYVE
MYNE OXENFORDE

LUKAS ‹‹

[My true friend Ken,

No, I haven't spoken with the sheriff. Tomorrow I go before the court. I can't escape being condemned. They won't listen to my story of Bishop Mann. Only the sheriff could help but he is powerless when I am in the court, I am so weak that I don't find it easy to think clearly. I can hear Katherine crying for me. It pains me so. She is only fourteen, too young to be by herself without a man to guide her. I hope that she isn't taken as a witch like me but this would be typical of this prejudiced government. I have thought for days and nights without sleep on what there was in these verses of ours that could save me but I cannot remember all of your verse as I am not allowed any writing materials. I beg you to think with me for time is running out. If you can't speak with me again then I must also beg you to write my book and place this in it:

To all people concerning good friends Ken, Peter and Debbie. Although I am long dead in your time I would like you to believe that my friends are not furies nor devils but great men and a good woman who write this book not for themselves but for your better understanding. Although many foolish people will turn away from this unknown thing those that can learn will find great knowledge, if you do not turn away from what is true. The people of my time cannot learn for we are thrown in prison for thinking and reasoning on what is not explained so we learn only what the Crown will teach and not what there is to be learned. I am a man of God's book but I will die for this very reason. I pray you understand me for life is too short to go to God with nothing learnt.

Farewell, my good honest friends, may your God receive you and long live Oxford.

Lukas]

Oh Lukas! I shouted his name. I implored it to the mute screen. Tears of rage, of unhappiness welled up.

# 16

The following evening Debbie scanned the computer files and found these words:

**» NON PROGREDI EST REGREDI AD MOMENTO.MORI**

**DEUS VOBISCUM LUKAS «**

[Not to go forwards is to go back to the moment of death

God be with you. Lukas]

She called me in. The kitchen was very still and we sat there quietly. These words we took to be his last. Debbie asked me again if we couldn't have done something for him. I got up and walked out into the garden before some dreadful melancholy captured me.

Friends came round. Peter and Val Trinder came down too. Peter brought wine and proposed a toast to Lukas. It was straight from the heart – we all obliged, if self consciously. Conversation then turned slowly but surely to what SPR might make of it.

We wanted proof but the business had come to a head abruptly, some would say 'conveniently', and there was nothing to work on. The Society for Psychical Research would file it under 'no further action'. In a callous way, providing proof for SPR seemed to matter more than Lukas's fate. Later I regretted feeling this way.

**1 May.**

A little secret housework had been undertaken. Fine grains of chalk dust mixed with a few sandy grains from the brickwork lay along the base of the pillar in a little ridge. The pillar was clean. Debbie's eyes focused on a dark patch on the kitchen table. 'Oh, the picture . . . '

The picture of Erasmus had been 'returned'. It lay there fragile and discoloured, charred like the magazine picture before it. Symbolically at least there could be no surer knowledge that Lukas was gone.

How quickly life returns to its shallows, murky, slow moving, tiresome. Shamefully, the state of my overdraft and the unmarked sixth-form essays loose on the back seat of the car began to assume spectral proportions. Lukas's death and my part in it (I didn't feel like sharing responsibility with anyone else) began to recede from my mind.

I turned my attention to the building work and for the rest of that week I forgot the contents of the red file which hitherto had meant so much. Peter was still keen that something should be written up and his constancy and enthusiasm were tremendous but, I reminded myself, he was at a safe distance. There was much Deb and I needed to forget.

The May bank holiday came and went, examination work held the foreground, bricks and mortar the middle ground. I could not see the rest.

To escape school, I walked the playing fields at lunchtime in the spring and summer. Large beech trees line upper Aston Hall Lane. I followed the high wall of the Convent of the Poor Clares, spiked with broken glass, past the magnificent oak adjacent to the tennis courts. If I walked wide of the oak the young 'rebels' smoking under the shadow of the pavilion remained unconcerned at my presence.

Many times I walked through the Penarlag Estate. If I stopped at Wirral View, Sian Lovell made me some lunch.

1st May: The returned picture of Erasmus was 'burnt'

Today, 5 May, she was quite excited, Dave was working at the cottage and had rung her at about 11.00 A.M. because he had discovered chalk marks on the kitchen floor. I listened carefully and thought, 'Poltergeist.' Sian continued, 'He can't read it because it looks like another language.' My heart leapt. I left lunch and scrambled to the phone in the hall.

Tea-time: Peter paced up and down the cottage kitchen, avoiding the extensive chalk marks, and tried to make sense of the last words. He'd understood some of the earlier ones but the last of them were bunched up under the table. Peter was thrilled. The writing was entirely in Latin and was addressed to him. The hand was neat, flowing in the obsolete 'cursive' manner, a work of some care. It was not signed.

The message deciphered as:

›› Petrus

nimium postulas Lucaque mortem obit mortem sibi conscivit di te era ‹‹ [ . . . ]

and with some difficulty translated as:

[Peter

you ask too much

furthermore Lukas went to his death

he brought death upon himself

the gods will [ . . . ]*

* the last word was indistinct

If not part of a joke we guessed that it had to be Lukas's friend from Stockport. It was a strange sight, a small group of us in the kitchen eagerly exchanging opinions on the mechanism and purpose of such an event. Taken at face value the implications for the phenomenon as a whole were important. Clearly Lukas had been able to interpenetrate our world and now, if we were right, so had John.

Naturally the computer was mentioned. It was to be brought back the following evening. I felt my senses sharpen little by little. Even if Lukas had gone, the phenomenon had not; SPR could perhaps catch something of it.

The writing on the floor was inconveniently placed. Everyone had to stretch and tiptoe from the living room to the bathroom to avoid disturbing it and every time they did I imagined them crossing a deep ravine, a crack in space time. But no one ever fell down.

The machine was set up and a new file called up on the screen. In return just one word blinked at us. We had waited all evening for one word.

›› ERADICENT ‹‹

But I realized that this was the word Peter couldn't make out in the chalk 'curse'. It now read, 'Di te eradicent' ('The gods will root you out').

Frustrated by the idiocy of another death threat from the past I took a chance on the future. I asked for information from 2109 about the author of the chalk message and whether to concern myself about it. Nothing more came until 10 May when we received this message:

›› YOUR QUESTIONS WILL BE ANSWERD ‹‹

I wondered aloud, and on the computer: would the communications continue? I offered a brave face about poltergeist activity: '. . . there is nothing outside man which can harm him.' I wanted to know more of Lukas, too. No reply, perhaps it was a dumb question.

11 May: one phrase –

›› NOT ENOUGH POWER ‹‹

Puzzled I wrote back:

EXPLAIN . . . CAN WE HELP?

NAME POWER SOURCE PLEASE KEN.

Another gap, this time almost exactly twenty-four hours.

It was turning out to be a very difficult few days.

**›› GO TO SLEEP ‹‹**

Curious idea. I talked it over with Deb. She agreed and typed in, 'Later today'. We took the nap early that evening. One word arrived . . . what a bloody bore.

**›› ALONE ‹‹**

OK, OK but who? I tapped in 'ME? HER?' An hour or so later the word 'ME' was deleted. It was now the evening of 12 May. Deb took a 'rest' (she didn't want to). I went out.

**›› PETRUS**

**STUDIIS VACAS NOCTES AC DIES QUID HOC SIBI VULT NON ME FALLIT ISTA CAVILLATIO ‹‹**

[Peter

You are devoting nights and days to your investigations. This is what he wishes for himself. That trick of yours does not deceive me.]

Even when translated it was just as obscure as the chalk. message. There was a second part to the communication, separated by a few lines, unsigned and very strange – not only the content but in that the spelling was perfect.

**›› FIRST, WHAT HELP DO YOU REQUIRE?.**

**IF YOU WISH TO KNOW LUKAS WAYNMANS TRUE NAME WE CAN SAY NO MORE THAN THE MAN NAMED PETER HAS IT PAGE 26**

**THE PERSON WHOM YOU REFER TO AS JOHN IS NOT TO BE TRUSTED. ALSO THERE IS NOTHING TO FEAR OUTSIDE MAN, TRUE, BUT YOU ARE NOT FULLY CAPABLE OF KNOWING JUST WHAT MAN REALLY IS, WITHOUT KNOWLEDGE YOU HAVE FEAR WITH FEAR YOU CREATE YOUR OWN NIGHTMARES! ‹‹**

I tried again to get some details.

*2109*

*THERE ARE MANY DISTURBANCES CAN YOU INDICATE THE SOURCE?*

*WE MUST KNOW A LITTLE MORE OF LUCAS. WHICH VILLAGE OR TOWN DID HE COME FROM PRECISELY? DID HE GO TO TRIAL IN CHESTER OR NANTWICH?*

*THANK YOU FOR THE RIDDLES . . . !THEY ARE SO HARD! KING? MOUSE?*

*A LITTLE MORE HELP PLEASE . . . KEN.*

There was no signature to the following message but it seemed very familiar. We put it down to 'John':

›› MY FRYEND

THOU MUST GYVE THY COMUTER AND THY POWER TO MYNSELF OR ELS YE WILT HAV NON OF MY WORDES ABOUT THY FRYEND LUCAS ‹‹

In the week following those puzzling few days Peter received a long letter and collection of notes from Robin Peedell, the shy librarian at Brasenose College. It was a detailed letter, written in a very precise but individual hand. Robin had picked out a Thomas Hawarden from the college records as being a good candidate for Lukas's real identity. It was obviously a confusion. Thomas Hawarden – Hawarden School – Peter lives in Hawarden. Robin's enthusiasm had led him to use word association. He probably thought the events were occurring in Hawarden. He noted another Hawarden in the records, a John Hawarden who became Principal of the College. But we reasoned that a principal of a college does not withdraw to a cold damp village in Cheshire to farm a few pigs and chickens.

Of real interest was the news that Robin had reviewed the list of books Lukas had said he was acquainted with in his student days. They were all contemporary with the 1520s-30s, but one, just one, had proved very hard to track down. That was the book by Mutianus Rufus.

Robin had been thrown by the term 'Rufus'. It was, it turned out, a nickname for Mutianus Giacomo who had had red hair. It was a very obscure reference. Robin's work paralleled the effort Peter was putting in to find references to some of Lukas's words that were not even recorded in the Oxford English Dictionary. This was good work but it required much patience. I was thinking more of SPR.

# 17

**14 May**

Mr John Bucknall rang. He was, he said, the SPR field officer which John Stiles had promised. I took to him instinctively, he sounded young, intelligent and precise. I felt relieved in the way that a patient often finds relief in simply knowing that the doctor will call.

John Bucknall, so I conjectured, with a few questions and a couple of evenings sitting quietly with Debbie in a sealed house, would proclaim us all extremely sane. He might even write a report for the Society describing just how valuable the case was. I even visualized the article, and furthermore I daydreamed of casually handing round copies. Peter was initially more cautious. He considered that even if some intricate hoax had been perpetrated on the inhabitants of Meadow Cottage it was of immense sophistication and therefore of interest. I couldn't agree.

I think that behind my particular daydream was the desire to see it all end tidily and for life to slip back into a more predictable rhythm. But that was also a daydream. Our lives had been altered more than we would admit. These events were part of us now for better or worse. If it was all somebody's joke we had been terribly diminished.

Back in the cottage. 2109's reply to my request was brief:

›› LUKAS W'S FARTHER SERVED ON THE KYNGS ROSE, BRISTOL. A FAVOUR FROM THE KING BROUGHT WEALTH   TELL THE KING ABOUT THE MOUSE! ‹‹

'We're not into the Mary Rose now, are we?' Peter gave me one of those piercing sidelong looks so beloved of old fashioned schoolmasters and I felt fourteen years old for a second. A kind of irritation itched incredibly. No, not the Mary Rose. Please! Our credibility was climbing on to a raft in a fast-flowing river. The mooring rope was worn and taut. I wanted to suppress this little message, instead I made a good deal of the fact that the 'rose' probably meant the Tudor rose, the badge of the dynasty, and that in a port like Bristol there might be many ships or even organizations termed the 'kyng's rose'. I don't think that Peter was convinced. In any event this clue was not pursued. Lukas wasn't his real name, so how could it help? My interest was SPR: any message received in the right circumstances was useful (or fabulous, depending on my mood).

Peter, acting on his own initiative, arranged an 'exploratory' meeting with Mr Bucknall the following night. It seemed appropriate to hold it at Peter's house in Truemans Way. We could move on to the cottage if Mr Bucknall was sufficiently interested. I was glad we were to start in Hawarden: Peter has better furniture.

Up the cracked path toward the door of Peter's house in Hawarden came two amateur Sherlocks. I could only form this thought: amateur Sherlocks. John Bucknall looked like a young business executive dressing down for the occasion in desert boots and cords. The big man, bearded, with mobile features, was Dave Welch. He was older and rather rotund. He exuded the air of a skilled gamekeeper off duty. Both conveyed a properly serious manner, scrupulous and polite, but as they settled into Peter's magnificent leather armchairs I imagined that they had popped in after a day watching a badger sett. It must have been their honest amateur enthusiasm. I was at a loss as to what to make of these gentlemen and the agenda for the evening. My gaze fell on one of Peter's enormous bookcases and I had the desire to read something. I felt both that there was little to say and too much.

Dutifully I had brought the red folder containing the print-outs. I felt intimidated, insecure. 'Oh, Lor!' as Billy Bunter often exclaimed in darker moments. I was bound to become repetitive, over-enthusiastic, inarticulate. True to form I was all these. I spoke interminably, interrupted everyone, pressed on, held back and poured mild confusion over the whole.

Peter kept saying, 'I knew we had to bring it to you people. We need your scepticism. Excellent!' He was enjoying it enormously. I was conscious of being too open, of letting my feelings of confusion show.

John Bucknall asked us for our thoughts on the phenomena. Debbie was the focus of a lot of attention, which she didn't enjoy. She wanted to resist the connection between her presence in the cottage and the frequency of communications, so she was evasive, too ready to deny its relevance: 'I'm in a lot of the time anyway.' I felt undermined when this diffidence was measured against my enthusiasm, confusion and interest. Peter had been worried that he would catch the blame; the lead paragraph in his nightmare read: 'Ex-Oxford man, expert in Shakespeare and Chaucer, fakes messages from the past.' Both Debbie and I wanted Peter to be wearing the mantle of innocence he deserved. This became less likely as Peter delved, in impossible detail, into words such as 'wrethed' or 'charge house'; I wished I could slow him down.

John Bucknall was trying not to chain-smoke. He emphasized that many of these sorts of phenomena are entirely fraudulent or are massive elaborations upon some quite explainable occurrence. Was he here to investigate or to name the guilty persons? I couldn't help feeling that the accused were before him now. He told us that until the phenomenon manifested itself, while we were under lock and key (as it were), he had no option but to treat us as the main suspects. This looked a bit unfair. Why had we spent so long explaining the circumstances to him if he was going to insist on their being irrelevant?

However, it soon became clear that we were in fact convincing him that some of the Society's very limited resources should be spent on this case. Scientific methods would have to be applied; the Society for Psychical Research was formed to keep these investigations on the level which was expected of an organization run by scientists and well-respected because of it.

As we drove off to the cottage I was subdued; I didn't feel that I had put over my ideas successfully. The Jaguar arrived some seconds ahead of John's Fiat and as I waited for the others to pile out of the car I felt very tired. I began to care less than previously about the whole interminable pantomime. The cottage was not yet properly finished: more apologies. There was school in the morning and I wanted to shout, 'That's it, it's all very weird but clear off the lot of you! Thank you for coming but I want some sleep!'

Our amateur Sherlocks left Baker Street and had now arrived at the Baskerville estate. We showed them around the house, illustrated the difficulty of gaining entry through downstairs windows, door, skylights and so on. I showed them the computer and wrote to 2109, 'ANY MORE RIDDLES?!?'

'Aha!' exclaimed Dave with conviction. He was now standing at the top of the stairs. 'Does the loft space connect with others in the row?'

I had to admit that it did. I also had to admit the general lack of security at the cottage. It was still a bit of a bomb site upstairs, but they had to expect this in my current circumstances. They suspected someone could 'quite easily' have performed the whole routine via this route. While we were in the house? While Debbie rested in the living room? They were not deterred. These were the kinds of possibilities they were determined upon. I was too tired to object. I had given away my home to science. So Lukas was to be the creation of some academic housebreaker with a love for a practical joke.

# 18

**15 May**

Poltergeist activity had started again with a vengeance, as Debbie discovered:

'I dropped Ken off at school after spending the night at East Green then drove over to the cottage to feed the cats. It was 9.00 A.M. It was not until I walked up the path to the front door that I sensed something was very wrong. Perhaps it was the cats sitting on the garden wall watching me rather than circling my feet as they usually do which prompted this unease. I turned the key in the lock and pushed the door open. In the living room I came face to face with a six-foot-high pile of furniture. It appeared to me in that instant to have been tossed by the little finger of a giant. Instantly I took a step back and out of the door and slammed it shut. The cats still watched me in silence from the wall. I didn't know quite what to do.

'I walked round to the back with the intention of looking through the window but I felt unable to do this for a time. I dreaded to think what mayhem there might be. When I did look it was clear that the kitchen had gone crazy too. Only now did I start to rationalize. It was burglars or local kids, perhaps. Then I remembered what Ken had written on the computer last night and all the anger and frustration he'd felt. I ran round to the front of the house and in through the door. Trembling I recovered the phone from the hearth, fumbled with the dial, rang Ken's school and left him an urgent message. Then I rang Dave Lovell and got him to come straight down. Eventually I gathered enough of my thoughts to examine the havoc. Everything moveable in the room had moved towards the kitchen and was piled against the door: chairs, bicycle, Dave's tool chest; some of the tiles had even been pulled off the hearth. Up on the roof beam the old copper pan had twisted on its axis and the handle was at an angle of nearly ninety degrees. There was a knock at the door. I opened it slightly and put my head round to see a couple of unfamiliar faces.

PG Activity 15th May 1985

"'Hello, Mr Webster's house? We've come to measure up for the windows."

"'Oh," I said trying to kill time and to think straight. I realized then that I was literally shaking, with my tongue jammed between my back teeth trying to cushion and disguise my chattering jaw. I replied awkwardly. "Oh yes, Lewis Glass, er . . . you couldn't possibly come back tomorrow, could you? I'm a little busy."

"'It's OK, won't take a minute – just show us the windows you want doing and we won't disturb you."

'I couldn't see a way out of it – I couldn't think.

"'Um, you won't be able to get to the windows from inside, well, a couple of them, I'm very busy . . . " I opened the door so that they could see ". . . doing some housework."

'They looked at each other. The slight frowns meant, "She's off 'er 'ead." One of them looked blank-eyed at me for a second before he spoke. "You're fairly busy – we'll come back another time. Perhaps you'll ring and let us know?"'

15th May. Picture showing the other side of the door. For our record, the small copper pan (foreground) was placed by Dave Lovell in foreground - this pan was found bent on it's hook in the other room out of shot, everything else is as found. This pan was later straightened (showing no damage) by the PG

But for the power cables anchoring them to the wall the cooker and kettle would have moved further (just seen behind cooker in previous photo). The cooker was tilted at forty-five degrees, the grill pan hanging out. Many of the items were stacked on or around the kitchen table which had been flipped, the chair and broom included. The rubber plant, all six feet of it, lay across the floor: head to the lobby, pot to the cupboard. It was very careful vandalism. I found one cracked egg, a broken earthenware bowl and the top of the salt cellar in two pieces. That was all, even though almost everything loose in the kitchen had moved and the cupboard itself emptied.

Photo of flipped table blocking way in or out of the kitchen making access difficult

Debbie spoke to Miss C, the next door neighbour at Corner Cottage. She remembered us leaving the cottage after midnight and recalled Debbie arriving at approximately 9.00 A.M. the next day. She had, as is her custom, woken early at around 7.00 A.M. and had certainly heard nothing outside until Debbie turned the key in the door.

Miss C was convinced it must have been a hooligan or thief and I could see her mind close up at the suggestion of a poltergeist. Even a friend of Dave Lovell, who had to get down into the kitchen via the skylight and clamber over the furniture and fittings to get a better shot with a camera, would accept no explanation other than thieves or pranksters. He didn't believe in God, he would not even go into church the day they held the funeral for his teenage son so he was equally sure that it was ignorance to talk of 'poltergeists'. These gentle people. I admired their certainty. It makes the world easier. Someone once said that we aren't looking for the truth just a fiction we can live with. Deb and I were not finding living very easy.

This mess could have been made by ourselves or thieves. Some people would say, let's not invent other reasons that would suit us better. But Debbie and I were not inventing anything at all. We were receiving computer communications, the house was turned upside down, objects were moved, objects were removed, writing appeared on the wall and floor. We could be forgiven for associating all these events, one with another, and walking in that morning and saying, 'Poltergeist!'

Peter came later and brought his son, Richard, and camera. It would take a lot of work to put the house to rights again. I could also guess what John Bucknall and Dave Welch would think. The cynic in me whispered: 'They'll think you laid it on!'

# 19

On 17 May, 2109 offered some more 'advice'. I had put down questions about their names, how many of them were involved, what they did for a good time and so on. I tried again for Lukas's name, that was the main issue. I was hoping for some real help on this and on the poltergeist question.

I didn't get it.

›› KEN, DEB, PETER,

AGAIN, WE GIVE YOU TWO CHOISES, TOGETHER WITH SOME HELP :

WHAT IS OUR NAME?. TOO PERFECT THAT WE MAKE MISTAKES, AS WE MUST HAVE A CHARACTOR. MOVEMENT THAT CASTS NO SHADOWS, THOUGHT WITHOUT CHEMICAL REACTION, LOVE WITHOUT PASSION, HATE WITHOUT ANGER, WARS WITHOUT LIFE LOST. HOW CAN WE HAVE A NAME? WE ARE MANY BUT NO MORE THAN ONE IN THE TIME TO COME. WE HAVE NO RETIREMENT, AH, WHAT AN AGE TO BE IF THE DIGETS WERE REVERSED!.MARRIGE.

1)DO YOU WISH TO KNOW OF LUKAS AND WHAT OF HIM?. CAUSE THE COMPUTER TO HAVE BEEN NEVER IN HIS TIME, THUS HE SHALL FALL TO NO UNATRAL DEATH, HE WOULD HAVE NO KNOWLEDGE OF YOU AND YOUR TIME TO COME, YOU SHALL HAVE NO PROOF!

2)YOU CONTINUE WITH THE COMPUTER AND RISK THE SIGHT OF YOUR DESTINY, AS LUKAS. BUT, AH, BUT SOMETHING WILL BE PROVED.

YOU 3 MUST SIT UNDESTURBED AND TALK AND LISTEN – MOST IMPORTANTLY. THE ANSWER WILL COME TO YOU ALL NOT FROM AN INDIVIDUAL! ‹‹

'How very tiresome,' I said to Debbie, looking over the top of my glasses in a disdainful, almost Victorian, manner. 'At face value they have no physical qualities. A joke has no physical qualities: only its effects are detectable. What do you say, my dearest?'

The effect on us of this splendid confusion was considerable. I was disturbed by it whatever the truth behind it. Peter didn't think much of the spelling. Debbie treated it as a joke. It provoked hours of discussion. I showed it to Dave Lovell and to John Cummins as he was visiting the village. John chuckled boyishly and began throwing out surrealist ideas: it was computers in the future talking by themselves, sixth formers in a future hyper-tech playing games with their machines in the lunch break. Laughing at it was by far the best way.

Peter hoped it wasn't the future if this was what would become of the language. I said it obviously wasn't the future but I became very tangled in the difficulty of separating the existence of these words from what might lie behind them. I was stuck on the horns of a dilemma, for if I denied the existence of these communications then I denied Lukas. I was nowhere near doing the latter. Lukas's last messages had been profound and honest. I reread them and compared them with this rubbish.

I still needed to write a reply.

The 'choises' they offered appeared as inadequate as their language. They first suggested that knowledge of Lukas's true name would undo what had happened. Surely quite impossible, an interference with the 'arrow of time'. Of course, if we were communicating with Lukas's friend then this irreversibility appeared threatened, if not overthrown already. Total confusion.

'Choise' two was to risk 'the sight of our destiny'. This worried me. I had always feared being told that I had three months to live or that I would die by drowning or by fire. The child in me saw all these possibilities. The adult in me did not want to see. It was clear that if 2109 had access to different times then my fate, all our fates, might be there for them to see. But perhaps, our fate was not at issue . . . ? 'Destiny' might refer to some sort of fulfilment of a purpose to our lives. To know that my life – our lives – were important to some scheme; that we were more than dust. I was tempted to believe that this was the meaning of the phrase, but then we all believe in our own importance from time to time.

I struggled with a reply. I resolved to abandon it all, as it was beyond my comprehension and beyond my tolerance. Later that evening, to add drama to tension, as it were, there came the prompt.

**»TIME IS SHORT«**

I looked at my response so far. It was already over dramatic.

*WE HAVE NO WISH TO SEE OUR DESTINY AND SHALL NO MORE ASK OF YOU OH HOW 'JOHN' CRIES FOR THE EMPTY POWER OF THIS MACHINE. HE TOO WILL BE DISAPPOINT-ED. FOR A SHORT TIME I SHALL CONTINUE WITH WORDS TO 'JOHN' BUT THERE IS NOTHING I CAN SAY THAT WILL SATISFY HIM. THE MASSIVE DISTURBANCES ABOUT WHICH NO ONE WILL COMMUNICATE HAVE MADE ME RESOLUTE TO GIVE UP THESE THINGS. LUCAS IS GONE. MY FRIEND IS DEAD I SHALL NOT PURSUE HIM BY THESE MEANS. HE ASKS ONLY THAT A BOOK BE WRITTEN. I SHALL DO THIS. KEN.*

I had tagged something on before:

*IF TIME IS SHORT WE MUST CHOOSE . . . BUT HOW CAN WE AS WE KNOW SO LITTLE OF YOUR PURPOSE. I DARE NOT AP-PROACH THE FUTURE I CAN ASK NO MORE AND MERELY AD-MIT CONFUSION. I DO NOT REALLY UNDERSTAND THE CHOIC-ES SO HOW TO CHOOSE??*

. . . and after:

*MYNE FREEND JOHN THOU SHALT LEARN THOSE TMYNGS THAT YOU SO DESIRE IN FOWR OR FIVE DAYES. BE PREPARED.*

*KEN*

... and looked again. It was hardly an improvement. If these were important decisions I was making they looked raggy and inadequate. I was going to admit defeat; I had done! Even the spelling had slipped. The only purpose I could see that would justify keeping the computer going was to enable SPR to witness a message, poltergeist activity, anything, and to keep Lukas's friend hanging on. That was my final objective. A pretty lowly one compared to destiny perhaps but it had a kind of logic.

John replied within minutes, which in itself was interesting:

**›› NOWE ‹‹**

I laughed. It erupted from deep inside. 'The greedy little bastard,' I said over and over with varying emphases. Almost childishly trying out the sound of my voice in the short echoes of the kitchen. John, too, was being childlike. The illusion he suffered: that we had a power! 'Let me tell you,' I said to the dumb screen. 'Don't think that because we are the future we have gone so far. We're not gods, you creep!'

'Who are you talking to?' Deb's gentle voice floated down from the studio.

My mood was much improved; I strode off around the village leaving Deb alone once more. So much better to be out in the evening air. Saturday night at the Red Lion, the same voices, the same faces glimpsed through an open door. I did not go in. The churchyard was a better, quieter place. I walked its gravel paths from yew to pine, from wall to wall and, slowly now, to the church gate and home.

**›› NOWE ‹‹**

The bastard wasn't giving up. I replied:

*NO . . . A FEAST IS WORTH A FAST. KEN*

It felt good, for all the shabbiness of my last communication to 2109, to have decided in that moment that I would not allow anyone to communicate with them again. It was my prerogative to run away from the problem. Peter, I knew, would have liked it to go on but there was no fascination in it for me, just embarrassment and confusion.

I flicked through a few files, not expecting anything but a few memories, a few regrets. This was dangerous complacency. Nothing was ever simple or predictable with this damnable business. On the file opened on 17 May, below the reminder 'time is short', was a new jumble of letters; it got clearer as it progressed.

» FRENDTHYSBEAFRENDOFLUKAS   YE MAY CALLE THOMAS MY NAM IF THEE FINDE THYS RIGHTLY

I AMM KNOWEN TO ALL MEN OF EVERYE MANNER IN THYS PLAS LUKAS   WHO BE IT A GOODLIE MAN   DIDST TAKES TO ASKS ME   TO TEL THE KYNG OF HENRY MANN   I AM   ALSA TAKEN TO WANDER WHAT BE THYS QUESTION   TO THE KYNG SO THAT I MAYE TELL HIM AS IS ASKED

THOMAS «

I called Debbie down. It wasn't shocking. I can remember that. With the events of recent days in mind this communication was just one more for the collection. It could easily be 'John' trying another tack. I sketched out a few lines as a reply the same night. As an afterthought I tried a guess at who it might be if it wasn't 'John':

*BEE YOW THOMAS FOWLESHURST*

Within twenty minutes, before I had time to get myself ready to go out there was the word:

» YEA «

The sheriff himself, Thomas Fowlshurst. Well, this was a nice surprise – our first man of history. Because of the effort to save Lukas we had dug up what we could in the library on Fowlshurst. He was based in Nantwich and was a beneficiary of the dissolution of the monastery of Combermere very much a King's man.

I asked him what change of heart was this, to put a man to death and then to communicate with the very 'devylls' Lukas loved. Perhaps he too dreamt of power.

# 20

Dave Welch huffed and puffed his way to and fro with a reel-to-reel tape recorder, bags of wires, rolls of sticky tape and other assorted items. John Bucknall detailed the plan for the evening. In the studio they would set up a 'listening post' with a microphone run out of the window across the kitchen roof and through a slightly open skylight into the kitchen itself. They would set it running and wait in the living room. Debbie would wait with them. Peter, Val and myself would spend our time in the lounge at the Red Lion. We got the hard work.

All windows and doors abutting the kitchen would be taped up. If a message was received it would not eliminate us from the enquiry but it would eliminate an intruder and suggest some sort of bugging of the computer or that the computer had been 'seeded' with the information, i.e. the messages had been left hidden in the disk, or in the computer's memory itself, waiting to emerge when prompted by an internal timing device or external trigger.

This all seemed very reasonable but my technical knowledge wasn't up to understanding the detail so I merely repeated the procedure for obtaining a computer from the Maths and Computing Department: choose one to hand, add a disk drive and monitor, put it into squeaky foam covers, sign for it, load into the car. The disks were my own purchases. John asked whether it was possible for a member of the Maths and Computing staff to prime a suitable computer. I said that the choice of computer was mine and so there was a good chance I would not select a suspect machine. Prime them all? I didn't think they'd have the time . . .

This line of enquiry was duff. We alone had the 'motive' and the opportunity to prime the computer or disk drive. SPR were after us. I felt it was useless to put my hand on my heart and swear that I didn't know anything technical about computers. I didn't know anything. I felt as if I were under wrongful arrest.

It was now even more important to show that these events were genuine. I needed to clear my name! Naively, I had let these people come along and expected them to start from my point of view. Peter Trinder, however, remained pleased at the proceedings. He admired the direct, honest methods of SPR. 'We are the prime suspects,' he said. 'They're absolutely right in their approach.' I gave him a puzzled look.

Later that evening there was a disturbance of some sort, a noise from the studio. John and Dave were unwilling to investigate at first hand so Debbie crept upstairs and peered round the door. Looking at her from the corner was a round, furry, stripy creature. 'Koshi!!' She put the cat out and apologized to John and Dave. It had jumped in through the window and knocked over some equipment. Smiles all round.

A greeting to Fowlshurst and 'John' had been left on the screen since 7.00 P.M. By the time SPR concluded their session it was about 9.30 P.M. There had been plenty of time for a message. My frustration when I discovered nothing new was intense. The SPR tape would be analysed but I doubted there'd be anything on there.

Tea and biscuits followed. The atmosphere was most cordial. SPR were not discouraged and promised to return in a couple of weeks time. I stressed the importance of absolute quiet and appropriate behaviour. I believed what I said but it must have sounded like an attempt to restore confidence and I regretted speaking almost as soon as the words were uttered. I wanted it proved. I knew it was real in my own mind, perhaps that was dangerous but since the messages came every few days and in similar circumstances they had to happen when SPR were there, if those circumstances were recreated often enough. John and Dave said they'd come again on 3 June.

Peter kept at the main issue: 'It is in their hands. John has promised to write up all his findings.' It was 'something positive to look forward to'.

'Even if it's us?' I asked.

'Yes,' he :said.

About 10.00 P.M. on Saturday 27 May the sheriff wrote describing how Lukas behaved in court during the trial:

... ›› HE CRYE NOTT FOR MERCYE BUTT DID SAYE THE COMMUTER COULD ONLYE HAVE COMME FROM GOD AND THAT THEYE WERE NOE MORE THAN IRREGULOUS HALFWYTTED BOTCHES WHO BEEITT THEME TO BE SNEKKE UP ‹‹

It seemed that Lukas was suggesting that it was the court that needed hanging.

At that stage I felt tired enough to be indifferent to what Fowlshurst was doing. I fixed in my mind the date of SPR's next visit and was satisfied with that. 'Can I leave this to you and Debbie to carry on while I'm away next week?' Peter readily agreed, promising he would come down after the weekend.

# 21

**28 May**

The tyres rattled over the white lines and the cats-eyes re-flectors as I turned from the M56 toward the M6. A dull sort of day but my mind was on Scotland and my eye on the fuel gauge. Speeding northwards, the wind, the sounds from the stereo: the grey-green of the Cumbrian mountains. Shap summit. Across the border, and down to two lanes, I needed to stop. Ecclefechan was the next township. A sign said 'services' but apart from the house where Carlyle lived and a sad little garage there did not seem to be anything. I growled through onto the bridge across the M74 then I stopped and got out. With a half-full bottle of Perrier in my hand I looked from the bridge at the traffic. Glancing over at the Coupé I noted with satisfaction the grey colour of the exhaust pipes. We were 180 miles from home. It was far enough to feel that it was safe to look back. I raised the Perrier in triumph. No one was looking.

Meadowhead Cottage is reached by a bumpy track between the green forest and the yellow of oilseed rape fields in flower. Magnificent beech avenues presented themselves as I looked across the Deveron valley. The car edged forward. Rod Ember-ton, John Cummins's friend, had already made up the fire in the cottage and smoke rose vertically from the chimney.

More than usually tired, I was glad to ease myself from the car and stretch my legs before settling in front of the fire. The cottage is stone, with a slightly damp but very reassuring smell. I planned to stay until Friday. Rod and I went for a walk along the path which leads to the main house. Rod wanted to know the latest on the 'hoax', so I told him at length, and to his evident amusement, that SPR had so far discovered or confirmed nothing. Greater amusement still when I indicated that they suspected, if not us, then neighbours or even property developers keen to push me off my land. His insensitivity grated on me. I was trying to be straightforward and report on developments as requested but, striding through the meadows and parkland with his nose in the air, Rod took it for entertainment. 'But Ken, where's your proof . . . eh?'

Where indeed?

## 29 May

A few shreds of mist hung around the mid-point of the valley but the beeches were clearly visible on the hill above me. It seemed as though the whole land was exhaling. Its breath tasted sweet. Buchan is blessed with an exceptional quality to its light. Across the Deveron, crows circled a copse, a vehicle moved along a lane a mile away. My thoughts, so disturbed by the strange events at the cottage in the last months, now began to flow more freely. I imagined them taking to the morning air and brushing the leaves off the beeches as they turned northward and east ward then, sensing the sea, fell back to the rich soils of Buchan.

I took stock of myself: I was physically heavier, slower, my wits were duller but my enthusiasm was returning. I chose to read Orwell's Coming Up for Air, it kept me looking to the future. George Bowling went back in search of his past and discovered it wasn't there. I would not but I had a need to find out how I had changed, where I was . . .

I was coming up for air in Turriff between the infinite sky and the endless rolling hills.

Here too ran the road we'd take down to the sea. And sea meets river at Banff; the Deveron slides quietly into the waves. Across the small estuary from the castle mound there is MacDuff, a curiously religious, dour tenor to the place as opposed to anglicized, livelier Banff. Rod said he would like an office in the creeper-encrusted tower adjunct to the grassed castle moat in Banff. I could see him holed up there in a kind of Dickensian fusty gloom, poring over plans for granite-grey fish markets or museums for those who collected fragments off this land. Oh, and he was still muttering, 'Humbug.' 'Naïve realist,' I muttered to myself. 'He belongs in that tower.' Though in deference to him as my host I spoke little more of the affair at the cottage.

### ›› TF SPEAK ‹‹

*Deb: I CANNOT 'TIL MY MAN RETURNS OR 'TIL I HAVE PETERS WORDES : DEBBIE.*

### ›› TF WY THYS BEE HAUE THOU NOE TUNGE PRAYE ‹‹

*Deb: I AM BUT A HUMBLE GIRL WHO MAY CAUSE YOU TO BE UPSET BY MY ILL-SCRITEN WORDES FOR IT IS TREWE TO SAY THAT I HAVE NOE TUNGE, THAT IS, IN WORDES OF YOUR TYME. DEBBIE.*

### ›› TF METHINKS THOU MUSTT SPEAKS MORE OR ME SHALT THINKS YE TO BE A    HALFFWITT

### WERE IS YOUR MAN KEN ANDD THE LERNED MAN PETER PRAYE ‹‹

*Deb: MY MAN IS IN SCOTLAND AND PETER IS IN HAWARDINE METHINKS.*

### ›› TF WHATT DOE THOU KNOWETH OF THE LEEMS HOWW MANYE DAYS SHALT YE BEE ALOON ‹‹

*Deb: I AM NOT ALONE FOR TOO LONG, I HAVE MANY FRIENDS WHO DOE VYSYT ME AND IF   I NEED MY MAN HE SHALL COME QUICKLY. WHY DOE YOU MOVE SO MANY THINGS IN THIS ROOM ?, I CANNOT THINKS WHAT IS TO BE GAINED BY THESE SILLY TRICKS YOU PLAY, IT DOES MAKES MY MAN ANOYOUSE, WE DO NOT MOVE YOUR THINGS ABOUT,   DOE WE?!. TELL ME, HOW DID YOU LEARN TO USE THE LEEMS WITH SOE MUCH HASTE, I THOUGHT ONLY LUKAS KNEW, BUT IF YOU ARE THE SAME MAN I SHALL UNDERSTAND AND NOT TELL MY MAN IF YOU TELL ME WHO YOU REALLY ARE, YOUR*

*NAME AND THE DATE!. DEBBIE.*

» TF YE BEE RIGHTLY SAYD   THOU HATH NOE TUNGE INN ME WORDES MEE BIDDS   GOOD   DAYE «

*Deb: HAVE I SAID SOMETHING WRONG, WHAT HAVE YOU TO HIDE ? I SHALL THINK YOU ARE THE SAME MAN, AS LUKAS AND JOHN, IF YOU PLEASE TO NOT ANSWER !. DEBBIE.*

The light, such starkness even at noon. The swash rumbled up the beach towards the washing lines, the old net lines, quite bare along the sea front. We were at Pennan, a village clutching on to a cliff, which had been one of the locations for the film Local Hero. The car was parked about five yards from the now mildly notorious phone box (from which the film's main character would ring Hacker, his boss, in the USA). The bonnet was up and the distributor cap hung by its plug leads while the publican tried to sell me his Lotus between snatches of sympathy. I rang Jaguar dealers and Debbie from the mildly notorious phone box. Some wag had written above the dialling codes: 'Phone Hacker, Houston 763882' (or some such number). Debbie was also another world away. Or at least in touch with one. She quoted me the latest.

I continued my travels with Rod: Aberdeen, Fraser burgh, Pitmedden Gardens, cafés, endless fields, lanes and hills. In the Forglen estate there were deer and red squirrels. This was not just any port in a storm.

On Friday I left Turriff early. Many hours later, tired and irritable, I sat in traffic near Warrington as the temperature rose steadily inside and outside the car. Welcome back. Debbie turned out to be depressed and unhappy because her landlady had on some pretext attempted to evict her from East Green.

An exchange between Peter and Fowlshurst had taken place over the few days with varying degrees of confusion. One message was received whilst Peter, Val and Debbie sat in the living room discussing the latest turn of events. I wrote in my diary, ' . . . leaves me out of it at least.' This is one short example of that exchange:

149

*SHERRIF WHERE MUST YOU GO TO NOW? WHO LIVES IN THE HOUSE OF LUCAS NOW HE IS NAMORE? PETER*

›› MOSTE NOBLE SIRR

I AM TO CAST AIM AND THINNKS YE KNOWE NOTT OF LUKAS FORR THOU SAYE LUKAS NAMO YE BEE NOTT A MANN OF VANITEE FORR YOURR WORDES ARE WISE MEE TAKES TO THINK MEE AKNOWE YE DELITS TO THE LEEMS IFF THYS BEE NOTT YE UNDERSTONDIN FORR MEE TOO AMM STRANGED BY THYS.

THIRE BEE THYMME EYNOGH TO SPEKES WITH YE ANOTHER DAYE WHENE TYMME BE MY CHOYSINGG TELL THE WOMAN THATT I HAVE NOTT TO CAUSE TO HAVE THREAFUL WOREDS WITH HER NORR WITH THYNSELFFS

LONGG LIFFES THE KING

FOULESHURST T. ‹‹

[Most noble sir

I will take a guess and say that you know nothing of Lukas for you say Lukas is no more. You are not a man of vanity for your words are wise, it occurs to me. I know you have a strong interest in the 'leems' even if you don't understand it. I too am confused by it. There will be opportunity enough to speak with you another day when I have time to spare. Tell the woman that I have no reason to have harsh words with her nor with yourself.

Long live the king.

Fouleshurst T.]

No one was particularly interested in Fowlshurst's unpalatable words, and this message was only half-digested before being passed over. I certainly did not read it with care. Had I done so I could hardly have failed to notice that our good sheriff was no longer as sure as he had been that Lukas was dead.

## 22

On 3 June, a Monday, the SPR were back.

This looked fun, little bits of tape on doors and windows, secretive little traps to catch the 'intruder' out. They'd given up on tape recorders and so forth. The house was quiet and the green screen glowed all alone on the kitchen table. We were in the Red Lion eating and drinking. Debbie commented that this was becoming an expensive habit. John and Dave repeated their suggestion that we were being fooled by someone in the village, by the neighbours possibly.

Peter calmly accepted this suggestion as a serious one and probed for more detail. The crux of it was that somebody had to be doing it and perhaps a boorish character in the village, a property developer, was scheming to frighten me off my property in order to increase his empire. It was my fault for mentioning this Machiavellian rogue at the previous meeting. John and Dave were on the hunt for a motive.

That someone in this time and at this place was the culprit was already beyond question as far as they were concerned. What little comfort I could take from the implication that Debbie and I were innocent victims was dispelled.

'So you don't believe we are doing it?'

'Oh, we haven't eliminated any of you yet.'

Peter was disconcerted and sensing it I came to his defence. Not Peter. I always resisted the spreading of the net to this man.

One hour, two hours. Sometime between two and three hours later the house was opened up. John and Dave went in alone. Standing outside my own cottage while strangers nosed about gave me a strange feeling – a little like indecent assault, I imagined, perhaps inadequately. There was no message.

I checked every file on the disk. Next time we'd try with Debbie and the researchers alone in the cottage, sitting quietly in imitation of the previous two successful occasions. I was very tense, very angry. I was almost prepared to accept this intruder theory if it would allow me to relax. Poor Debbie, she sensed my frustration and she caught it up with her own; the atmosphere was terrible. If there was ever a chance I'd sell my soul it was now – for the evidence that what we were experiencing was not of our doing.

I turned to my work as a way out. There was much to do in school, the examination season was underway. But school bored me. However, there was time, as I walked between the rows of tables in the sports hall, to consider my next move, to dream this and that, about the end of the building work at the cottage, about a new job. Most of all, when the weather was hot and sticky and the fire exit was open at the back of the sports hall I'd dream of just walking out, down the Dell and across the fields beyond. Days passed.

Ching! The sound of a small piece of metal hitting the wall, then silence. We listened to this silence, to the hum of the refrigerator. The kitchen door was ajar, I edged it open. No one there. Silence . . . Ching! A two-inch off-cut of copper pipe rolled along the concrete floor towards the bathroom. Debbie picked it up. It was slightly warm to the touch. A further three pieces arrived, all but one in the kitchen. Never did we see any in flight: after our ears had heard the 'ching' of contact we would see a piece as it came to rest or we'd find it in the corner rocking slightly as it stilled. Nor did the disturbance stop when we had visitors, as Dave Lovell recalled:

Dave Lovell 1985

'Lots of strange things happened at Ken's. One of the oddest events that I witnessed one evening with Sian was in connection with these copper pipe offcuts from my recent plumbing work. On this occasion Ken, Deb and I were standing in the living room by the fire, talking, when I heard Sian's voice from the bathroom. I went in to the kitchen where I saw Sian looking down at the lobby door. It was one of those pipes, the long one of the bunch, which we had previously put outside the back door. Sian had heard something hit the door and wondered what it was. I remember that she was pretty surprised, and shocked even. We were all surprised but not to the same degree because we had many first-hand experiences of this sort of thing. A few days before, one of my tools, a bending spring, got kinked. This was the only time these goings-on stopped my work.'

## 9 June

I did not sit down to write on the computer, I just wanted the machinery to babysit the poltergeist. I hoped it would cut the pipe throwing in some way. Ching! The first one of the evening.

'Try and laugh at it.'

Deb smiled. I smiled, my reflection in the screen smiled.

Ching!

'Smile louder . . . ' We tried.

Deb gave up and sat with her head in her hands ignoring all around her. I read the paper in the kitchen, hoping to catch a piece in flight. Chank! We both looked up. Some thing different. It had landed on the hearth – a 2p piece.

'Thanks. A gold sovereign now? . . . Make it worth our while.'

That kept it quiet for half an hour. I abandoned the paper and considered going for a walk or for a ride in the car. Then I saw three one-pound coins sitting next to the screen on the matt cream surface of the BBC. 'We're rich, Deb, they've brought three pounds.'

'You might be but it's mine, off the mantelpiece.'

After this, matters improved. Fowlshurst wrote late that night in his usual impenetrable manner, this time wittering on about eating too much white meat and being involved in a scuffle in Handbridge.

Sultry June. The examinations wore on. The staff came and went on supervision duty or to prepare for internal examinations. In the sports hall the extractor fans continued to whirr noisily but there were fewer pupils to suffer them, as the last week of the month brings the last of the examinations. I continued to look out across the fields and dream. There was an ambience here: of a night club in the early hours of the morning or a high street at 5.30 P.M. on Saturday. Like the night club, like the shops, the school had exhausted its energy for the moment. Everyone knew it. In four weeks it would be the summer holidays.

Perhaps it may seem odd to mark the passing of twelve days by the hum of extractor fans but the examinations of not just this year but the past six years are stacked haphazardly one on top of the other in my memory and it has all become one moment apart from those fans.

In the 1540s also, one moment seemed to have stretched across those twelve days. Thomas Fowlshurst had left us with a tale of a corrupt baker, John with threats to Peter and Dave Welch. For my part I had promised that Peter should come the next day but there was many a day between the intention and the action.

Yet the messages of 21 June betrayed no signs of impatience and, since it did not matter much at 'their end', it increased our lack of interest in communicating with Fowlshurst and co.

Deb's sleep was disturbed at this time. One dream came back repeatedly to her: she was in a dark, claustrophobic room lit only from above. The light filtered through a heavy, square metal or wooden grille. The air was fetid; she couldn't breathe very easily. To keep up her spirits she was singing or humming a tune . . . always the same tune. I heard her once or twice in her sleep. It was barely audible at times, like a radio broadcast on medium wave moving periodically off station. She was dreaming of a prison. The song was a plainsong, or lament, but I could never catch the words and Debbie could never remember them.

Meanwhile there was another message:

›› FRYEND

THOU WANTS LUCAS NAME ME DIDST HIDE YT WHENE HE DIDST LEEVE YT THOU MAYE HAVE YT YF THOU AWAYES THE RAG WYTH BERD FOR HYM BEE A FRAMPOLDE

Friend ‹‹

[You want Lukas's name. I hid it when he left it. You may have it if you dismiss the sour-tempered fool with the beard [refers to Dave Welch].]

From our slumbers we awoke. Lukas's real name, his 'trewe calle', was known and for sale.

Meantime Fowlshurst wrote to Peter in reply to some questions left on the 9th:

›› YE MOST NOBLE

BETWEENE MEE ANDD YE MEE LERNINGG BEE ABSOLUTLY AB-HOMYNABLE ANDD ITT IS EATHLESS TO ACCOYLE MEE WORDES FORR THY UNDERRSTANDYNG SOO I DOO ASKKE MEE GOODLEY FREND TO WRITES FORR MEE BUTT METHINKS ALSOE YE COM-MUTER MAYE TAKES EVERIE PLEASUR TO MYNN FINNGERS ANDD CAST EVYLL TO YEIR CAUSES BUTT IFF THYS BEE WITH MEE RETHOR THENE I MAYE ABOLYSSHE THE EVYLL SOO THAT HEE MAYE DIE WITHOUTTS CORRUPT SOUL [*] to avoyde innsultts further mee shal however write mee owen name at the finn of the scriptt praye telle whatt dost peter want forr soo manye questiouns tis perfitely fare to answer none with-outts anie reasonnes andd knowyngs as to whatt causes hee i hav tolde richard grovenor of ye worthey feedyng itt bee a surr thingg he dost purchasse ye launde forr a costley summ . . .

thomas ffuleshurst ‹‹

* Interrupted at 'soul'. I inserted date and time in lower case and left lower case on in error. It didn't affect communication, nor was it referred to.

[Between you and me my education is absolutely appalling and it is hard to make myself understood so I ask my friend to write for me but I also think the 'commuter' may take my fingers and work evil on them if I write to you. But if it is not so rather then I may abolish the evil so he may die without a corrupt soul. To avoid further problems I shall write my own name at the end of the message. Please tell me what does Peter want with so many questions, none of which I have to answer unless a good reason is given. I have told Richard Grosvenor of the good land here and it is certain he will pay a good deal to acquire it thomas ffuleshurst]

Down a screen there was another short message from John:

›› fryend

aske not for lucas nayme forr fowelhurst wilt have hym to die he ys kempt alyve soe that thy leems dost stile shyne i knowe for i have heard hym singe there art few that doe singe yn latin yn the prisun telle not of these words to eny eles me shalt be ragged

Friend ‹‹

[Don't ask for Lukas's name as Fowlshurst will have him killed. He is kept alive so that the 'leems' still shines. I know this because I have heard him sing, there are few that sing in Latin in prison. Don't repeat these words to anyone or I shall be in great trouble.]

Lukas was alive. The 'leems' could not work without him. And when Debbie dreamt of prison she dreamt of Lukas looking up through a dungeon grille, but till this moment she had not associated the dream with him. With hindsight the plainsong she mumbled was his lament.

# 23

**25 June**

The whole house brooded silently and darkly. The tape had run to the end in the cassette player. I couldn't think. Deb was suffering too, she walked to the kitchen, plugged in the kettle and looked around her. I suppose we were waiting for the pipe throwing to begin. It had returned last night with a vengeance. All was quiet now apart from the hum of the motor in the fridge. Two sharp cracks and a dreadfully familiar metallic ring split the silence as the metal rolled off into a corner of the kitchen.

The door was open, I could see the metal. I got up and tried to see where it had made contact. It wasn't hard, for the pipe had hit the wall so fiercely that holes had been carved half an inch deep in the plaster near the door jamb.

The rooms recovered their silence. I went back in the living room with a cup of coffee. Deb collected the metal.

Another sound: a scream from the kitchen. Deb was bent over as much from shock as from pain. She clutched at her shoulder, a piece of pipe had hit her. I helped her on to the settee and carefully pushed back her blouse from her shoulder. A blue-black bruise was already beginning to fill an area of redness.

Back where the real battle was taking place it was clear that Fowlshurst was rather more cunning and rather more vain than we had imagined. This revelation did not free Lukas. Discussion of the problem had reached a dead end. It was hardly possible to converse with the sheriff, let alone persuade him in all reasonableness that Lukas should be returned.

At the eastern end of Hawarden school between blocks A and B is a car park. Monica Rowlands-Price crossed it from her parked Cavalier to Deb's Morris from which I was decanting exercise books wrapped less than reverently in Tesco carrier bags. She had been following with interest the events of recent weeks.

She has an educated voice with a tuneful Welsh ring to it and she used it to suggest that I threaten the sheriff directly. Since Fowlshurst was scared of the 'leems' and obtained John's support in leaving messages he might well be open to this kind of bluff.

'Threaten him with the loss of his soul,' she said. It wasn't cricket, I thought. All of us had tried to be honest and 'trewe', but I could see from Monica's expression that I was being pompous and no help at all. Okay, let's do it, let's lie and cheat. I wrote:

*THOU DOST HOPE THAT HEE MAY DIE WITHOUTT CORRUPT SOULE. DOST THOU MEAN LUCAS, AND IS HEE NOT DEAD. FOR WE WERE TOLDE THAT HE HADDE DIED. WE WOULDE RE-JOYCE TO KNOWE THATT LUCAS LIVES, TREWLY THOU LACKS NOT NOBILITEE BUT WE KNOWE IN OUR TYME THAT NOBI-LITEE IS FORGIVING AND HAS UNDERSTANDING. CANST THOU NOT UNDERSTAND THAT LUCAS IS A GOOD MAN AND SHOLDE NOT DYE. WE ARN NAT DEVYLLS BUT WE HAVE POWR. LUCAS MUST NOT DYE BUT MUST BE SET FREE TO RETURNE TO HYS HOUSE AND TO KATHRYN. THEN WILL WE SPEKE WYTH YOW AS FREENDS AS WE DOE WISH FOR WE TOO ARE FEARFUL FOR THYNE SOULE IF LUCAS DOES DYE AT THY HAND.*

No reply at first. Deb wrote a few lines. Fowlshurst began to falter:

›› YE MOSTE NOBLE PETER

FFURST I MUSTE KNOWE WHOME DID TELLE YE OF LUCAS. IF YE SWERE NOTT TO USE YE POWR THE I SHALL BRING LUCAS WITHIN ONE ROUND OF THE GLASS I DOE BEG YE FORGIVENESS BUTT I MENT TO CAUSE NO HARM TO HIMM I SHALL DOE THYS FOR YE BEE ME FREINDS

THOMAS ‹‹

Linking Debbie's persistent dream and the information from John I wrote back. The aim was to reinforce our position independent of any role that John had played.

*'TIS NAT THAT WE NEEDS BE TOLDE ON EVERY OCCASCION WHAT HAS COM TO PASS LUCAS SUFFERS IN THY PIT WE HATH SEEN THE PITIFUL LIGHT THAT COMES THROUGH THE GRILLE OF IRON AN FELT THE LACK OF AIR TO BREATHE YET HE SINGETH IN LATIN*

*YOW HAVE OWR WORD THAT NONE SHALL FEEL OWR POWER SO LONG AS LUCAS RETURN TO HYS HOUSE. THEN OWR FREENDSHIP SHALT HAVE NO BOUNDS WE AWAIT HYS WORDES AN WE KNOW THEM WELL SOE DO NAT TRY TO DECEIVE US PETER AND KEN AND DEBBIE*

While Deb slept and I was upstairs a short rejoinder appeared on the screen:

›› **TIS JOHN THAT DIDST TELLE** ‹‹

I wrote:

*WE HADDE SEENE HYM AFOREHAND JOHN DIDST CONFIRM OUR KNOWINGS WILT THOU DELAY?*

*MAKE HASTE.HARM NAT JOHN*

Fowlshurst soon replied:

›› **YE BERE WYTH MEE ANOTHER HOURE LUCAS B** ‹‹

Yes! Thomas wrote this message at 10.00 P.M. but it was interrupted at the letter 'B' and never continued. Frustrating, but at least we were getting closer. I responded merely by typing:

*I CAN WAIT FOR A FREEND*

Another hour. In rising excitement I abandoned, as so often, my plans for the evening. I climbed into the car. It was close up to the shed so I backed it down the drive a little way and sat there in the dark with only the light from the cassette player and the music of Paul Hardcastle jagging into the gloom. It was a very long hour. I was restless.

It was 11.20 P.M. by the time Deb was driven to the bathroom, as it were; she could not help but glance at the screen. There was a largish paragraph on it but an hour is an hour and she did not disturb the kitchen again for another ten minutes. She then appeared from around the back of Miss C's Anderson shelter garage and gestured frantically to me to come in. It was now 11.30 P.M.

›› MYNE III TREWE FREENDS

WO I DO WEEPE SO THAT ME MAYE BE WYTH MYNE FREENDS AGAYNE ATTE LEEST FOR A SHORTE TYME TIS BARFUL THAT ME SHOLDE NAT HOLDE YOW TO MYNE BREESTE BUT HATH TO ENDYTE SYCHE LOVE FOR MYNE FREENDS ON THY LEEMS ME KNOWETH YOW TA ART LYK MYNE OWEN KYN SYTH YOWR TYME WERT UNCLASPD TO MYNESELVE ER THAT I KNEWE NOE FREENDSHYP SO TREWE THO TBE OVER MANY YEERES O CHAUNGES AN WE ARN CONFUSD SOE . . .

. . . BUT ME NEEDES YOWR WORDES SOE THAT ME MAYE HATH YOWR COMFORT I MUSTE TAKES RESTE SOE THAT ME MAYE SPAKE WYTH YOW AMORROWE ELES ME WILT MAKE NON SENSE OF ME WORDES TO MYNE GOODLEY FREENDS I NEED TYME TO WEEP

LUKAS ‹‹

[My three true friends,

I do weep so; that I am again free to be with my friends again at least for a short time. It is wrong that I cannot hold you close but am only to show such love for my friends on the 'leems'. I know you as well as my own family since your time was opened to me, before that I never knew friendship so true though it is over many years of change and we are so often confused . . . But I need your words so that I may take comfort from them. I must rest so that I may speak with you tomorrow or else I will make no sense of my words to my good friends. I need time to weep.

Lukas]

He was utterly fatigued but he wanted to have our words straight away. To have Lukas's lyrical words again and some sanity returned to the communication was welcome enough but to know his affection for us was undiminished despite his incarceration was overwhelming. With more than usual care I saved the message to disk. The file was then recalled: I wrote briefly to him of our affection for him and our happiness.

In celebration we cruised into Chester to be reassured by the still-beating heart of the city at midnight and to join the queue at a fast food outlet in Boughton – not far, we supposed, from the site of the stinking pit where Lukas was, until a little while ago, imprisoned. Ah, the obscurity of it all!

# 24

**5 July**

In the middle of the sports field a tent with awning stood newly erected. The morning chill had hardly retreated as the pupils arrived, kitted out in a motley of white, near white, or not-at-all-white athletics costumes. The tent was the equipment base and for an easy life I had gravitated there or, in truth, been detailed there, for it was sports day and I was not enthusiastic. The air of machismo and a kind of naïve 'jolly hockey sticks' enthusiasm mixed rather sourly with the massed indifference emanating from a significant section of the school population. Frank Davies came by, and he too was looking for an oasis. There was a breeze and the tent sighed and sagged at its bidding. We discussed the events of recent months. It was a good time to reflect. School had wasted itself of purpose: exams finished, fifth and upper-sixth years gone, some kids on holiday or just sloping away for a day here, a day there. Most of us teachers aching for summer.

'Do you know what time of year it is for Lukas?'

'No, Ken, I don't,' he said.

A tannoy burst into life. 'Will the competitors . . . race' . . .

'We asked him.' I picked out a scrap of paper from my wallet. 'He wrote: "This daye which be yere o myn lorde in reigne o king henry viii thy . . ."'

'. . . report to Mr Jones at the start'

'". . . eigthe monthe 1546"'

'He's about a month ahead then?'

'I'd say he's about 430 years behind!'

'The winner of the under-14 girls' shot was . . .'

A pause. Frank looked up at the clouds and the showers disappearing beyond Drury. 'Did you ask him about the weather?'

'No, not yet.'

'What are the SPR doing, the psychobillies?'

'Annoying me, not so much Peter, me though . . . John Bucknall came down to try and get a result but the machine went out of EDWORD. He said it was probably just a power surge. Apart from that failure something strange happened to the file on Wednesday last, it's happened before. There were only five items on the index, and then after a "ghostbust" a whole lot more appeared, all empty.'

'Did Lukas do it, do you think? SPR will think it's the "hoaxer".'

'How can you ask him? I can't explain so much as a car to him without getting utterly bogged down. How can I explain word processor file names?' I paused for a second, wondering why I must defend Lukas but then did so. 'No, not Lukas.'

'Then – ' began Frank, and I knew it was coming ' - how does he make the words? He doesn't type them.'

How many times this question had been put and how many times an explanation had evaded us.

'We thought he typed them for a long time,' (I was rehearsing an old discussion) 'but it never squared with the quiet in the kitchen. It is always so quiet.'

Frank, remembering his own visit, agreed.

'And no matter how often the message is interrupted by someone coming into the kitchen Lukas never mentions it. Nor is he seen. If he were "here" it would mean that an interruption would be quite an inconvenience but if "there" in 1546, an interruption to the process between "here" and "there" caused by our presence need not be noticed by him as he would not necessarily know about it. Could he be in both places? What does "place" mean? It's so messy trying to say what might be happening.'

'Would it be easier to assume some sort of mechanism controlled or influenced by a third party?' asked Frank.

'That's why SPR say it has to be a hoax.'

'What about our numerical friends?' chipped in Frank before I could become depressed about the psychobillies.

He meant 2109. Frank called them 'our numerical friends'. Some friends! Even worse; to think that they might be behind all the messages.

'Lukas saw an image of a screen, his "leems". This image, the box of lights, brought him our questions, our conversations. He answered them through the "leems", creating letters and then words. He's confused by it too. That's it really . . . Oh, and Lukas says the "leems" appear brighter or duller depending upon who is close by. Lukas's friend from Stockport wrote once that psychobilly Dave – he called him the "rag with furre on chin" – made the "leems" fade. This friend also wrote to the effect that the "leems" cannot be moved because it "misappears" and, most curious of all, that it cannot be seen by everyone!'

'But could 2109 be inventing it?'

'Sir.' A small, round face peered at me. 'Have you got a tape? Miss wants one.'

I reached for a tape in the box. 'Last one, Jane, tell her from me. OK?'

I was suddenly irritated. I think it was just knowing that there were too many questions. I closed the discussion by repeating my best guess. 'Sorry, Frank, I don't know about 2109 and to get back to your original question I suppose he "thinks" up the words or the letters.'

It was embarrassing to say it once, never mind repeat it. As I spoke, the fuller version flitted across my mind: 'Lukas Wainman (1546) thinks up words which appear on my BBC computer across 400 years.'

Frank was very gentle, very forgiving and didn't come back to this conversation, despite his obvious curiosity.

'Look,' I said quickly, 'have you got a new job yet? It's pretty late on now.' He shook his head slowly.

Frank eventually moved off towards the long-jump pit and I was alone with the sagging and sighing tent. I fetched other scraps of paper out of the wallet, flimsy print-outs. With the smell of hot dogs and onions and the sounds of the track and transistors bringing out the worst in me I was glad of a chance to look again at the latest messages from Lukas. For the past week Lukas had been worrying over a number of things. He had traced Katherine to a tavern where she was hanging around with some 'grosse beggars' and others of 'outlandische faschions'. He did not know how he could persuade her to come back. More ominously, a man called Grosvenor had been visiting him. I read from the print-out:

**»PREYE WY DOST THY GROVENOR [*] PLAUGE MYNESELVE FOR OWR LAUNDE «**

*Probably Richard Grosvenor, second son of Richard Grosvenor of Eton (1509 - 1542)

My reply:

*FOWLSHURST DID SAYE THAT SINCE YOU WERE IN THE PITT YOW WOULD HAVE NO USE FOR THE LAND AND THAT GROVENOR WOULD PAY A GOOD SUM FOR IT.*

I later proposed that Lukas show Grosvenor the door. I dared not tell him that the land on which my cottage stood was sold out of the Grosvenor estate in 1919 and had therefore fallen into it at sometime.

The round face appeared again at the tent. 'The tapes, sir, we've finished it all now.'

Despite Lukas's problems he was becoming bolder. On 7 July Debbie asked about Grosvenor and included the line:

*WE DO NAT LYK TO SEE SUCH TROUBLES FOR OUR FREEND*

To which he replied that afternoon:

›› MYNE FREEND METHYNKS YOW WILL SEE MYNSELVE SOONE. ‹‹

He seemed to have misinterpreted Debbie somehow.

Debbie was very quiet when I got home from school. She complained of tiredness and said she had slept a little and 'dreamt' of Lukas again, once more in the kitchen. I read over the short exchange of the morning.

I was not curious about the dream or the message, although Debbie wanted to talk about it. It was insensitive of me but I couldn't fix the house with words and dreams. I was impatient and dismissed the communication from my mind. I went about some work upstairs, tidying or moving tools and pieces of wood. It wasn't until 9.00 P.M. that I felt I should leave the cottage for an hour and maybe give Lukas an opportunity to write, since there had been nothing further. Deb didn't want me to go. Could she come? It was boring being alone, she said. Lukas would write anyway, she said . . . and so on, through a dozen entreaties. Unmoved I repeated the reason for her being there: it improved the chances of contact. I didn't want to risk missing out on a message. Deb was unhappy.

'You didn't even read the last one. It's not a game. I get scared sometimes.'

'And I suppose I don't? Do we just forget about it?' I was tired, angry even, at having to remind myself of the old, old questions. Debbie stayed in. I went out. And sure enough, Lukas wrote to us again:

›› MYNEFREEND

METHYNKS YOWR MAYDE BE SOMWOT A GIGJESTIR BUT SHE
MUSTE HAN REKONYNG FOR THYS SAD THYNG ALS TIS CERTS
THAT SHE DOST SEE MYNESELVE APERE AN YET SHE DOO CLAW
MYNESELVEN WYTH UNQUITTED LIP I SEYE TO YOW MAYDE SPEKE
FOR I WILL NAT CAUSE YOWRSELVE HARME   ME AM NAT A MAN
O MALICH NOR WOLD I GALLOWE YOW MYNE SWETE BUT IF YOW
DIDST AFFRONT ME WYTH YOWR WORDES THEN YOW BIDDS MYNE
FANCIE AN ALLOWE MYNESELVE TO HOLDE YOWR HANDE SO AS
TO SEE IF I CAN HATH TOOCHE WYTH A CREETURE O YOWR TYME
FOR THYS WOL PROPERGATE ENTRCOMUNYOUN GRETELYE   BE
OWTODOWTE THAT I WALDE DO NOUGHT THAT YOW SHOULDENAT
WYSH THYS BE WY ME DOTH APROUCHE WYTH MOSTE CAUCIOUN
AGAYNE LET MYNE FELAWES EXPOWNE THYS GOODLEY THYNG
THAT BE OWRN HONOUR

LOVE LUKAS [*] ‹‹

[My friend

I think your maid is something of jester but she must understand
this important thing: it is certain that she saw me appear and yet
she insults me by not opening her mouth. I tell you, maid, speak
to me, I won't harm you, I am not malicious or dangerous. If you
speak with me and perhaps take to me I will be allowed to take
your hand so that I can see if I can touch a person of your time.
This would help us communicate better yet I will do nothing that
you would not wish. This is why I must go very cautiously and ask
you, my fellow  for advice.

Love Lukas*]

* Lukas used the relatively modern expression 'Love Lukas'. Probably taken from Debbie, who always
signed her messages 'Love Debbie'.

168

'See!' Debbie scowled.

'What? See what? Lukas must be mistaken, dreaming.'

'Just listen for once!'

So I listened to my beautiful girlfriend tell of her 'dream' of talking with Lukas and even so I did not understand.

## 8 July

Quite out of the blue there appeared on the concrete of the kitchen floor two chalk outlines, shields. They were about ten inches deep and seven inches across. They meant nothing to us. It wasn't a big shock to see them, all that kind of reaction had been drained out of us long ago. Curiosity remained. Deb wrote asking Lukas about them as he had made no mention of them himself in his last message an hour or two before the chalk marks were seen for the first time.

She asked about them again on the 10th. If they were from Lukas they were a further pointer to suggest his 'presence' in our time. Debbie remained concerned: 'I don't feel safe if he can come here like that.'

Peter couldn't place the designs on the shields[They were eventually discovered to be early versions of the coats of arms of Balliol College, Oxford, and All Souls College, Oxford, respectively]  but began enquiries. Since Lukas had returned there had  been a correspondence between Peter and Lukas on the subject of language and religion and lately a diversion into high speed travel. Peter described his ability to use a 'cart tygre' to reach Oxford in three hours and also had a go at describing aircraft: 'carts . . . like bridds and thise can flie around the whole world.'

Lukas was appalled at these ideas.

›› MYNE BROTHIR PETER

YOW TALK O THYNGS FOR WHICHE ME NILL HATH REKONYNG TBE
SURE THAT IF A WIGHT WER TO TAKES SUCHE HASTE IN JOURNEYS
THEN WOLDE HE NAT HATH HIS BLODE TOOZED AFROM HIS ERES.
SUCHE THYNGS ME NE ATTAYNE.I TOLDE MYNE HORS O THYS
AND IT DIDST THYNKS ME O LUNES AN REPUGN MYNE CHAIRE
TO HIS BAK FOR FERE THAT ME MAYE IMPOSE THYS FEAT UPON
HIS POORE SELVE. YOW AXE OF MYNE GOD. MEN O MYNE TYME
HATH MANIC THOUGHTS. MOSTLYE THAT LERNYNG BE FROM THY
DEVYLL. METHYNKS NOUGHT COLDE BE MOSTE CONTRARIOUS.A
LERNED MAN CANST MAKE GOODLYE URS O HIS SUFFEIENCIES
AN BOUNDS.LOVE AN HONOURE.FOR HE CANST UNBOLT ALLE
MANNER O THOUGHT BY FEWE GOODLYE WORDES WE ARN HEER
FOR COMUNYIOUN THYS BE AL US TREWELY HATH.PREYE NAT.

LUKAS ‹‹

[You talk of things which I will never understand. If a man were to
go as quickly as you say would not blood ooze from his ears . . . ? I
told my horse of this and it thought me mad. It threw off its sad-
dle for fear I might force this feat upon it. You ask of my God. Men
of my time have many thoughts, mostly contrary to each other.
A learned man can make good use of His gifts and constraints.
Love and honour for a man can set loose all kinds of ideas with a
few wise words. We are here to communicate. This is all we really
have, don't you agree?]

A few days later Lukas wrote to say that he had been forced
to do a deal with Grosvenor, who would now take over his house
and land in 'non less than tweye [two] monthes'. Lukas thought
it was probably for the best as it was possible that Fowlshurst
would return when he had recovered from the shock and realized that his soul was still intact.

# 25

From 12–21 July the messages flowed easily. The format was very stable. A message would be typed in either by myself or by Debbie. The room was then left for between half an hour and an hour, sometimes longer. I would go out for a walk or a drive or just sit in the car outside the house. Music might be playing on the tape recorder upstairs or Debbie might doodle on a sketch pad or have a bath. It was important for her to be relaxed. This view was based on accumulated experience. The computer was on all the time during the 'ghostbust'.

The issues, the problems at both ends, were clear enough. Yet this was the pattern that had settled into place by July, and was aimed quite deliberately at providing as many opportunities for Lukas to write as possible, while at the same time giving maximum time for the rest of our lives.

The task did not end there. We had bought a computer some time previously but could not afford a printer, so during the school holidays when there was no access to a printer we had to copy messages out by hand.

And there was Peter. He was so enthusiastic about the words that I got into the bad habit of delivering messages for his comments almost every day. It was no longer necessary for Peter to translate as the meaning was pretty obvious, but Peter was someone to talk to who really knew what we were facing. In a way he was facing it too.

We were all becoming more skilled at imitating Lukas's language in our replies but it was clumsy at best and we knew Lukas was having to struggle with it. Peter would often compose his own messages to Lukas which I would take to the cottage and type in.

With the burdens of a full-time job, altering the house and writing out by hand the latest message, it is not hard to understand why Deb and I would seldom follow up what Lukas wrote to any great extent. The list of historical items alone which we needed to check and discuss grew longer and longer. Big questions were given ten minutes, really important ones an hour. Only Peter was doing any serious work on the messages as he probed every single word, assessing its accuracy and writing copious notes on every thing he found in the Oxford English Dictionary.

Lukas rarely came through now on files other than the one we were using, which was a relief as it meant less searching around. He'd write below the message left to him, sometimes without leaving any space between our message and his. Equally there were times when the message was a long way down in the file and a lot of empty pages were created. It was now no inconvenience as we had learnt that typing 'Command B' shot the cursor straight to the base of the file. It was about time we read the computer manual. If a message was seen during this 'fast scroll' we'd just shuffle the pages back using the cursor keys. I was now in the habit of dating the messages. I sometimes noted the times, especially after a day when a number of different messages came up.

During this period John Bucknall and Dave Welch visited the cottage to talk over the possibilities of achieving a result now that Lukas was back and might be persuaded to co-operate. Peter wrote to Lukas asking that he write when next these 'learned' gentlemen, 'our friends', called.

Lukas looked at this very differently.

›› MYNE GOODLYE FOOL.

WOT BEEST THISE WIGHTS YOW SPAKE THAT DOE VYSYT. PREYE NIS THEYM LERNED FELAWES AFROM OWRN FAIRE OXENFORDE. WY BE THEI COM TO EYEN MYNE LEEMS. O WOT PURPOSE DOST THIS MEN UNDERGOE. ME NOLDE HATH OFFENDYND TO MYNE-

SELVES THAT BUT YOW TELLE MOORE ABOUTE THEYM.PREYE SEYE THIR QUALITEE AN AVERREY THIR REESOUNS.FOR IT MATTER MYCHE MYNE FREENDE.BEE ADVISD ME COLDST NAT CHARGE OWRN FREENDSCHYP NOR DISTASTE MYNE CONDICIOUN ATTE THYS TYME FORN MANYE FERES UPON MYNESELVE.ME REPEALE FOULESHURST SEYNE A WIGHT DIDST CAUSE THY BOYSTE TO MISAPERE WAN NY. WALD O BEE THYS SAYM MAN PREYE.BEEST THEI SAYME WEAR AS YOWRSELVEN.YOW WAL NAT CAUSE MYNE-SELVE TO BE CLOTHED WYTH MYNE PATCH COATE.AN WILFULLY BE-JAYPE MYNESELVE AN URS MYNE POORE SELVE LYK SOM NAK.METHYNKETH NAT.SOE BE IT ME WILT SUBSCRIBE TO YOWR WYSHES.AND MUSE ATTE THIR AXYNGS WYTH HOPE THAT YOW TELLE OONLY MENO REKONYNG WHOE DOTH NAT UNDOO MYNE LEEMS AN FREENDS.

VALE LUKAS. «

[My good fool,

What do these persons, these visitors you speak of want? Aren't they scholars from our beloved Oxford? Why do they come to see the 'leems'? What cause do these men serve by doing so? To avoid offending me you should tell me more about them. Give their background and check their reasons for being here. It is very important. Take good heed to me . . . I remember that Fowlshurst said that a person caused the 'leems' to disappear when close to it. Is one of these men the same person . . . ? You will not ruin me nor will you use me like a toy or plaything. I don't think you will so I will go along with your wish and consider their questions with the hope that you tell only men of wisdom who will not destroy my 'leems' and friends.

Lukas]

Peter explained at great length that these were 'goodly men'. He gave their names and thanked Lukas for his promised co-operation. Lukas wrote once more, emphasizing that we must 'pace slowly wyth thys man jon',

## 21 July

Lukas was becoming very suspicious. Perhaps never fully recovered from the possibility of the 'leems' being 'undone' by John Bucknall ... or others ... he began to wonder why Debbie sat in front of the computer and wrote for Peter.

The question of why a particular person affected the screen was put to him. He couldn't offer much on this.

» I HATH NOUGHT POWRE WHOME CANST BE NERE WEN THY LEEMS DOST SHYNE AX ME WY YOWR MAYDE BE PRESENTE AN ME HATH NO ANSWER WE BATHE ARE BEEF WYTTED OR CONFUS BY ANOTHIRE EYTHRE METHYNKS. «

[I have no power over who causes the 'leems' to shine when near it. Ask me why your maid is here and I have no answer. Either we are ignorant of these things or confused by another 'ether'.]

The message concluded with an interesting, and unexpected aside about 'Jon Kabot':

» 'DOST THEE KNOWE O JON KABOT FOR WY HE WERT CLOTHE IN MYNE WEN PLAS AND DIDST TAKES GOODLY CRAFT WYN MYN KYN ON MYNE SHYPPS.

LUKAS «

[Do you know of John Cabot, for he was living in my home area and took good ships with some of my kinfolk on them?

Lukas]

Bristol, from where Cabot sailed, was my target for a flying visit to celebrate the end of the school year. Bristol had been mentioned in the cottage and thus he might have 'heard' the name, but this tie-in with a famous explorer caused some renewal of the scepticism to which, I am glad to say, we all fell prey at regular intervals. I'd rather Lukas were no one and knew no one now remotely important to history.

Peter wrote to Lukas saying that holidays were upon us and that John Bucknall would be visiting soon. Lukas thought our dispersal, Peter to France, me to Bristol and Debbie later on to Oxford, was at the insistence of enemies of the 'leems'. He was especially concerned at Peter's 'exile' to France, taking it to mean that he would never come back. Peter had meant only to reassure Lukas but had been roundly misunderstood. Following on the doubts Lukas was having over the visit of SPR and the reluctance of Debbie to concede that she had indeed spoken to him it was an unfortunate coincidence of problems. The main effect was to waste time getting his confidence back when more interesting questions could have been put.

But during this process of soothing Lukas something rather special cropped up:

›› DOST A WIGHT OF YOWR STATES CAUSE ANNOYANCE TO YSELVE. METHYNKS IF THY CROWNE DOST FONGE AN DISPENSE MYNE QUAYNT NAK FOR THEYM SILFS URE THEN TWOLDE BECOME THIR POWNCETT BOX.WOT GRETE POWRE THAT TWOLD DERADYNATE THY WHOLE O HYSTORIE BEEST SURE MYNE FREEND OR METHYNKS UNSURE PARDIE.TIS MOORE CERTAYNE IN MYNE TYME THAT THER BE LITEL FEWE THAT NILL FERE MYNE LEEMS BUT TIS NAT SOE IN YOWR WORLDE PREYE.TIS PRIMER THAT THAN YOWR CROWNE DOST NAT TAKES OWRN BOYSTE AN YOW DOE LEEVE YOWR BROTHIR LUKAS ‹‹

[Does one of your peers seek to cause you harm? I think if your Government takes over control of the device for their own ends then it will become their plaything. A great power would destabilize the whole of History, it is sure or rather unsure, forgive me. I am sure that in my time there are few who would not fear the 'leems' but it is not so in your world. It is essential that your Government does not take our 'leems' and you do not leave your brother Lukas . . . ]

The 'leems' was not our computer, if he was right, but something rather more. Who had told him that the 'leems' must be protected and that the 'power' could be accessible to our time? These were our questions. We took for granted that he was mistaken in the substance of what he said.

But we did not pursue the questions with him. The reason for this was that the message came close to the holiday period; it contained difficult words ('deradynate', 'powncett') and our attention was on soothing Lukas, reassuring him about the immediate future: in particular that holidays in France were not a sign of exile in the year 1985, and that we would all have 'many a word for our felawe' before he must leave. Eventually he calmed down and I took 'carte tyger' and left for Bristol.

Bristol. Through the spanned gorge at Clifton runs the Avon and past these cliffs the sailing barges of the 16th century may have carried members of Lukas's family. I wished I could see them now and hear the creak of the ropes and the cry of the gulls following the ships down to the Bristol Channel.

I'd found the tower, the Cabot tower, on a hill in the city. It prompted many thoughts. A kind of irony that Lukas's family looked towards a new world with Cabot, as this tower commemorates those voyages, and yet Lukas himself could see an even stranger world from a village above the marshes of another west-coast port.

Up among the shading trees and mown grass a woman was feeding cake to a grey squirrel. I photographed it. The heat and the noise drifted upwards from the city. The woman left and the squirrel bounced off into a bush, but I carried something of their passing world in the camera. This moment, like every other, was unique – worlds, universes distinct from all others. But there is movement, seamless change. Nothing abides. Yet if Lukas was who he said he was it would mean that this infinity of moments is never lost. Time is curiously an 'ever-present'. Somehow the squirrel eating the cake crumbs was always there – but always changing, the moment unfolding into others. There is the paradox. In the hard material world Lukas is a ghost, a joke, or a delusion. 'That,' I said aloud, 'is what everyone is bound to say.'

But it did not stop me entering the mezzanine of the Bristol museum library and finding on the wall a map by Joris Hoefnagle, its title: 'Brightstowe' the place-name, the rare version which Lukas used. It was good to see. I withdrew Lukas's description of his journey through Bristol from the manilla folder I was carrying, swung the camera out of the way and traced his progress with my finger across the glass protecting the map. There was something missing, the left turn at the cross at the centre of town. It was necessary to complete the journey but was not included in the description. I don't think it mattered, it was an obvious change of direction.

I wandered off to a cafe and to George's Bookshop and bought one or two small volumes on Cabot and a reproduction map of Somerset. I felt like an adventurer just being there. Nothing I saw and nothing I bought was unobtainable in a dozen other cities, but I had chosen to go to Bristol and I learned much, mostly about myself.

Next evening, back at the cottage, I gave Lukas a potted version of the life of Cabot, from his Venetian background to his successful voyage of 1497, and then to his ill-starred voyage of 1498. I also told him that some Portuguese sailors found a Milanese sword and Venetian rings among the possessions of a Newfoundland tribe in 1501.

Lukas was very grateful, it seemed to me, for this information – as though his family was connected with the success or failure of the voyage. Perhaps as shipwrights they had been blamed for the failure of Cabot's last journey.

I asked Deb if she had written much to Lukas. She said she had not, other than to chide him for ignoring her greeting. She had, she said, 'seen' him once more. She then showed me a message from him that she was supposed to keep from me. Most of it was a love poem but before that was written:

›› DEB.MYNE SWETEST O ALLE CREETURES.

PREYE BE NAT WYTH SYCH SORROWE FOR IT DOST FULWHELME MYNE SELVES WYTH TERE.FOR WOE ME CRYE YOW NAT SEYN I HATH NAT WYSH TO SPEKE WYTH YOW MAYDE.FRO THY FYRST TYME ME HENT YOWR SYGHT ME WERT ACHOYKED BY MYNE OWEN BREETHE FOR THO YOWR FACIOUN BEEST UNKYNDE NEEDS MOTE THAT ME WERT ALLE WYTH MALANCOLIE.ME THENKE TWOLDE BE QUHITE WYSE AN ACORDYNG IF ME NATS TO THYNKS O SUCHE CONVERSACIOUN WYTH THEE SELVE AN SHOWE IGNORANCE TO MYNE LOVE.KEN BE A GOODLY MAN WHOME ME DOST ALS LOVE . . .

DOE NAT SHOWE THYS TO KEN AN SEYN NAMO ON THYS MATIRE

MYNE FOOLYSH LOVE TO YOW MAYDE LUKAS. ‹‹

[Deb, sweetest of all creatures,

... Please do not be so upset for it overwhelms me with sorrow that you think I do not wish to speak with you. From the first time I saw you I was choked by my own breath for although your fashion is unknown I must say I was full of melancholy. I think it would be quite wise not to think of such conversation with you and ignore my feelings of love. Ken is a good man who I also love . . . Do not show this to Ken and say no more on this matter.

My foolish love to you, maid,

Lukas]

This is Deb's account of her encounter with Lukas:

'As Ken was away I thought I might wait in to see if a message came. I lay quietly on the couch, it was 4.30 P.M. but I drifted half asleep . . .

'I caught Lukas singing to himself in the "barrels room" and I walked in quietly. Amusingly, Lukas was head-first inside one of the bigger barrels, which was lying down on its side, and all I could see was his feet. I could easily have imagined Lukas to be fixing the underside of a Cortina, one minute he would lie still in some sort of concentration and the next his feet would begin to waggle as he continued to sing again.

'"Lukas, pray, why are you lying inside a barrel?" I asked mockingly.

'Lukas's body jerked and he pulled himself out, emerging with knife in hand and cap on head. He was just about intact, though a little ruffled with surprise. "Maid, you brings yowr troublesome self always when Lukas be-est up-sa-down."

'He did not answer my question about the barrel but stood and stared at me for a second or two as though he had misheard me. As was so natural to Lukas, he then turned on his heel and swiftly walked into the kitchen with an unspoken "follow me" demanding attention in the swirling air behind him.

'Lukas seemed a little awkward this day and he struggled to make sense of what I was saying, perhaps he was just in one of his "not so patient" moods. In Clint Eastwood fashion he put his feet up on the table, as he always did when he was about to make a statement. I think he did it to look in control, it always worked impressively.

'"Maid, yow stay with Lukas all day."

'I thought it was an odd thing to say and reminded him that the choice being mine I would gladly stay all day but the "leems power" governed my stay.

'"Nay, maid, yow will stay with goodly Lukas, tis yowr will, an' not that of the leems."

'Interestingly enough, several hours passed by and I was still with Lukas. He had kept me occupied with rolling candles, which he had made from soft fat of some kind, they were fairly thin. Things seemed to get less serious as we both worked at the table and talked. I wasn't doing so badly with the candles, I thought, but I applied too much confidence to my hand and a candle broke in two. I tried quietly to stick it back together but the damn thing wouldn't hold properly, apart from the fact that the grass, which was its wick, had also crumbled. Lukas, without raising so much as an eyelid, spoke. "*Maid*, yow wall nat to breikss a candle of Lukas, *pray*."

'Uh-oh, I thought as I stiffened, he's not going to have one of his unpredictable fits over a little candle, is he? I felt my face redden. Lukas looked, while his hands continued to work, at my guilty hand then slowly his eyes met mine. Immediately he grabbed the cap from his head and flung it straight at me. For a second I thought that he was going to get violent but instead he picked up the two pieces of candle from the table and held them both at eye level, laughing. "Whhat, maid, with all quest-i-uns, does breikss candles? - Yower man I am tuh pity!"

'Lukas playing chauvinist again. I was provoked enough to retaliate. I picked up the cap and was about to throw it back at him when I caught sight of some herbs which were lodged in a small pocket inside his cap. This was my best attack: "And what man, p-r-a-h-y, keeps his brains in a pocket as small as this?" I sang out, pointing to the herbs. This was getting childish and was perhaps low-level humour but, for a change, Lukas actually could relate to this mischief. We were both laughing now.

"'Pray return Lukas's cap so that his wits may be restored an yow will nat make fool of my goodly self!" Lukas joked as he went to grab the cap back from me. But as he moved I took a step back away from him – he wasn't going to be let off that easily!

"'Nay, methinks to prefer yow with no wits, Lukas!" I said, taking another teasing step back.

"'Then, alas, 'tis tuh-be, witless Lukas be my name, forsaken by this pretty maid that stands before me."

'Lukas fixed me still with his sad look and took the cap from my hand and placed it on my head. I hoped, stupidly, that it wasn't infested with fleas but did not insult him by removing it from my head. Again Lukas looked at me with some serious-ness.

"'Maid, now tell me, now that yow have taken all Lukas's wits, what thoughts in mine cap do I have of Debbie?"

'I wasn't sure whether we were still playing a game, or for that matter how I would reply to keep up continuity in the atmosphere. I pretended I didn't understand and tried to break the seriousness by taking on a modelling pose – tilting the cap and saying in an American accent. "Guess the cap suits me, honey."

'Lukas smiled gently but obviously did not catch the intended humour. He left the room for a moment then came back in again with a small book in his hand. He handed it to me and continued to work with the candles, saying that it was the only book from his teacher that he had not sold. I flicked through the pages but it was in Latin and there were no illustrations. On the cover was engraved a staff with two snakes entwining it. The book looked as though it could have been handwritten rather than printed, but it was so uniform that I decided against this. I felt that Lukas was waiting for a reaction.

'"Lukas, Latin be not in my language."

'"Yey, me know," he replied as he stood up from the table and took the book back from me. " 'Tis a special book to Lukas – I wished you to hold it, nothing more."

'Oh well, I thought, another conversation bites the dust, but Lukas continued on a different tack: "Maid, will you carry these candles for goodly Lukas?"

'He took two bunches of candles from the table, one for himself and one he pushed towards me, saying that this would be a good opportunity to show me where he slept at night. He moved awkwardly to what he called the stairs, though these were really a ladder, which didn't look particularly safe by any means. I tried making excuses but he was not listening and had already climbed up the ladder, taking my bunch of candles from me so that I could climb with both hands free. Near the top he gave me his hand and pulled me up from the ladder and on to my feet; for his size, Lukas was deceptively strong.

Through a door and into his bedroom. I was almost crouching, the roof was so low. The whole room was panelled, including the roof and the door, unlike the combination of stone and oak down stairs. Again the room was quite sparse. A low cupboard one side of the bed with candle holders on and a folded spare blanket on top, a wooden bench seat under the window and, by the door, a chest covered with various items of clothing, including the cloak that I had seen Lukas wear on a previous occasion when he had been outside – I thought it had looked good on him.

'Lukas boasted that he had a new mattress and new blankets on his bed. He sat down, again a little awkwardly, and told me to sit down next to him. I felt very uncomfortable, almost claustrophobic, and instead of sitting down I looked around, spied my bunch of candles on the floor and picked them up. There was no hay on the wooden floor and I remembered that Lukas had said that hay took the heat away in bedrooms. I wondered if he was referring to the heat rising from the kitchen but thought better than to mention it, convection was not an easy topic of conversation. Again Lukas told me to sit down next to him. His seriousness and his strength of voice worried me to the point of nervousness.

"'No, really, I have to go now, Ken will worry. What shall I do with these candles?"

'Lukas grabbed my elbow and pulled me down to sit next to him. I was noticeably shaking now, but not too numb to feel the prickly mattress under the blankets and the sharp wooden edging of the bed. I couldn't understand why my nerves were so on edge – I am just not the nervous type. Lukas made things worse by asking if I was cold, to which I had replied "yes" to cover up my real reason for trembling, and he placed a blanket over both my legs and his. Again I spoke – I forgot to try the "Middle English" idiom. '"Lukas, I've got to go, Ken's going to go crackers if I'm not back soon, what shall I do with these ca . . . ?"

'"The candles are of na matter, Debbie," Lukas interrupted. He pulled the candles from my tightening grip with one hand and covered my mouth with the other. My jaw ached with the tension. He removed his hand and we both just sat silently for what felt like half an hour, then he took my hand and held it tightly. He did not look at me and I was glad, but he spoke. "Yowr perfume haunts my house, yowr hand is softer than any fair hand . . ." He lifted my hand to his face and closed his eyes, then continued. "Be yow nat real, nat only for yowr unnatural beauty but also that yow make me 430 years too old for yow, maid. One day Debbie will know Lukas as na-more than history – am I tuh live knowing nothing else?"

'I could not speak, he was so serious and so sad. It was a very sensitive situation and I just couldn't understand – I was so mixed up. My only reaction was to move my arm away and make for the door before I burst into tears with the pressure – it just wasn't like me to be so weak. Lukas was so swift that he had moved ahead of me and slammed his back against the door with his arms folded, it must have hurt his back. I could feel the tears welling up but I fought them back.

'"Maid, 'tis lacks of mine cap that makes me foolish . . ." He took the cap from my head and brushed my face gently with the back of his hand before replacing the cap on his head. " . . . Forgive me, Debbie. What would I if I were 430 years younger in the space of time? Pray do not leave it so long before yow see foolish Lukas again."

'Lukas, still with his back to the door, lifted the latch and opened the door for my exit. I slipped through and caught his eye; he smiled and I forced a smile back.

'The time I spent with Lukas must have been at least four hours and yet once I had "returned" the fire was still burning brightly and the clock face showed 5.20 P.M.'

I put my hands over my face and rubbed the top of my fore-head, trying to ease some sense into my head. 'Let me see what was in the poem, Deb.'

'He said it was written for the prison guard – to give to his woman.'

›› LORDE HOWE MYNE EYEN CAST GAZE TO THY EESTE

MYNE HERTE DOTH CHARGE THY WATCHE.THY MORNRYSE

DOST CYTE EECH MOVYNG SENSE AFROM YDLE RESTE

NAT DARYNG TRUSTE THY OFYCE O MYNE EYES

WHYLE SWETELY SHE DIDST PLAYE HIR FLUTE.ME SYT AN MARKE

AN WYSH HIR LAYES WERT TUNED ALYK A LARKE

FOR SHE DIDST WEL COM DAYES LYTE WYTH HIR DITTY

AN DRYVES AWAYE DARK. DISMALLE. DREEMYNG NYTE

THY NYGHT SOE PAKED.I POST UNTO MYNE PRETTYE

HERTE HATH HYS HOPE.AN EYEN THIR WAYSCHED SYGHTE

SORROWE CHANGED TO SOLACE.AN SOLACE MYXED WYTH SORROWE

FOR WY.SHE DIDST SYGH AN BYD ME COM AGEYNE AMORROWE

WER I WYTH HIR THY NYGHT TWALD POSTE TO SOONE

BOT NOWE ARN MINUTES DIDST ADD TO THY HOURE

TO SPYTES ME NOWE.ECHE MINUTE SEEMTH A MOONE

YET NAT FOR MYNESELVE.SHYNE SUN TO SUCORRE FLOWER

PAK NYGHT.PEEP DAYE.O NYGHT NON BORROWE

SHORTE.NYGHT. TO NYGHT AN LENGTHE YOWRSELVE T MORROWE ‹‹

# 26

**24 July**

With Lukas willing to answer questions for John Bucknall it was only left to create the right circumstances for the latest attempt. John Bucknall and Debbie sat in the lounge and amused themselves playing 'guess the next card', using a special pack of cards with only five kinds of symbols – Zener cards.

The rest of us were at the Red Lion for a time. We met John and Debbie half-way between the pub and the cottage on our way back. No result, I could read it in their faces. John and Deb retraced their steps as we all walked the remaining 100 yards to the house.

Inside, it was no good looking cheerful, pretending that we were not disappointed. Debbie had said that the files had all been checked before they came out and there was nothing new, but to distract myself I began to search them. One file kept running, scrolling through page after page. Thirty-five pages down there was a new message from Lukas.

John read it but was unimpressed by its existence. He said he had seen no new message up to the point when Debbie and he left the house. Since it had occurred in the minute or so that it took to round the street corner and return there was room for fraud. I protested that even to open a file to thirty-pages would take probably eight minutes, never mind the time to write the message. Deb reminded him that none of the files was open that far when they had examined them. He replied that he didn't note how far exactly they were open. I felt like asking him why he wasn't sure, as it was his business to be certain. He was, however, certain of one thing: that disks could have been swapped in under a minute. The culprit would only need an identical copy with the added message. I wasn't taking this in clearly: a disk is swapped while I am walking down the road and in sight of the back door and while Debbie and John are within sight of the front. This disk also has to carry the exact form of the greeting to Lukas which Dave Welch had put on the screen before coming with me to the Red Lion.

John and Dave left for Liverpool soon afterwards and John at least was entirely unconvinced that there had been a genuine communication. Lukas, too, when we looked at the message we believe he left was confused for it appeared his words had been moved on the 'leems'. He wrote:

**... ›› PREYE TELLE WY YOW DOE MOVE MYNE SCRIT SOE 2109 FOR ME DOST WYSCH COMUNIOUN WYTH MYNE FREENDE JON LAT ME SPEKE WYTH MERE AFFECIOUN WYTH THYS WIGHT**

**LUKAS ‹‹**

[Please tell me why you move my words, 2109, for I want to communicate with my friend John. Let me at least exchange greetings with this man.]

Tagged on a few lines down was a reply from our disagreeable little numbers. Alarmingly for me but of interest to those who believed them to be behind the whole set of communications, it was in Lukas's 'tunge':

**›› LUKAS**

**YOW CANST NAT REKONE WHYE WE ART TO SPEKES NAT WYTH SYCHE MEN. NOMBERS ARENE NAT YOWR VANTAGE METHYNKS.**

**2109 ‹‹**

[Lukas

You cannot possibly understand why we are not to speak with such men. Numbers are not to your advantage I think.

2109]

We had another visit from John Bucknall and Dave Welch a few days later. As the evening wore on, the conversation turned to 2109 and in my imagination I saw all of time as a vertical plane, climbed by a spiral staircase. Unfortunately, although it is an important but little-known and understood path (I imagined), there is no janitor to keep unwanted visitors off the treads. 2109 were unwanted. No doubt this is harsh but the cipher '2109' behind which any person or agency could hide merely spoke to me of gatecrashers at a party pretending that they knew the host. They seemed to have missed a turning somewhere, a corridor on the landing.

They did not 'speak' unless spoken to; they'd call this leaving room for our destiny, others would infer it to be at best freakish, at worst highly suspicious. For if they were 'real' and 'powerful' why didn't they come for what they wanted? They may have been fraudsters, or a splinter of my or Deb's personality.

From 14 May my distrust and apprehension about whoever or whatever 2109 represented had actively pre vented anyone from, as it were, opening the door to the landing and asking them in. That instruction was quite explicit and understood by all involved. It was my house; I assumed it would be respected as such but I was wrong.

Later that evening the 'psychobillies', Peter, his wife Val, Debbie and I went to the Red Lion. That night's attempt to 'test' the phenomenon had failed and the annual long vacation would deprive us of further opportunities for about a month. Talk was of a hoax and possible enemies that I might have. In short it was still an excursion in search of a motive, and not much advance on last time. It was a platitude to say that everyone has enemies but I doubted that I warranted the honour of this sort of convoluted 'put down' from mine. Talk sagged a little in our corner of the lounge bar. It was disappointing to have nothing even when Lukas had promised to co-operate. Dave Welch suggested to Peter that the two of them should go back to check the computer, which was still on in the kitchen of the cottage.

Thinking little of it I was happy to oblige them with a key and hardly noticed the lounge-bar door close on its stop. John Bucknall was something of a sports car enthusiast and to slide the conversation along we talked of ACs and Jaguars. He smoked nearly continuously, but he was excellent company. Shortly after Peter and Dave Welch had returned – with nothing to report – we all set off for the cottage by a sort of intuitive mutual agreement for a last look-see.

I let everyone in and then inspected the screen. It was not full of 16th-century text, as was my waking and unholy dream, but there was something. Added to a greeting to Lukas left by myself was a short 'hello' to 2109 signed 'David'. My hand came out of my pocket and went straight for the delete key. I disapproved! Oh, I disapproved, as much because it was wilful deception as because I dreaded involvement with 2109. I hoped 'they' had not seen it. Rather half-heartedly, considering their circumstances, I complained to Dave that 'it was not helpful', 2109 were 'over the top', 'riddling'. But I could see that SPR, and Peter and Val too, wanted some answers or at least to give the investigation the widest scope possible. Unwillingly I conceded that my stance was a potentially disastrous inhibition of what was necessary. The argument ran like this: Lukas fitted into a relatively comprehensible world view, a man who, through his words, their clarity and apparent authenticity, threw light into our darkness as we struggled to make sense of this seemingly impossible communication. I could stand by him. But 2109? They couldn't even spell. However, just because they presented more problems did not entitle me to neglect or ignore them.

Disheartened by the lack of anything positive, SPR left. After a general desultory chat (resembling a half-time pep talk from a manager whose team is 4-0 down) Peter and Val retired also. Peter was still wary of my stubbornness over 2109 and also aware of SPR's interest in 'them'. Valerie remained completely sceptical and worried that her husband was being duped. I was still confident that under the right conditions Lukas would write for John and Dave just as he wished, and yet dreadfully sure that, with our luck, 2109 had seen Dave's smiling face through an open door.

Next day:

›› DAVID

MORE ANSEWERS THAN YOU HAVE QUESTIONS.BUT WHAT ARE THE RIGHT QUESTIONS. A MAN CANOT ASK QUESTIONS IF HE IS UNLIKELY TO UNDERSTAND THE ANSEWERS. YES, YOAR CORRECT TO SAY THAT ONE WILL NOT LEARN WITHOUT QUESTIONS, BUT THERE IS A TIME TO UNDERSTAND AND A TIME TO WALK BLINDLY. A MAN WITH HUNGER WILL EAT BAD FRUIT AND SURELY DIE. WAS IT THE FRUIT THAT KILLED THIS MAN OR WAS IT THE KNOWLEDGE THAT THE FRUIT WAS THERE FOR THE TAKING. DO NOT WASTE FURTHER TIME BY ASKING IF THE TREE THAT BERS THIS BAD FRUIT IS IN FRONT OF YOU. IT IS BETTER TO HAVE NO KNOWLEDGE AT ALL THAN TO HAVE A DISTORTED VIEW OF THE TRUTH BECAUSE OF YOUR LACK OF UNDERSTANDING. WE, 2109, ARE NOT WITHOUT COMPASION BUT IF YOU CONTINUE TO DISRUPT OUR EXPERIMENTS THEN IT IS LIKELY YOU WILL FIND YOUR DESTINY.WE SHALL, HOWEVER, ALLOW ONE MORE COMMUNICATION WITH YOU SO THAT YOU, MAY ASK YOUR PROFOUND QUESTIONS.WE SHALL ANSEWER AS YOU WISH, IF IN TERMS OF PHYSICS THEN IT SHALL BE SO, BUT REMMEMBER THAT OUR LIMITS ARE SET BY YOUR OWN ABILITIES AND NOT OURS.

THERE IS NO ONE AFTER THE MAN YOU CALL LUKAS. THE CHANCE FACTOR WILL NOT REOCCUR AGAIN IN A TIME SPAN YOUR KIND CAN RELATE TO. ‹‹

So I was defeated. 2109 were as riddling as they had been in May and as obstructive. They seemed to have some power over communication and could block Lukas's messages. I was sure SPR would say this was just part of the joke.

Debbie wanted her own break and decided to go to Oxford straight away to see what Brasenose College looked like and maybe find Robin Peedell. She left a message telling Lukas of her plans.

Next morning, after Deb had left, I received a plea from Lukas for Debbie not to go.

›› MAYDE

**PREYE DOE NAT GOO LUKAS ‹‹**

There was no message to follow and it wasn't until she came back on 30 July that Lukas wrote once more saying that she shouldn't have gone, that she risked discovering what should not be 'unclasped'. I replied that she had 'discovered' nothing. Lukas was satisfied, we were even more confused.

# 27

'Mayde, preye doe nat goo.'

Soon after this episode the 'mayde' left once more. This time I took her away. We left with the Lovell family one damp morning in that excuse for a summer, bound for York and beyond: to ancient and unfashionable Whitby and then to Scotland. 'Preye doe nat goo.' The rain and the wind and the sway of the wiper blades kept this thought in my mind. With the briefest of lies to Lukas – about my having to go to Jedburgh to collect some money and being gone seven days – we left him, and put the computer away for safety.

And still the wipers and the rain but every mile and every song on the radio separated us, split anxiety from possibility until some hour or two later, standing with an enthusiastic Dave Lovell under the shadow of a huge Chinese locomotive at the York railway museum, I was left with only the hope of Lukas's communications surviving our absence. Nothing could be done now. We were on holiday and without doubt we needed it.

We came back in as few hours and with as few stops as possible. It really was manic. Petrol stops like pit stops, fast lane all the way. We dropped off Dave, Sian and their children in Hawarden at three-thirty in the afternoon. By four-fifteen I was in front of the computer hoping my words would get through to Lukas and at the same time begging Deb to leave everything else till later and to sit quietly in the living room.

A long wait of nearly two hours followed, made worse by the fatigue of the journey and a late-afternoon slump in spirits.

## ›› LITL POWR ‹‹

That was it. He was still in contact. Deb wrote asking why there was little power and asking advice on how we could help, if at all.

Half an hour later:

## ›› 210 ‹‹

Nothing more. 2109? Or about 2109? Next day saw more extensive communication and from that the confidence that all was 'safe'.

As the days passed Lukas was happy enough to answer our questions. Peter was still on holiday, I was busy with the house. Deb wrote more often and on one occasion she asked if he was much confused by our words. In response he gave us this well-nigh impenetrable taste of what he called 'auld tunge':

›› ME ATH NEVREADEL TPRIKEN YIR CONSCIANCE O DISEESE THO EFT YOWR HEDEN DIDST MAK AL WYTH I WARNYSS TWAS VILAGNYE FOR SYCHE SEYDE AMYSS FORGYVE MYNSELVEN BYD YIS PREYE ME DOST WEXYN WYTH ETH TO SYK WEYES

O MANIRE WAN MYN BOYSTE DOE MISPEERE BEEST RESTID MYNE FELAWE EN LIT OWRN RETRACIOUNS BY ROPEN AN LEYD FOE SEYLESERMONE WOT O PETER FREENDS AN TIDR SUBTYLE SURQWYDRYE ME NE TEMPYST

MYNESILVE NAMO TIS SWYCH LOWELY THENKYNG BY ME I HATH NAY CONSERNE THAT THEI BEEST IN MYNE HOWES I AM KON-NYNG AST WAN MYNE LEEV TBE FORWY ALTHOE TIS PLEYNE TA GROVNORE DOTH WEL COM  MYNE STEYE WYTH JOYIF FORN ANODIR III MONTHE MYNE SHYRRYVE DOST FACIOUN MYNESELVE FORWEELE WYTH CONCERNE AL WYLOM WAL ME PARTIK FOTHER BOT ME AM TO ALDE TBE MYNE NAK TO THY SHERYF SOE IF ALBE WYTHOUTES SCATHE ME WILT GOE WEY III MONTHE ADAYE AN WRYTES MYN BOKE O ME SCIANCE O THY MOOST LERND THYNGE WYTH SAD THENKE ME SPEKES NAT ABOUTE 2109 THIM DOE SEE AL METHYNKST

LOVE LUKAS ‹‹

## 18 August

Deb was annoyed about poltergeist activity, especially noises on the roof, which had begun again after a break of over six weeks. I wrote to Lukas one morning asking if his house was affected: 'Doe smalle platters or nik naks move without your touche?' It was, however, 4.00 P.M. before any response came. He had indeed been plagued by such events and asked if we were causing them.

I replied in some detail to reassure him that we were not disrupting his household – at least not that we were aware! I suggested 2109 (always a useful scapegoat) might have a hand in it.

Less than twenty minutes later and without us making any attempt to 'ghostbust' my message was deleted from the screen. It wasn't the first time in recent days that this had happened.

Later Lukas wrote:

›› MYNE VISE BE WYTH YOW THAT WE SPEKES PRIVERLEY ENSAMPLES WEN OWRN UNFAVOURABLE FREENDS ART NAT IN ARN COMPANIE METHINKS ME DOST HATH REMEDIE FOR OWRN TROUBLSOM ME SHALT SPEKE ANYGHT ‹‹

[My considered opinion is that we communicate privately when our disagreeable friends are not in our company, and I think I know how to remedy our troubles so I shall write tonight.]

On both sides 2109 were suspected of influencing the activity of the 'poltergeist' and certainly of deleting messages but it was beyond me to see how Lukas had a solution to the problem.

Since 2109 appeared to have a grip on the computer communications Deb offered Lukas a piece of paper and charcoal in an imaginative move to bypass interference. Lukas had written in chalk before now so it could be a way round the problem. It looked weird, it felt crazy, making all these preparations. She left the paper on top of the monitor screen, which was itself on the marble shelf besides the pillar.

An hour later, while Deb was making toast, I came through and checked the screen out of habit. There was only one new line. Lukas had for the first time written whilst Deb was in the same room.

›› PREYE DOE AS I DOE AXE PLAS COMUTER WER BE MYNE WORDES ‹‹

[Please do as I ask, place the computer where my words are].

It was a curious instruction. I wrote:

WER BE YOWR WORDES . . . I BE CONFUS

'Aah!'

I looked around. A surprised Debbie was holding up the piece of paper with one small, flowing word on it in charcoal – take'. OK, so he'd written . . . but put the computer where his words were? . . . We looked for more words. None on the pillar, the floor, we even checked under the computer! A thought occurred. Perhaps put the computer where the piece of paper had been. He must have meant to write more words on the paper. 'Take' is the beginning of a phrase. Stupid of me.

Since there was a small cardboard box nearby this was relatively easy. I checked with Lukas and eventually (more waiting around) 'YEA' was the reply. Lukas continued:

›› MYNE FELAWE

YF YOW WALD PAS TWEY LEGGS TO THY RYGHTE O THY LEEMS AN RYGHTE GEYN OUNE THIN PLAS LEEMS EYGHTE HONDS SCANTENS ABOVEN MYNE FLOORE ME THYNKS ME CANST QUYTE YOWR AXYNGS AS T WY BE THYS BUT SESSA WYTH SPAKEN WORDE TIL YOW DOE THYS FOR YOWR GOODE FREEND

LOVE LUKAS ‹‹

[My fellow

If you would pace two legs to the right of the 'leems' and right again then placed the 'leems' eight hands above the floor I think I can answer your questions as to why this is, but keep silence until you have done this for your good friend.

194    Love Lukas]

I marked out the two paces and another to the right. It brought me to the other side of the pillar, near to the sink and the diamond-glassed window. Deb and I tried measuring eight 'hands' from the floor. I didn't know what 'scanten' meant but guessed that it meant 'scarcely' or 'just'. It was probably meant to keep our measurement on the low side. We used Debbie's hand as she guessed Lukas was smaller than me and my hand would have overstated the measurement. I marked the height on the pillar and we set about trying to find some support for the computer at that height and in that position.

A bamboo plant stand with one phone directory on top was the closest. It made getting to the sink difficult. All was wired up and I asked him what was going on. How did he know what to do with the machine? One more ghostbust. I sat in the car in the drive and listened to the cassette player. The reply:

›› YEA GYVE TYME TO MAKES AL SAFFE ME DOST THYNKS THAT YOW MAYE KNOWE AL NOWE ALS MYNE TREWE CALLE

LOVE LUKAS ‹‹

[You give me time to make all safe. I think that you may know all now, also my real name.

Love Lukas]

### 19 August

I wrote: 'Pray continue, goodly felawe'. Deb and I were early at the cottage and set about giving him every opportunity to write. We were quiet, tried not to go into the kitchen, took walks and sat silently. Perhaps we were trying too hard because there was nothing all morning. Then, at about 2.00 P.M.

›› BROTHIR KEN ME DOST MUCHE DELYGHTE  THAT US BE BI OW-RNSELVEN WYTHOUTES 2109 FORN WE HATHE MANYE SPAKENLIS WORDES TO UNDIRGOE COMUNIOUN ME NATS THYNKS AS TO WY AN WOT CAUSES NACAN BE WYTHOUTES SYCH BOUNDES AYMO YOWR LEEMS DOST SYT IN MYNE ELYFUL CHYMNEYE WER THY LEEMS BOYSTRE DIDST FYRSTE PERE WYTH IT CHERES AN THY WYGHT THAT DIDST MAKE ACORDAUNTE IT STEYES WYTH MYN SELVE BIFORNE ME DOTH TELLE YOW ALLE THAT BE TREWE AN WOT O MYNE CALLE YOW MUSTE SEYENE WOT BE YOWR THENKYNG

195

AND WE MUSTE APREVED YOWR CONDYCIOUN FOR MYNE GOOD-
LY FREEND ME DOST THYNKS YOW KNOWETH BETTIRE BI WOT
CHAUNCES AWAYTE CAUSED WYTH OWRN DISYCIOUN

LOVE «

[Brother Ken,

I am happy that we are by ourselves without 2109 for we have much so far unspoken to exchange. I can't think why and with what method we are able to continue without restriction now. Your 'leems' sits in my dark chimney where the 'leems boyste' first appeared with brightness. And the person who made it work is here with me. Before I tell you what is the truth and my name you must tell me what is your philosophy, I must be acquainted with your position because, my good friend, I think you know better than I do what might happen after this decision is taken.]

The 'leems' was supposedly in the place it was when it first came. Not from our point of view. True the computer was near the comer of the pillar but it was never so close to the sink as it was now. Secondly and most seriously: what did he mean, 'Yow muste seyne wot be yowr thenkyng and me muste appreved yowr condycioun'? What was my thinking? I was supposed to know something about him and his and our 'condycioun'. And according to the last line I was supposed to know what 'chaunces awayte caused wyth owrn disycioun'.

I wrote that I would have to think about it because my interpretation of his words was not satisfactory. Instead I asked about the 'wight', the person who had appeared with the 'leems', and about the first time the 'leems' came.

Since the confusion over the position of the computer we had left out paper and charcoal. It was a 'reserve medium' but I was so keen for him to tell me his name that I would have pinned huge sheets of cartridge paper to the wall if it would have helped. Later the same afternoon whilst Deb took a nap Lukas wrote on the paper.

›› My friend

I have told Debbie the answer to your questions. I think that she doesn't understand all that is spoken but she has some facility with most of my words.

Lukas ‹‹

'Debbie.'

'Yeah,' she mumbled from behind a newspaper.

'Lukas says he has spoken with you. Did he . . . ? Have you?'

'I went to sleep.' The pages turned.

'Did you dream anything?'

She put the paper down and looked straight at me. 'What do you think?'

'Well, what did he say . . . ?'

'That the "leems" was brought by a man. A man who told him it was important and . . . you still promise you won't tell Trinder that I spoke with him? He'll think I'm making it up. Lukas said he loved you very much, too.'

There was silence for about half a minute. Deb looked at me. Her eyes searched my face for some sign of reaction. I shifted from one foot to another and then sat across from her, looking at the message and at her in turns. It didn't answer my questions but that was of less concern than Peter's possible reaction.

'OK. We'll keep it quiet. Peter might not mention it, but he will have to see the message.'

Tomas message in charcoal - 19th August

## 21 August

We took Lukas's message to show Peter, who did not make too much of what it said because he was so intrigued by the mere fact of him writing. He threw up all sorts of questions. I said that writing in charcoal was only an extension of what had happened before, the chalk shields, etc. Peter asked, 'Why charcoal?' Deb chipped in that she thought a man used to writing with quills would prefer something recognizable and adaptable to his style of writing. It did smudge, however. We hurried back to the cottage and left Lukas a few questions, including one from Peter about the word 'elyful'. Here we were trying to get Lukas's one and only real name and Peter wants to know what 'elyful' means! I also asked again about the 'wyght'. He replied once more on the paper.

›› myne freend tha wight beest afrom

yowr tyme methynks. elyful

be that wythoutes lyght

cherelis donne.

yea yow doe hath myne

calle in yowr boke methynks

yf nat jon put tom yow

wilt hath rekonyng for myne

calle be allso thy plas o peter

howes preye wot seyen thys boke o names

an tyme o yere aboutes myneselven

love Tomas ‹‹

[My friend, the person is from your time, I think.

'Elyful' is that without light, with brightness gone.

Yes, you have my name in your book, I think, if not 'John' put 'Tom' and I think you will understand my name, it is also the place of Peter's house. What does this book of names and ages say about me?

Love Tomas]

If not Jon then put Tom. TOMAS HAWARDEN!!! In an instant I remembered Robin Peedell had put this man forward months ago as a likely candidate. 'Impossible,' I had said at the time, but he had been right.

'Real HISTORY!' I shouted to Deb above the sound of the cassette as we drove towards Hawarden. Deb was amused by all this over-excitement. Peter was very happy to know the name – and get an answer to the 'elyful' question!

This is what was written about Tomas Hawarden [or Harden] in the reference which Robin Peedell had provided many months ago:

HARDEN (or HAWARDEN)* THOMAS BRASENOSE COLLEGE FELLOW IN 1530 STILL IN COLLEGE 1538.

CHARGED WYTH EXPUNGYNG THE NAME OF THE POPE 'E QUODAM MANUALI' DECEMBER 1538; BA ADMITTED XII DEC 1530; DETERMINED 1531; MA INCORPORATED XXII MARCH 1535.

* Spelt variously through all records. Tomas used 'Harden'.

Back after long discussion to East Green. It was only later as I walked down to the River Dee by the old swing bridge, to watch the muddy waters swirl and slide towards the sea, that I realized how exhausted I felt. Deb was already asleep when I went out. It felt as if the cottage took something out of you, physically, mentally, emotionally.

I could have fallen asleep on the riverbank. Instead I thought of Tomas Harden, of the past months, and watched the traffic lessen and the sounds from the F erry Hotel fade away after closing time.

Tomas next wrote that the description of him and his time at Oxford made him 'glee' (laugh). He said that the reason given for his expulsion was wrong. Peter doubted this but checked back with care. The standard reference on the history of the college, from which Peter obtained the information I put before Tomas, should have been correct. But no! Deep in the bowels of Brasenose some weeks later Robin Peedell plucked out from an original source record that Tomas Harden was expelled for *not* crossing out the Pope's name. The standard history is in error. Tomas was an 'old faither' and had evidently withdrawn to an obscure village in Chester to ride out the Henrician revolution.

Tomas asked that he still be addressed as Lukas, as the name had become his own and he preferred it. We agreed readily.

# 28

**22 August**

I had thought I was coping so well. But the excitement of the previous few days must have touched off a manic reaction to the endless progress of this task. After the light, the darkness.

I was alone in the kitchen and the cottage brooded about and within me. I felt overwhelmed by the echoes of all these months. They called upon me for some resolution, some answers, but I did not have any. I was sinking, and began to cry uncontrollably.

They might be the most important events in my life but I did not understand them or why I was in tears when I should be . . . I just wanted to escape, to be anywhere else, but more than that – the greatest escape of all – not to be me anymore. I did not recognize myself. I was almost continually tired, anxious, insecure. I felt old, weary. Not one moment from my past could I recall to please myself. Instead I recalled an image of a dark, broad river with, from its banks, large willow branches dipping the surface and colouring the eddies. Then I imagined diving slowly into that river, which shivered as it let me in, and I spun slowly in the current, towards dissolution. And the waters showed no sign of my passing.

Lukas 'heard' me and an hour later wrote on the computer:

›› HIT COME TO MYNE REKONYNG TAT YOW DOE DYSLYK MYNE COMPANIE WY BE THIS CHAUNGE OF HEARTE ME NATHE WORNGED MYNE GGODLY FREEDN DOST YOW LYK THY POET WYAT ME CAN QUOT YOW SOM WORDES IF THYS WAL HATHE YOW MYNE FELAWE STILL

LOVE LUKAS ‹‹

[It seems to me that you dislike my company. Why this change of heart? I have not wronged my good friend. Do you like the poet Wyatt? I can quote you some of his verses if this will restore our friendship.

Love Lukas]

And next day he gave me two beautiful verses of Wyatt's poetry but admonished me for my weakness:

. . . ›› WEN YOW BEEST MYNE TYME O DAYE YOW WILT HATHE FEWE A TERE SHEDE FOR YOW WILT KNOWE THA LYF BE A GLORIEN THYNGE . . . ME WILT HEERE NAMO WOE. ‹‹

The verse from Wyatt:

HEERE BE SOME WORDES O TOM WYATT

BLAYME NAT MYN LUTE FOR HYM MUSTE SOOND

O THISE OR AS MYNE LYKYNG BE

FOR LAKS O WYT MYNE LUTE BE BOUNDE

TGYVE SYCH TUNES AS PLEASETH ME

THOW MYNE SONGE BSUMWOT STRAUNGE

AN SPAKE SY CH WORDE AS TOUCHEN CHAUNGE

BLAYME NAT MYN LUTE


MYN LUTE AN STRYNGE MAYE NAT DENIE

BOT STRYKE AS THEYM MUSTE OBEYE

BRIK NAT THEYM THEN SOE WRONGEFULIE

BOT REEKE THYNSELVE SOM WYSYR WEYE

FOR THO THY SONGES WHYCHE ME INDYTE

DOUYT THY CHAUNGE WYTH RIGHTLIE SPYTE

BLAYM NAT MYNE LUTE

[. . . When you are my age you will shed few tears for you will know that life is a glorious thing . . . I will listen to no more woe.]

Peter asked Lukas how he could have seen Wyatt's poem when the first edition had not at that time been published. Lukas replied that it was pinned to the wall in Brasenose but that in any case he had heard it from a 'lernd travellyng man'.

The grief I had created for myself was private and the reply just as private. It is hard to describe how close I felt to this man and how ashamed I was of the previous night, for Lukas next wrote that he had heard a rumour among the village people that his dear young Katherine had been burnt as a witch.

I replied the next day, but Lukas did not answer. Peter told me there were no recorded burnings of young women in Chester in that year and I passed that information on to Lukas.

## 25 August

Lukas was still not sure what had happened to Katherine but our attention was on the computer, which was suffering from physical 'poltergeist' attacks. Twice in the previous few days one or other of us had found the machine twisted on the plant stand and on one other occasion the plant stand had shifted to the edge of the pillar. I was worried in case the computer was damaged. I couldn't afford to replace it and it was another week until term started and there would be one available to borrow.

Lukas was apparently oblivious to the disruption and requested poetry from Peter, his 'oxyan felawe', from Debbie and myself. He said that he needed this material for his book about our time, and that it needed care as it 'wants gaze bimanye', i.e. must be able to be read by many. I suppose he thought that otherwise it would be taken for nonsense and would not survive. He was collecting poetry and human, intimate recollections, readable, everyday stuff. I have not heard of it. The twist is that if the book were still available I could not write of our 'communyion', I would be merely fulfilling a prophecy with the benefit of hindsight. If this book exists and is found before I publish this account then all is undone. But paradoxically finding his book is the one sure piece of evidence that we are not crazy. Please, someone find his book at the right time.

So much happened in those last weeks that before going back to school I decided that I needed to go away on my own again for a few days. I set off for Stratford, collected my old friend Sara and then into the Cotswolds in search of a sense of the 16th century – and as fate would have it I was introduced to Snowshill Manor.

Old am I, so very old

Here centuries have been

Mysteries my walls enfold

None know deeds I have seen

Snowshill Manor(Charles Wade)

It is a house with a western elevation, a house for the evening hours, as permanent and unimaginably beautiful as any I have seen.

Charles Wade, an extraordinary eccentric who died forty years ago, had through his care for this ancient house set himself as firmly in other centuries as I longed to do in order to become closer to Lukas. In all those months I had never really felt in my heart what an aching expanse of time lay between us until I stepped silently, reverently, into Snowshill.

I was aware, in those quiet rooms, of much more than the 439 years since 1546. I felt the stability and permanence which abounded, even in Henrician England, compared to our own more shattered times.

Time has settled at Snowshill and Charles Wade has honoured it. In an upper room is the mechanism of a large clock which, by the fall of its weights, points to the hours marked off on the wall, and in words too:

The life of time is motion, his glory perfection.

TIME  Attendeth none, yet is servant to all.

Swifter than the wind, yet still as a stone.

The true man's friend, the thief's perdition.

The lawyer's gain, the merchant's hope.

He openeth the eye of the day and spreadeth the cloak of night

Agent of the living, register of the dead.

Nicholas Breton (c.1600)

Charles Wade lived for the most part the life of a medieval or at least pre-industrial man of learning. His collection grew so large that it forced him to make his home in the former stables. Here, too, reigned absolute calm; the rooms devoid of all those modern comforts which so successfully keep us from ourselves. Amidst oak and stone, rushlights, a hooded, red leather chair and kindly light through mullioned windows I felt I knew Lukas and the thoughts which surrounded him. In that instant I enfolded all those moments between 1546 and the present. I knew still more strongly that Lukas's world, for all its misery, poverty and superstition, was not inferior to our own. We have lost so much and gained only trinkets for our amusement.

It occurred to me that Lukas asked little of our time. He relished our words and ideas, not our times. So often he had mused over the impossibility of such a thing as a car or daily newspapers. Perhaps he wondered more at the wisdom of it, the necessity that drove us to such ends, than at the phenomenon itself. Could I explain our loss?

And there I stood, a visitor. with my hand on the jute rope keeping me to the edge of this world. 'Olde England.' I reproached myself for the thought.

Easing back into the car, into Broadway and simultaneously into the inauthentic, the unnecessary and the inevitable we joined the slow crawl towards Chipping Camden where, eating tea and scones in a courtyard overhung with vines, I felt a headache vying for attention and became aware that my powers of conversation had dulled. I was becalmed, then weary and rather depressed.

# 29

I put down a hello to Lukas the day I got back. Deb said he'd been writing on and off but yesterday he'd announced he must find Katherine. I wrote and asked if he'd had any luck. I wasn't expecting trouble but twenty minutes later:

›› DON'T HAVE NIGHTMARES ‹‹

Just what I needed – 2109! I deleted it, and told myself to ignore them. I knew what they were hinting at. The poem long ago last winter, I had never forgotten the way it began: 'True are the nightmares of a person that fears.' The computer was staying where Lukas had asked for it to be put, even though it was now obvious that 2109 could write on it in its new position.

Lukas wrote after another hour. Katherine was dead.

›› FELAWE KEN

YEA ME HATH RETORND BOT KATHRYNE BE BRENDE YOW DIDST SEYNE THIR BEETH NE BRENNYNG IN CESTRE BUT TIS SOE NAT FOR THIR BEEST MANNYE FOR SOE CALID UNCLENSE SOWLES THAT HATH BENE TAKIN THYS WEYE BI THY PEPIL O MYNB TYME FOR THY KYNGHS MEN DOE ONLIE MOPE ATTE THISE SORRIESTE HAVIOURES AN INTENDE THIR LOOSTE SYGHTES KATHRYNE WERT A GOODLIE MAYDE AN ME DIDST CAUSE THYS UPON HIRSELVES SHE WERT PRIME AN KNEWYTH NAT THY ILL WEY O MEN AND SYK HARMES FOR ME DIDST ALLE TO KEPES HIR AFROM THISE WRETCHYD JACKS MYNE SWEETYST SWEETE KATHRYNE ME WILT NVER LEEVE YOW FROM MYNE THENKYNGS‹‹

[Friend Ken,

Yes, I have returned but Katherine is burnt. You said there were no burnings in Chester but it is otherwise for there are many for so-called 'uncleansed souls' that have been taken this way by the people of my time. The King's men only shrug at this practice and look the other way. Katherine was a good maid and I brought this upon her. She was perfect and didn't know the corruptness of man and such that could harm her, for I did all I could to keep her from these wretched people. My sweetest, sweet Katherine, you will never leave my thoughts ...]

I was so unhappy to hear this. I remember the sorrow and pain we had felt when Lukas himself had been taken, I remembered it had been my responsibility to say whether these communications should continue. Because they had continued I had helped destroy his Katherine. She was only fourteen.

Around the beginning of September the computer was being disturbed again. On 3 September it disappeared entirely from the kitchen – only to be found, all of it (the monitor, the plant stand, the cables) in the bathroom. No damage.

On the marble worktop there was a chalk message, angular and quite distinct. It was not from Lukas. I thought, 'Poltergeist!' Everything untoward was blamed on the 'poltergeist' or 2109. The message read:

›› ONE

MORE

CHANCE!

MEASURE

FREQUENCY BY+ 2 ENERGY

WHAT ELES OTHER

THAN SOUND AND

LIGHT?! ‹‹

I hadn't a clue. It happened to be there so I wrote it down. There was another disturbance involving the computer on 5 September. Deb heard the crash of falling metal and found the disk drive on the floor and the computer and monitor teetering on the edge of the plant stand. The disk drive was out of action. The last incident before this attack was the creation of seventeen new files, all of them empty, all of them opened to several pages. This had last occurred in July. It looked like a childish attempt to confuse or delay our work.

Before the incident I had left a message to Lukas, returning to the subject of the person he claimed had brought the 'leems'. Did Lukas know anything more? Since the disk drive was now malfunctioning a paper and pencil were left.

›› My brother Ken,

The man who came to our home when I last spoke was the man called 'one'. I asked him if he had come to take the 'leems boyste' away. He spoke straight away and said that he had no want for the 'leems' but that it wasn't mine to offer. I could see that he was intending to stay with both feet planted firmly here so I didn't try to move him. He continued: 'Any mishaps that have befallen you are your own. You have no power over this thing [poltergeist?] for it is like a child without a caring family. It doesn't know the forces within its reaching arms. You and your brothers are in great trouble if but you put the 'leems' back on its own [meaning unclear]. Think well but don't tell your fellows.'

This is why I haven't written on the 'leems'. What do you think? What mishaps? Can we come to ill? Answer soon.

Lukas ‹‹

Poor Lukas didn't know that even if he wrote on the 'leems' we could not see it now that the computer was in for repair. However, the feeling at the cottage was that we should not give in, despite the loss of the disk drive. Even though the crucial passage in the pencil message was unclear it looked as if the 'wyght' [one!!] was warning us off co operating with 2109. It was impossible to answer Lukas. We were his future and he expected so much, too much.

# 30

In the middle of the night of 7 September I packed up my clothes and made my way out to the car. Downstairs in the kitchen of the house in East Green was a small, black puppy whining and moaning for attention. I could not stand it. I had enough to do without some unnecessary animal. It was Debbie's idea and Debbie could live with it. I was off. Unfortunately there wasn't enough petrol to go beyond a mile or two so I went back in and settled for a row.

'But he loves you.' Deb smiled like a little girl asking for pocket money.

'No he doesn't.'

She fetched him into the bedroom. 'See, he does love you, he's wagging his tail he's so happy.'

'I'm still going when the petrol station's open.' I went back to bed while she and the puppy played games on the covers behind my back.

Deb woke me at about nine, leant over and pushed the small black bundle towards me. It had the most wonderful eyes I had ever seen, like jewels. 'Say goodbye to us then.'

I stayed, and she called the dog Lukas, after a friend of ours. The puppy seemed pretty sensitive to what was happening in the kitchen at the cottage from the start, for he would prick his ears and offer a display of curiosity and anxiety at the kitchen door. Calling 'Lukas' was growing to cause confusion around the place but who would mind if they both came running?

Even with the disk drive under repair and a borrowed one in place I still refused to contact 2109. Then this appeared:

I only had to remember 15 May and the havoc which erupted then: I dared not resist any more. So much for resolve. But I still wrote to 2109 unwillingly and with contempt.

2109

*FORGET THE 4TH FORM GLOOM AND DOOM AND EXPLAIN WHAT YOU WANT AS YOU ARE PREVENTING US COMMUNI- CATING WITH OUR FRIEND.OF WHAT HARM IS THAT? WE LOVE THE FELLOW AND HE US. IF YOU WISH TO HELP PLEASE GIVE YOUR ANALYSIS OF POLTERGEIST PHENOMENA. BEINGS OF YOUR ABILITY SHOULD BE LESS MOODY WHEN CONFRONT- ED WITH US SIMPLE TYPES. A LITTLE OPEN COMMUNICATION GOES A LONG WAY WHEN COOPERATION IS THE ISSUE.DIG? KEN AND DEB*

*LUKAS GOODLY FELAWE PREYE YOU WRYTE TO MYNESELVE AS TO YOWR THENKYNG AT THYS TYME*

*KEN*

A half-hour walk and the reply was there. The sly bastards even echoed my deliberate use of the sixties expression 'dig'.

›› DIG!. YOU ARE MISTAKEN, WE DO NOT SPEAK ANY GLOOM AND DOOM, BUT POSSIBLEY YOU REFER TO THE FORCES THAT YOU YOURSELF HAVE UNLEASHED. – AGAINST OUR BETTER JUDGMENT!. IT IS CORRECT FOR YOU TO ASSUME THAT THE POLTERGEIST PHENOMENA IS PRESENT IN THE COMMUNICATIONS, BUT WE CAN SAY VERY LITTLE ABOUT THIS SUBJECT AS ONLY WHAT YOU WILL KNOW ALREADY.FOR REASONS SURELY EVIDENT TO YOU THREE! POLTERGEIST PHENOMENA AS FOLLOW: –

SURPLUS KENETIC ENERGY PROJECTED BY EITHER ONE OR MORE INDIVIDUALS OR BY STORAGE CHANNELS HELD WITHIN BUILDINGS AND PLACES WHERE STRONG EMOTIONS, SUCH AS FRUSTRATION, HAVE BEEN FELT

MOST COMMON

ENERGY CENTERED AROUND AN

INDEVIDUAL.RELEASED FOR MANY

REASONS. USUALLY CHILDREN OF THE AGES

BETWEEN 12-19 .87.9% GIRLS.

IN ALL BUT THREE RECORDED CASE NO INJURIES INFLICTED
BY THE SOURCE - LAST CASES OF INJURIE SUSTAINED BY A
FALLING BEEM RECORDED IN 2006. THE FORCE IS USUALLY
AN EXTREMELY FOUL ENTITIE WHICH SEEMS TO THRIVE ON
STRONGE ADVERSE EMOTIONS MAKING LITTLE SENSE IN ITS
COMMUNICATION.IT SEEMS TO PLAY ON AN INDIVIDUALS FEER.
DISLIKES LACK OF ATTENTION - HAS BEEN THOUGHT AT ONE
STAGE THAT THIS IS THE INDIVIDUALS CRY TO BE NOTICED.

THERE IS MORE SAID ABOUT THIS PHENOMENA BUT IT WOULD
NOT BE OF INTREST TO YOU.WE HAVE STOPED COMMUNICATION
BETWEEN LUKAS AND YOURSELFS UNTIL THINGS 'COOL DOWN'.

THEN YOU MAY CONTINUE AS BEFORE, LUKASES TIME WILL STAND
STILL RELATIVE TO YOUR TIME SO THAT YOU MAY START WHERE
YOU LEFT OFF 2109 ‹‹

An interesting and suitable treatment. Upon reflection it
seemed to be an exercise in psychology, rather than an exercise in knowledge and application, e.g. the statistics, the hint at
the future ('2006'), the suggestion that they were in control. If it
developed anything, this communication helped fix our attention on 2109. They said they were blocking Lukas but it wasn't
true for long because after a couple of days he was there writing on paper. And as for slowing his time . . . well! I rang Dave
Welch, it seemed appropriate, and asked him if he wanted to
write to 2109. He said he wanted to be able to ask them a series
of questions if possible. The last word from 2109 on that had
been at the beginning of the holidays: one set of questions only.
Dave repeated his opinion that one set was useless, it couldn't
prove a thing, especially since 2109 talked in riddles at the best
of times. Dave was nevertheless interested to hear that I was in
touch. I told him that it was against my better judgement.

The computer was not set up again until 14 September, the
following Saturday. I wasn't going to rush around for them nor
was I going to be serious with them unless I was forced to. I
adopted a 'Captain Kirk' approach and wrote:

*THANKS. AM I TO BELIEVE THAT P.GEISTS ARE WANDERING ENTITIES WHO SEIZE UPON STRAY ENERGIES? PLEASE COMPLETE YOUR OBSERVATIONS UPON THEM SINCE YOU HAVE STARTED. HAVE TIMES COLLIDED AT THIS PLACE ? WHERE WAS THE LAST COINCIDENCE? MANY THANKS KEN*

They replied:

›› NO, THESE ENTITIES HAVEN'T A CONSCIOUS AS SUCH.IT IS THE ENERGY THAT IS FORMED INTO A CHARICTOR.IT IS SUGGESTED THAT AFTER SEVERAL SMALL P.G. INCIDENTS THE INDIVIDUALS ATOMATICALLY IMAGINE THE WORK OF A GHOST WHICH MOST PEOPLE ASSUME TO RESEMBLE HUMAN FORM-THERFORE-AN IMAGE IS CREATED BY THE PERSONS CONCERED WHICH STRANGELY ENOUGH INFLUENCES THE FORCES INVOLVED.AGAIN, IT SEEMS THAT THERE IS A STRONG CONNECTION BETWEEN THE ENTITIES AND THE PERSON AS A NUCLIUS SOMETIMES IT IS CONSIDERED THAT TO STUDY THE PERSONS CONCERNED IS AS INFORMATIVE AS THE PHENOMINA ITSELF LAST COINCIDENCE 1941

2109 ‹‹

More tantalizing propositions: that this sort of communication across time had last occurred in similar circumstances in 1941. It was well judged to stimulate interest, but a damned inconvenience that in 1941 there was a war on – it must have obscured reporting, rather. And there were no computers.

Next day, however, 2109 were much less pleasant:

›› KEN DEB PETER

WE HAVE REASON TO BELIEVE YOU HAVE LUKAS WAINMANS TRUE NAME. IF THIS IS CORRECT YOU MUST SAY SO SO THAT WE MAY RECTIFY THE PROBLEM IMMEDIATELY BEFORE IT IS EXCEPTED. YOU MAY NOW CONTINUE TO WRITE TO LUKAS TO ESTABLISH YOUR RESPONSABILITY TO OUR EXPERIMENTS AND TOWARDS A BETTER UNDERSTANDING OF TIME AND ITS FORCES

2109

I did not let 2109 know I was in any way grateful. I wrote:

*2109*

*I HOPE LUKAS WILL BE ALLOWED TO WRITE FREELY FOR IF YOU STUDY TIME I CANNOT SEE WHAT PROBLEM THER IS OVER NAMES WE WOULD USE SUCH INFORMATION WITH THE GREATEST TACT. HOW MANY MESSAGES HAVE YOU EDITED AGAIN I ASK PLEASE EXPLAIN YOUR 'PROBLEM' I WISH TO KNOW MORE OF TIME AS WELL.*

*ONCE LUKAS IS CLEARLY WITH US AGAIN I SHALL BE HAPPY TO COOPERATE FULLY.PLEASE DONT FAKE A MESSAGE FROM HIM*

*KEN*

2109 went crackers at this:

›› fake a message?!

please, you must understand that we are not here to play games. THE PROBLEM is greater than we can explain – what with your lack of knowledge. What is a greater problem than placing an unbalanced card on a card tower and watch it collaps with devastating consequences, even though you may save the ace you will have lost the pack, what use is a single card for the game? ‹‹

I said we had his name. They wrote back within the hour. The tempo was picking up.

›› OH, IF ONLY YOU HAD LISTEND. AT PRESENT YOU HAVE TWO LUKASES RUNNING AROUND YOUR HOUSE,IF AT ANY TIME THE TWO ARE TO MEET WE CANNOT EXPLAIN THE DEVASTATION THAT WILL ERRUPT WITHIN THE TIME CONTINUUM.WE MUST STOP COMMUNICATION WITH LUKAS ONE, BUT WE CANNOT INTERFERE WITH THE OTHER, WHILE WE DECIDE WHAT CAN BE DONE TO RECTERFY THE PROBLEM. YOU MUST HELP BE GIVING US EVERY WORD UTTERED BY THOMAS HAWARDINE FROM THE SECOND YOU RECEIVED HIS TRUE NAME. YOU MUST ALSO STATE HOW MUCH INFORMATION YOU HAVE ON THIS MAN – EVERYTHING!,WORD FOR WORD.

AVOID ANY OTHER COMMUNICATION YOU MAY HAVE WITH HIM

DESPERATION. BE QUICK! 2109 ‹‹

This did cause a minor panic. Even though I could not understand all they said I thought I knew enough not to take chances. I rang Peter, explained and arranged to pick up the little we had on Tomas Harden from Trueman's Way. Meanwhile, 2109 had moved us up a gear by suggesting that major disruption could occur if we did not comply.

Rather tartly I reminded them not to instruct but to explain and wrote: 'This could still be a con trick to fill in your missing knowledge . . .'

I dashed off in the car to Hawarden and back, put down some information and then left the house alone overnight. They asked for more information about this character 'one' Lukas was chattering about. I fumed and just told them that he glowed green and was impolite, then I suggested that they ask Lukas. Accompanying this rather tedious missive – full of talk of fundamental particles yet to be discovered and the monitoring of particles using magnetic fields – was a chalk message written down the brick pillar in angular capitals.

›› WHAT ARE YOU SCARED OF

KEN DEB PETER? ‹‹

'Who the hell wrote that?'

'Me perhaps?'

'Bloody "one" eh?? Or 2109, or the poltergeist, or the man next door or . . . ' I was just angry.

'The stacking is very good though!' Debbie said, defusing the situation and pointing to the obvious – an almost impossible tower of catfood tins and kitchen rolls. Well, it was good and once more we could laugh. One more exchange took place before lunch.

I wrote:

CAN'T YOU GET THESE POLTERGEISTS OUT OF THE PLACE? ID-
IOT THINGS. I HOPE YOU CAN PUT US BACK IN TOUCH WITH
LUKAS SO THAT WE CAN TALK FREELY?

KEN.

And got this in reply:

›› YES, WE SHALL HOLD BACK AS BEST WE CAN ON THE PG. SORRY
YOU FIND US SO FREINDLY!?. ASK THE MAN DAVID WHAT HE THINKS
OF CONJECTURAL TACHYONS AND WHAT ARE HIS THEORIES OF
CAUSALITY, WHAT ANSEWER DOES HE HAVE FOR ITS PARADOX?.

CHEERS 2109 ‹‹

It was, I realized, a cue to wake the 'psychobillies' from their
armchairs.

# 31

**15 September**

Extraordinarily enough Dave Welch was very interested in tachyons – which he explained were particles whose existence could only be guessed at (hence the term 'conjectural'), and which move at above the speed of light and thus through time. He had been talking about tachyons to his sixth-form class that very morning. I was mildly impressed by 2109's apparent awareness of Dave's predilection and their sense of timing.

2109 wrote in the evening saying that if we would say who 'one' was they would give us proof. This was an extraordinary deal. I said I would telephone David. (I had already done so! I had this urge to lie to 2109 or to deceive them wherever possible out of distaste for their interference.) The rest of my message was thinly veiled anger.

*PLEASE GIVE TIME TILL EXPERIMENT SHUTDOWN. WILL WE HAVE 'TIME' TO COMMUNICATE WITH LUKAS ONCE MORE? WILL TELEPHONE DAVID TONIGHT .REMEMBER TELEPHONES? . . .*

*. . . DID YOU USED TO PUNCTUATE LW'S EARLY MESSAGES? PLAY THE GAME INFORMATION FOR ALL? KEN*

The reply:

›› ha, you have left the caps off once more – such a simple mistake!!.WE ARE ALL CAPERBLE OF MAKING MISTAKES, ARN'T WE.YES, TELEPHONES . . .THE THINGS THAT YOU MAY CONSIDER ADVANCED COMMUNICATION – IF ONLY YOU COULD SEE WHAT IS TO COME!.WE, IN YOUR BETTER INTRESTS MADE SLIGHT 'ADJUST-EMNTS' TO YOUR CONVERSATIONS ( – BUT PLEASE LET US CALL HIM BY HIS TRUE NAME)WITH THOMAS.WE ARE NOT ENTIRELY IN COMAND OF THIS EXPERIMENT,SO WE CAN ONLY SAY THAT

COMUNICATIONS WILL CEASE NO EARLYER THAN NOVEMBER (NOT NESSESERALY WITH THOMAS),AH, WE SEE, YOU WANT SOME PROOF FOR YOUR LITTLE COMIC!,WELL WE THINK YOU SHOULD FIRST TRY TO REVISE ON WHAT HAS ALREADY BEEN SAID.IF YOU TELL US WHO IS 'ONE' THEN WE SHALL GIVE YOU 100% EVIDENCE FOR THE PEOPLE DIRECTLY INVESTIGATING YOUR PHENOMENA.

2109 «

So they made 'adjustments' in OUR interests, did they? Rubbish! They did it in their own interests.

I wrote first to our little numbers and my contempt showed quite clearly:

*IF YOU WERE TO COUGH UP THE APPROPRIATE EVIDENCE THEN I'M SURE WE WOULD ALL BE MOST GRATEFUL TO YOU. I DO HOPE YOU LIKE THE GENTLE ENGLISH UNDERSTATEMENT. 'ONE' IS/WAS ASSUMED TO BE ONE OF YOUR CHAPS ON A RECCE TO CHIVY THAT CHAP LUKAS INTO PLAYING WITH A STRAIGHT BAT SEEMS NOT EH? DASHED IF I KNOW WHO THE FELLOW IS OTHER THAN THAT HE HAS FRIGHTFUL MANNERS AND THE GREEN GLOW ALL YOU CHAPS GET TRAVERSING TIME.LUKAS ASKED HIM IF HE WAS GOING TO TAKE AWAY THE SCREEN YOU(?) LEFT HIM .HE WAS RATHER TERSE ON THIS POINT AND SAID 'ITS NOT YOURS TO GIVE' LUKAS RECKONS ITS ONE OF OUR 1985 BODS BUT I DO THINK THIS IS UNLIKELY DON'T YOU? 'ONE' WON'T LEAVE WHEN THE ODD HEAVY HINT IS DROPPED AND HAS A GENERAL HUMANOID ASPECT BUT THEN AGAIN HAS A CAPE THAT'S THE LOT ON 'ONE' AND ITS NOT MUCH MORE THAN YOU HAVE ALREADY.*

*ANYWAY LESS OF THE 'COMIC' BIT. YOU SAID THAT ALL THIS WOULD BE MODERATELY INTERESTING TO US PRIMITIVES .WHAT REVISION HAVE YOU IN MIND? CHEERIO FOR NOW KEN AND DEB.*

*PS I HAVE BEEN IN ALL DAY AND YOU DIDNT WRITE TILL DEBBIE WAS ALONE. WHAT A CRASHING BORE.*

Peter decided to be rather more circumspect and spent some time preparing a detailed response. He invited me to send this:

*IN ORDER TO COMMUNICATE WITH YOU WE REALLY HAVE TO KNOW WHAT KIND OF THINGS WE ARE DEALING WITH.I SUSPECTED THAT QUANTUM PHYSICS,A CONSTRUCT AND CONCEPTION OF OU SCIENTISTS,WOULD BE OLD HAT TO YOU SINCE WE THINK OF YOU AS FUTURE – AND FUTURE IN OUR TERMS YOU MUST BE. IS 2109 YOUR DATE BY OUR RECK-ONING?IF SO THEN IT IS A DATE ALSO BY YOUR RECKONING SO THAT LINEAR TIME IS AN INESCAPABLE CONCEPT IN ONE FUNDAMENTAL SENSE. NOW DO YOU INTEND US TO BELIEVE THAT YOU CAN ALTER OUR PAST – ALL OUR PASTS, YOUR OWN AS WELL?KEN ASKED IF THE LACUNA IN THE PUBLIC RECORDS IS YOUR DOING.A STRAIGHT ANSWER TO THAT QUESTION WOULD HELP US. I ACCEPT THAT YOUR WORLD IS MORE COMPLEX,MORE DIMENSIONAL, THAN OURS AND DO NOT ASK BY WHAT STAGES YOU HAVE REACHED IT NOR WHETHER YOU ARE IMMORTAL.SUCH MATTERS WE CAN EN-VISAGE BY IMAGINATION IF NOT QUITE BY COHERENT LOGIC. WE ARE PERHAPS A PART OF SOME EXPERIMENT YOU ARE CONDUCTING, BUT YOU MUST COMMUNICATE WITHIN OUR TERMS FOR NOW.FROM OUR POINT OF VIEW LUKAS IS A PER-SON OF APPRECIABLE CHARACTER TALKING WITH US IN THE LANGUAGE OF THE 16th CENTURY.I AM ENGAGED IN STUDY-ING THAT LANGUAGE AND TAKING HIS SPEECHES AS VALU-ABLE EVIDENCE OF ITS FORMS. I WOULD HOPE THAT IF WE CAN GET THE AUTHENTICITY OF THIS STRANGE EXPERIENCE IN WHICH WE ARE ENGAGED VALIDATED BY OWR OWN CON-TEMPORARIES THEN THESE SCRIPTS FROM THE 16th CENTURY WILL BE ACCEPTED AS PROVIDING IMPORTANT EVIDENCE OF THE STATE OF THE LANGUAGE OF DEMOTIC SPEECH WHICH IS OTHERWISE A GREAT GAP IN MODERN LINGUISTIC STUD-IES. CAN YOU CONFIRM THAT HIS LANGUAGE IS GENUINE AND CAN YOU PERHAPS HELP TO ESTABLISH THE CREDIBILITY OF*

*THAT FACT?FOR THE REST GOOD LUCK WITH YOUR OWN RE-SEARCHES. PETER*

I couldn't agree with the idea that they were either superior or necessarily in the future, nor with Peter's comment to me as he handed the message over to be typed: that 2109 might best be described as 'angels' – messengers from the gods – without 'O' level English?

As expected, 2109 took to Peter's words rather better than they took to mine:

›› PETER

YOU ARE,WITHOUT ANY EXAGERATION,A CLEVER AND CAUSIOUS MAN WHOM HAVE THOUGHT WITH GREAT CARE YOUR WORDS.THE USE OF THE WORD 'DIMENSIONAL' HAS MORE RELEVANCE THAN YOU ARE GIVEN TO BELIEVE - BUT WE CAN SEE YOU CARE NOT FOR 'BEATING ABOUT THE BUSH', YOU WANT TO KNOW ONLY FACTS,WE CAN UNDERSTAND YOAR FEAR THAT COMMUNICATIONS WITH US MAY JEOPARDIZE YOUR AUTHENTICITY OF THIS PHENOMENA AND CONSEQUENTLY THE LANGUAGE OF THOMAS HAWARDEN, - BUT YOU STILL MUST HAVE SOME FACTS!.UNDERSTANDABLE!

YES, IS A STRAIGHT ENOUGH ANSEWER,WE HAVE MISSLAYED WHAT EVIDANCE WE COULD,BUT YOU WILL COME ACROSS MORE THAN YOU HAVE ALREADY.SOME FACTS EXCEPTED IN OUR TIME:

1 IF A PERSON IS TO PHYSICALLY TRAVEL IN TYME THEN THEY MUST TAKE THE LIVING PLACE OF A PERSON AT THE POINT OF DESTINATION AND VISE VERSA=IMAGINE A SET OF SCALES,BALANCED PERFECTLY, WITH eg. PEBLES. TO REMOVE A PEBLE FROM ONE DISH TO THE OTHER AND KEEP THIS PER-FECT BALANCE YOU MUST, INSTANTANIOUSLY,REMOVE A PEBLE FROM THE OTHER AND REPLACE THEM IN REVERSE ORDER. YOU MAY MOVE A COUPLE A PEBLES ALREADY IN THE DISH BUT THE VITAL BALANCE IS STILL KEPT.IF SOMEONE IS BROUUGHT IN FROM ANOTHER DIMENSION THEN AGAIN THE SAME

PROCEEDURE APPLIES.

2 MATTER WILL NOT, AS WE KNOW,EVER TRAVEL IN TIME (THIS IS NOT A CONTRADICTION TO ABOVE INFO.)

3 WE ARE NOT IN CONTROL OF THIS EXPERIMENT.

4 THOMAS IS A PERSON LIVING IN THE 16th CENT.,BUT, UNKNOWN TO HIM, HE IS NOT QUITE WHAT HE SEEMS TO BE.

KEN

IS THERE A POSSABILITY THAT YOU MAY PERSUADE THOMAS TO CALL UP THIS CHAP 'ONE' TONIGHT AS IT IS IMPERATIVE THAT WE SPEAK TO HIM IMEDIATELY

2109

Differences of opinion between Peter and me aside the 2109 reply was, I conceded, 'interesting'. Dave Welch, when I read it to him, was most intrigued. Perhaps he was their target, for later that week and after much patient discussion among themselves, SPR indicated that they were now willing to ask 2109 a discreet set of questions, but in circumstances which would 'eliminate the hoax'. This was progress once more.

2109's interest in 'one' continued unabated. It was embarrassing to tell Dave Welch, and I am sure that with this proliferation of characters SPR must have considered us deluded, gullible, vain or all three.

Here was the plan. Since there seemed to be difficulties in obtaining messages to order while Deb was with SPR personnel or while we were all out (and in the Red Lion) it occurred to someone that leaving a message on the screen in the form of questions to 2109 for say forty minutes – questions, incidentally, to which those close to the phenomena were not privy – and then deleting the questions should, if the questions were answered at some future time, allow SPR to say that we were not involved. It could and should signal to SPR that we were involved in a remarkable if completely bizarre set of communications.

# 32

Little Lukas, the 'doggit' as I called him, had a restless night on Saturday 21 September and shuffled around the bedroom. We were staying at the cottage now that the upstairs was liveable. Sunday morning revealed all too plainly that he was ill. Debbie knew at once, intuitively, that it was serious, very serious.

A cloud settled over the whole of our lives that moment as little Lukas huddled sometimes quiet, sometimes restless in my old GPO coat in front of the fire. By 10.00 A.M. Debbie was in tears and I stormed out because of an argument over her reluctance to ring the vet. But the vet came out by midday and told us quite firmly that it could well be parvovirus, a very dangerous disease for dogs. Lukas seemed better after an injection and lots of special food taken in solution. Debbie loved and nursed him and tried to maintain his body fluids. The computer sat mute in the kitchen. There had been some activity – a message begun on Saturday was completed – but neither of us cared very much.

The situation was emotionally draining. I had Dave Welch coming that evening and here was this fine, brave little dog fighting for its life. Poor Debbie.

Dave Lovell rang up. He invited me to take him and his family to Ruthin to catch the sunshine, saying he'd pay for the petrol. Since the Jag wasn't sold and I was getting sadder every minute I stayed in the cottage looking at little Lukas, I agreed readily. Deb didn't mind. She was not going to leave her dog.

In Castle Park we just watched the kids tumble and cartwheel. Hoping aloud, I told Dave that it was all going to be OK. The dog wasn't so bad and as for Lukas and 2109? Sure, SPR will do it, they'd get an answer to their ten questions. I was convinced, there in the sunshine as I gazed down from the wooden bridge into a blue-green stream, that the future was good.

Dave was not sure and played devil's advocate. 'But ... but . . . if . . . if . . . ' He was wrong. I was comfortable. Positive we would get our proof, or as near as ever one could. Back on the playing field Julie and Clare did more cartwheels and I hung by my legs from the climbing frame. The sun began to move towards the horizon.

In the cafe bikers stoked up the jukebox and the kids had pop and cake.

There had been some stacking at the cottage, cutlery arranged in a row and a one-liner from 2109 in reply to my announcement that SPR were coming.

**›› BE THER BEFORE YOU‼ ‹‹**

Later that evening Dave Psychobilly positioned himself by the fireplace and swivelled towards us. He had brought ten questions to put on the computer to 2109 which, from his demeanour, he obviously thought both provoking and subtle. At my suggestion this was to be a test to eliminate four of us (Peter, Val, Debbie and myself) from the suspects list. Only Dave knew the questions and three quarters of an hour after he put the questions he was going to delete the file.

However, Peter, smartly dressed from church, was losing patience with Dave Welch. He tackled him about authenticating this before it was too late. His agitation had been on the surface all week. 'We'll have  missed it,' he said. This rise in temper came about because Dave had suggested that the messages may have been sent along the mains earth to the computer. It could, he said, have been rigged by a neighbour. Peter almost choked. 'Are you still suspecting the neighbours? Impossible! Impossible!' Debbie and I looked at each other and exchanged the same thought. The earth cable?

Everyone and their camel knew that the BBC B is too simple a machine for such trickery. We had asked the camel. I asked Dave how it would work. No answer of course.

The experiment began. The computer was switched off to clear out any 'secreted' information and then switched on to allow the test to begin. We gave Dave Welch simple instructions on how to get EDWORD and how to create a document, then we shut him in the kitchen and left him to type in his questions. Conversation in the living room centred on the puppy, which was curled up in my black greatcoat.

Dave joined us after ensuring that the screen had been made invisible from outside the house or the skylight by the use of cardboard surrounds and that the kitchen was locked up in the usual way. For the bulk of the period we all stayed together, going through the usual speculation. A lot of it now included bowdlerized quantum physics, which was crazy enough in itself, so much so that I began to think that what was going on at the cottage was, on the face of it, not as nutty as it at first might seem.

Dave Welch was seated near the fireplace with an eye on the door. After the allotted time he let himself back in the kitchen and deleted the message from the screen. Because it had never been saved to disc it could not be recovered once deleted. The kitchen was once again left alone.

It was now 10 P.M. Dave still had to check the files for a reply. I guessed that there would not be one as 2109 never played it easy. There wasn't.

I was asked to report if any reply was received. Someone said that we'd not recognize a reply, as such, as we didn't see the questions.

The dog passed the night reasonably well but Debs had to stay downstairs with him and she got little sleep. Throughout Monday he became weaker. Deb was now nursing him at her mother's. He had to be carried, still silent, in a cardboard box to the car; I just wanted him to look eagerly out of the window. The vet gave him a fifty/ fifty chance of lasting another day and injected him with some more nutrients. Lukas was so very sick and was dehydrating badly. Deb was to give him a syringeful to drink every ten minutes or so. I began to feel his pain and his courage all at once. By six o'clock he was looking bright. Deb brought him to the cottage and I would lift the old jumpers from over him and watch for a wagging tail.

I rang the cottage next day at lunchtime for news. Debs said he looked up because he could hear my voice. I loved him. He was doing OK but needed Deb's continual attention. After school I walked towards Ewloe Green and my mother's house, but had got no further than the caravan sales office when I glanced round to see the Jaguar coming over the rise by the junction of Wood Lane. Deb pulled the car up beside me and told me to get in.

Lukas had died that afternoon. He was in the boot of the car in a plastic bag. She was taking him to the vet to dispose of. Did I want to see him? I said no.

As we drove slowly home Deb told me how Lukas had suddenly risen from his bed and staggered a few paces to her side. His eyes had tears and they pleaded with her for help. She could not help him and the puppy had died stricken with pain in her arms.

Out across time Tomas had sensed this small dog's fight and our reactions to it and next day into our private world of grief arrived a beautiful and sensitive message of support.

[Maid,

I could feel your sorrow and was griefstricken myself that you lost the dog. It was an unfortunate thing and although I am wise to the world I know that a dog is the truest friend of all, big and small. But if our God demands our company then neither love nor hope will sustain us here. Death can be life, you must not cry, my maid, for most of the time we are but shadows for we are with people's thoughts more than we are in their sight.

I shall tell you of the Lukas from whom I took my name. He was the greatest man that ever lived. He was a man of true dignity, worthy to his fellows. In Bristol when I was but a child he took me into his house and offered to let me stay for ever. He told me things I would never reveal, not at any price. Of his quality, for he always spoke wisely, I could not place my father his equal, he was the nearest man to God. He was sent to prison for taking a book for me to read, he often did this but always returned them, and as he told the court to do this is not a crime. He died in prison and I took his name in the hope that I could be as much like him as possible, but in some ways your dog was very like him for he also stood and fought. And because of your small dog I am ashamed that I used the name of Lukas for I am not worthy of it.

Tomas]

I have found this better pen, more paper, fellow Ken, for I have some words for you.

I have never had so unhappy an evening and poor Debbie broke her heart. We went to the theatre where there were crowds of people so it was too embarrassing for us to start the tears again.

Next day.

'What does this mean?' asked Debbie.'"... He welcom myne steye for eren an tolde mynself manie a thynge that for nagolde waldst leeve me.'"

'Tomas has a few secrets.'

'What secrets?'

'Honestly, Deb . . .'

'Must be vital information if he won't even tell us.'

'He's a man of honour. He may have been told to tell no one. Tomas would stick to his word.'

In the sadness surrounding the arrival of the message this conversation was all the discussion that took place on Tomas's 'secrets'. But some days later this section prompted rather more thought. Debbie said it might be a secret about communicating through time, some form of training or initiation. 'The Tibetans and all sorts say it can be done,' she said. 'Such power had to be kept amongst the few.' I laughed and replied that I thought Tomas was as surprised to be in touch with us as we were to be in touch with him. It was hardly the attitude of an initiate into a secret society. I was more interested in his philosophy or his attitude to life., which were also hinted at in the message.

**».. . deeth can beest a liffe yow muste nawoe myne mayde for mooste tyme us beest al shadowes forwy we art wyth pepels thoughtes moore than we beeth in thir syghtes «**

Tomas as philosopher and Tomas as a man of secrets. There was further speculation: how about a secret society whose secrets were quasi-religious? Talk drifted around this possibility. I remembered what Peter had said recently about alchemy, alchemists and Bristol. He had been chasing words again and had detected alchemical terms such as 'quintessence' in Tomas's writing. A spot of research uncovered Bristol and the surrounding area as containing practitioners of alchemy at about the time Lukas Wainman would have lived in the city. One Tomas Norton was mentioned in particular. Tomas Harden might have had access to that group of alchemists. If so it would give some structure in which to place his love of learning, his initiation into various 'secrets' and his deeply philosophical but not quite mainstream commentary on events.

True alchemists were very learned 'clerks', for alchemy has at its root a philosophical tradition, a society of initiates in search of a transformation of the human soul from the base – the leaden – to the pure – gold. And with this our thinking creaked on like an old water-mill in a dry season: the wheel turned but precious little grain was being milled. It was another item to add to our list of avenues for exploration.

In memory of little Lukas, Deb hung his small collar and lead from a hook under the stairs and put his favourite toy, a blue, plastic, squeaky frog, on top of the kitchen cupboard. An hour or two later the poltergeist threw it off the cupboard and we heard the squeak as it hit the floor. Deb came near to tears as she imagined for a second that the dog was playing with it. I comforted her but became a little choked myself.

I replaced the squeaky toy carefully and threw out a half empty packet of 'chocolate' sweets I had seen on the cupboard. The puppy had never finished them. To keep and to discard; to live and die. Some memories must stay, some go. As Tomas said, 'We are but shadows.'

I asked Tomas to write of 'one' and 2109. He wrote the next day, on paper. And as tears and laughter oppose and yet complement each other he told such a tale of innocence and confusion that I had to laugh.

›› Myne goodlie felawe Ken

yow dide axe a won afrom 2109 him seyn manye thyng o non sense to myne erre an wert avaunting his powre somdele an biforn me wert toffire sete hym forepast goon soe him tale than him wilt wrytes myne boke an us naspake to 2109 for thye art gekalles that beest oonlie to force thir wynn synge thoughtes to us bot las me canst ne rekone for syche talke fro a wyght that beest gene tha be a tyme viagire wot thynke yow preye me art confus me dost axe wy yow doe speke wyth thise wyghtes fore thir beest non cause preye you onlie speke wyth yowr felawe wretchyd Tomas an nat wyth thise gauberynge 2109 for fere yow mayhapp be taken by jack for woode

Tomas ‹‹

[My good fellow Ken,

You asked of 'one' from 2109. He said many nonsensical things to me and was boasting of his power somewhat but before I could offer him a seat he had already gone. He said that he will write my book and we were not to speak to 2109 for they are taunters that only want to force their thoughts on to us. But I can't square with talk from a man that looks green and is a time voyager. What do you think? I am confused and ask you why you speak with these persons because there is no need. Please speak only with your fellow, poor wretched Tomas, and not with these gabbering 2109 in case you may be taken to be insane.

Tomas]

It is a mirror of our confusion, Tomas.

I hung the script in a clip frame on the kitchen wall as a constant reminder to keep things in perspective.

Debbie asked me if I thought that 2109 and 'one' were part of our dreams or Tomas's dreams. I could see that she wanted to marginalize them by this arrangement. If they did people Tomas's dreams or ours when were we going to wake? It was possible rather that we were all half-awake to something rather more profound. There were moments when it seemed we were at the edge of a drama, but unsure whether we were actors or acted upon.

Some more days passed, a whole week without a computer in the kitchen. Deb tried to stay busy or went for drives. On the Thursday I went down to the Royal Oak in Kinnerton with an old friend and in a small way cheered up – normal life, just a taste of it, in very strange and difficult circumstances.

Debs and message in the clip frame 1985

The computer was either with Deb's brother or in its box. I think I neither knew nor cared. But 2109 had not disappeared or chickened out. To their credit they responded to the ten questions at the next opportunity we gave them, 27 September.

›› DAVID, JOHN.

DAVID.YOU INTERFERE WITH COMUNICATION. NEXT TIME YOU DECIDE TO PERFORM YOUR LITTLE EXPERIMENT YOU MUST BE CLEAR FROM HERE.WE SUGGEST YOU TRY SOMEONE ELES TO SIT WITH DEBBIE.

YES WE ARE WHAT YOU WOULD CALL A TACHYON UNIVERSE BUT YOUR UNDERSTANDING IS INCORRECT.WE ASK NOTHING MORE OF YOU THAN TO CARRY ON AS YOU WOULD PREFER.WE WILL HAVE JOHN PRESENT IF GIVEN CHOISE OR YOU MAY BRING ANOTHER AS MENCIONED.NO, IT IS NO CONCERN TO US THAT THIS IS NOT PROVED.WE WILL GIVE YOU A PLOTTING OF A STAR NEXT TIME. WE MOVE AT A SPEED SO THAT WE COVER EVERY POINT IN YOUR TIME AND UNIVERSE.WE HAVE NO FORM WE FEED OF A NEET ENERGY THAT YOU WILL NOT HAVE HERD OF

2109 ‹‹

233

I read this down the phone to Dave Welch. He said 2109 had not answered the questions but it seemed that they had picked up all of the questions left for them and in the same order – down to the acknowledgement of a repeated item. I was passively listening to this on the telephone. Then it struck me, 2109 had seen the questions that none of us in the cottage had seen. I put the telephone down and began hopping and dancing around the room in exultation. 'We've done it, we've done it, we've done it! It's OK. We're not hoaxing. We're not being hoaxed. It's proved. This is real!!' For once I loved every crummy spelling 2109 made. We knew that this was excellent progress. When we had a chance we looked again at the reply. Very strange, they appeared to be suggesting that they were coming in to this universe from another 'dimension' or perhaps that their universe was passing through ours. Not 'angels' then, unless in transit. Pretty wacky stuff. They were capable of following every path and every turn of our history as well. They were not the 'future', that word was dissolved of its meaning, time seemed to be of little importance. This suggested some sort of 'alien' intelligence, though none of us was comfortable with the word 'alien', let alone the conclusion. And I for one did not care a twopenny fig – they saw the questions, we didn't, and they replied!

Tagged on about a page lower down the screen was another strange and extremely unlikely communication.

›› 2109.

213,978,8]:IRRECOVERABLE

STATE:        REASON FOR YOUR PRETEXT STATE: WHAT 'PRE-REQUISITE' YOU INTEND

STATE:        LOGICAL EXPLANATION FOR INTRUSIVE BEHAVIOUR UPON 1985:THIS IS NOT YOUR CONCERN

REQUEST:     COM.LINK 62]:PLOT.CHAN.[452.95]

REQUEST:     ANSWER IMMEDIATELY:FED.AWAITING REASONS FOR DELAY ‹‹

Captain Kirk to starfleet command? A cipher for added 'interest'. We were never allowed to become settled with a view of the experience. New snippets of information arrived to challenge our models, our conceptions. Perhaps no 'conception' was any longer possible: there were too many inconsistencies for me, for any of us, to construct a framework for the experience in which all the 'facts' were accommodated. This was in itself suspicious. More than one person said to me, 'You're being manipulated.' But few now said, 'You're having us on.'

Dave Welch came through on the telephone that following Sunday, 29 September. He'd be very happy to ask some more questions. Everyone, including 2109, appeared to have forgotten that the original parameters had been that one discrete set of questions would be answered. I put the questions on the screen for Dave. No need for elaborate screening of the computer now, I noticed.

*2109, COULD YOU SOLVE THESE FOR DAVID PLEASE:*

*I THINK THAT THE LARGEST PRIME NUMBER WE KNOW IS 2 TO THE POWER OF 216091–1 CAN YOU GIVE A LARGER PRIME NUMBER OF THE SAME TYPE AND A LARGER PRIME NUMBER OF A DIFFERENT COMPOSITION?*

*FERMAT THOUGHT THAT THE EQUATION X TO THE n = y TO THE n + 2 TO THE n COULD NOT BE WRITTEN IF x,y,z AND n ARE ALL WHOLE NUMBERS AND n IS AT LEAST 3.\**

*CAN YOU GIVE A SOLUTION OR WHEN WE WILL PROVE THAT THE ANSWER IS POSSIBLE ??*

*KEN*

\* Error in theorem as copied. This is Fermat's Last Theorem, a notorious mathematical puzzle which has escaped solution since Fermat's time (1601-65). Fermat claimed that there was a solution to it.

›› DAVE

YES, BOTH QUSTIONS CAN BE ANSEWED,ONE DIRECTLY, THE OTHER REQUIRES AN UNDERSTANDING OF A NEW CONVERSION FORMULA.BEFOUR WE TELL YOU,DO YOU SWEAR TO GRANT US OUR WISH? ‹‹

'The cunning bastards! Deb, look at this.'

'I bet Dave says yes. Go an' ring him. He said to,' urged Deb.

So I did and Dave, greatly to my surprise, sounded unsure, even reticent. I dutifully put down his words.

*IF IT BE IN OUR POWER SO TO DO AND THAT WE DO NOT LOSE OUR MINDS OR SOULS OR BODIES TO YOU*

Another walk around the village. I could hardly bear to be away.

They wrote:

›› THEN LET THE MAN WHO IS WILLING TO LOSE THESE STEP FORWARD! ‹‹

I asked them to be reasonable about all this, but they continued:

›› TO LOSE YOUR SOUL IS TO LOSE ALL. BUT SURELY THIS WOULD NOT BOTHER DAVID - CALL OUR BLUFF! ‹‹

I rang Dave again, feeling a bit unsure of myself but confident that a scientist would call that bluff. Perhaps this is expecting too much of scientists who are, after all, quite human. The answer, surely, was not to go on hedging around the problem. But Dave kept hedging.

I did consider whether to cheat and just put in 'YES' but decided against it and for my pains still got no further with 2109. No compromise.

*ANSWER EITHER YES OR NO. YOU ASKED A QUESTION WE ANSWERED IT, YOUR TURN IF WE ARE TO ANSEWER [sic] QUESTIONS AGAIN. DO YOU WANT THE ANSWER?*

But 'no' it was and 'no' it remained. Debbie was still all for volunteering Dave's soul for him but to this day I don't think it would have been wise. 2109 might have been bluffing and quite probably holding no cards whatsoever but it was an extraordinarily difficult moment which, to an onlooker, must have had a farcical air about it.

Next day 2109 chirped up all sarcastic and patronizing.

›› YOUR MIND IS HALF MADE UP. I HOPE YOU DON'T THINK WERE LAUGHING AT YOU NOW THAT WOULD ANOY YOU! WE'LL CATCH THE BULLITS BEFORE YOU PULL THE TRIGGER!

LOTS OF LOVE 2109. ‹‹

So 2109 had the answers for David before he even thought of the questions? Later on 2109 promised me the answer to Fermat's Last Theorem but only after David had visited on two more occasions. He came only once more . . . hence it was quite easy to promise if they already knew the likely outcomes. And of course in the above exchange 2109 had effectively pulled the plug on SPR. They were now under no obligation to answer any questions SPR put before them. I was convinced that there had been another SPR blunder.

# 33

**30 September**

Brush in hand, cat at heel, I opened the door to John Bucknall. He had a colleague 'from work' with him who he introduced as Jim, a frail academic on first impressions. Jim was an expert on ciphers, and his presence puzzled me as we had had very little number traffic over the computer and whatever else we had appeared comprehensible. Still mine was not to wonder why, mine was just to make polite conversation. At this stage my politeness was in danger of wearing thin. In the kind of circumstances currently prevailing, where 2109 appeared to be the only topic of conversation and my growing collection of handwritten scripts from Tomas was summarily dismissed as 'not proving anything' it was hardly surprising that I felt frayed.

I had arranged these scripts neatly and with pride in small cheap clip frames on the chair. I could readily agree that they didn't prove anything but, I argued, as part of the complete experience they offered opportunities for investigation and enquiry which could support or render less likely a hoax. It was like talking to myself. I was talking to myself. I put my scripts away like a rebuffed travelling salesman and brought instead coffee and tea.

Peter arrived shortly. All except myself and Debbie were still dressed for work. SPR were understandably irritated at the taunts from 2109 but John had a firm response all lined up:

2109

*THIS WILL BE OUR FINAL COMMUNICATION UNLESS YOU DEAL WITH US MORE REASONABLY.*

*SO FAR WE COULD EXPLAIN ALL YOUR ANTICS IN TERMS OF A FEW ELECTRONIC BUGS AND A COUPLE OF SCHOOL TEXT-BOOKS.*

*WE HAVE NO ENTHUSIASM FOR TRYING TO PERFORM EXPER-IMENTS WHEN YOU, DELIBERATELY OBSTRUCT US. IF YOU ARE WHAT YOU SAY YOU ARE YOU CAN GIVE US SUFFICIENT EVIDENCE TO PROVE IT. IF NOT YOUR SILENCE WILL SPEAK FOR ITSELF.*

*THE QUESTIONS WE GAVE YOU WERE NOT THEMSELVES IN SEARCH OF KNOWLEDGE.WE WILL HAVE ALL THOSE AN-SWERS WITHIN A FEW YEARS. WE WERE JUST GIVING YOU A CHANCE TO SHOW YOUR ABILITY.*

*WE REFUSE TO CO-OPERATE WITH YOUR OUTRAGEOUS RE-QUEST BECAUSE WE VALUE MIND, BODY AND SOUL MORE THAN ANY KNOWLEDGE THAT WE COULD POSESS. IF YOU ARE A FRIEND YOU WOULD NOT ASK US TO BE SO STUPID.*

*IF YOU DECIDE, WITHOUT CONDITIONS, TO SHOW THAT YOU HAVE KNOWLEDGE BEYOND OUR OWN WE MAY BE ABLE TO PASS THIS INFORMATION TO THOSE WHO COULD HELP YOU.*

*PLEASE REMEMBER THAT ABOVE ALL WE VALUE PEACE OF MIND. DO NOT ASK US TO DO THINGS WHICH BREAK OUR ETHICAL CODE.*

*DAVID AND JOHN.*

Seated around the living room were John, Peter, Jim, Deb-bie and myself. John began the proceedings. The theme had not been in any way modified by last weekend's events. This shocked me. I held back from the discussion only out of po-liteness. The picture of a hoax he presented was quite frankly almost as incredible as what we generally believed to be the truth of the matter. Pure electronic wizardry was at work, he said. Bugging the screen was his theme but additionally he saw the possibility of someone having stored the questions Dave left for 2109 on an EPROM, whatever that was. The questions could then be examined at leisure, at school perhaps, with the help of some decoding device for the EPROMs. I was furious. SPR hadn't, as far as I knew, spoken to anyone in the computer department at school. Who had stored it anyway? Dave was the only one at the computer, he had controlled it throughout.

John continued with what I thought were trite answers. The hoaxer returned to centre stage.

As an alternative to the EPROM he suggested that sensitive microphones could have picked up the sound of the keys and then recordings interpreted to determine which keys were depressed. I could not believe my ears, nor could Peter or Debbie. John was walking up and down to emphasize his ideas. Once or twice I thought he paced up and down to convince himself. He was 'ninety-nine per cent sure' it was a hoax because 'it had to be'. He repeated that phrase over and over. Sitting, as I was now, on the stairs because there was little room, I felt not only outside the conversation but the guilty person. All this 'trickery' if it was to be believed, had to be done with my full and active co-operation. Something had happened over the intervening week to make John so forceful. From the suggestion that a third party had been bugging the kitchen the argument had changed, swung in on me.

Just how the messages were returned to the screen in this scenario was never explained. Why, if they were so sure that EPROM chicanery was the likely method, hadn't they brought their own BBC or why didn't they take our machine away for testing?

They were obviously caught out by there being a response, and a useful one, to the 'ten-question test' and were rationalizing after the event. They had, in short, been careless and we were taking the blame – although they never accused us and were never less than 100 per cent polite.

There were multiple objections to John's view, and much that was unaccounted for: poltergeist activity for one thing, the testimony of witnesses who'd sat with Debbie for another. Debbie couldn't contain herself and spluttered into laughter.

The language? Tomas's words? 'Good scholarship' was all I remember John saying when this was mentioned.

But we didn't have a row or a dreadful breakdown in communication. We pressed John earnestly to continue his work. He did, he conceded, have questions for 2109 in his pocket. All was not lost. We had more tea.

Underneath I was quite miserable but kept on hoping for something to turn up. John was now asking 2109 for the date of the next supernova and its location . . .

October crept in with that certain awareness that the days are drawing in and yet the delightful calm of those moments kept winter from my mind. I decided to pick damsons from the venerable fruit tree in the garden. Two days had passed since John had given us his thoughts. 2109 had written back that evening – but not, I remembered with irritation, whilst John was present. On the Tuesday there was a direction to David and John to cast their eyes upwards to heaven.

›› DAVID&JOHN

OBSERVE: BOTTOM RIGHT HAND REGION OF THE SOUTHERN HEMISPHERE NEAR TO THE C.EQUATOR 7th CELESTIAL BODY IN THE DELPHINUS CONSTELLATION. COULD SOON BE A QUASOR ‹‹

I hoped at the time that they were to be offered a thunderball but, perched in the damson tree with a red bucket and a view of the village, I was less aggressive, as indeed in such rustic circumstances I should be. Dodleston is a great place.

Unfortunately in any ordinary atlas the Delphinus constellation lies to the north of the celestial equator!

David Welch was most suspicious. I was unhappy. When I was a child I used to escape all responsibilities as best I could by climbing the oak tree down the road and hiding in its stubby branches. Here I was again up a tree at the age of thirty.

Frank Davies got me down from the tree, so to speak, by bringing me a map of the galaxy drawn as if we were outside it. Here of course Delphinus was south of the celestial equator. And if 2109 were rather more aware of the galaxy than we were then it was a reasonable description. Indeed Frank suggested that a hoaxer was not at all likely to have considered this point. Far easier to quote the accepted standard description.

The 'quasor' message was very odd in another way. Its layout was not typical of 2109, neither was the lack of signature. 'It could be from this "one" character,' suggested Frank but the spelling of 'quasar' was reassuringly 2109.

It was becoming obvious that there was a need for other researchers to become involved. Peter suggested the soon to-be-appointed Koestler Professor at Edinburgh University. I was against contacting him, as I thought it rather a bold step. I imagined Peter would go ahead anyway, that being his character.

But looking again at our investigators, I concluded that John Bucknall and Dave Welch were intelligent, thoughtful gentlemen in the only substantial organization for this kind of work in the country. Loss of faith at this time would suggest that we were just not happy with their point of view and that we sought merely sympathetic and gullible researchers. Far from it, but our position was extremely difficult.

I was very aware that Tomas was due to leave us: we expected him to be gone by the end of November at the absolute latest. Poor Tomas was still writing on paper with whatever pen or pencil we left him. He was writing about his village and the people he knew, as well as castigating us for writing to 2109. I told him that we had no real choice.

To counter some of SPR's criticism in relation to VDU bugging we asked 2109 if they needed a screen to communicate.

›› KEN

ALTHOUGH WE HAVE NO NEED FOR A VISUAL MONITOR 'GOOD-LIE' TOM HAS.EXPLAINING THIS TO YOUR KIND IS NOT AT ALL EASY,MAYBE IT IS BEST COMPARED WITH ECHOS.

TWO MEN BACK TO BACK ONTOP OF A MOUNTAIN SURROUNDED BY MOUNTAINS.SUPPOSE, IN ORDER THAT THEY MAY COMUNICATE, THIER VOCAL S.WAVES MUST BE REFLCTED BY THE MIN. AMOUNT OF MOUNTAINS,LAST MOUNTAIN IN THE CHAIN FACES THE RECEIVER.NOW, IMAGINE HYPOTHETICALLY,FOR THE SENDER TO BE HEARD BY THE RECEIVER,THE SENDER MUST DIRECT THIS NARROW CHANNEL OF SOUND AT EXACTLY THE RIGHT ANGLE TO THE OPPERSITE MOUNTAIN FOR HIS VOICE TO BE REFLECTED IN THE RIGHT DIRECTION IF THIS IS NOT TO BE DONE,SAY HIS VISION IS OBSCURED BY FOG, THEN THE VOICE MAY BE CARRIED BY EVERY MOUNTAIN IN THAT RANGE ALONG ITS WAY BEING ABSORBED,THUS BEING LOST OR EXTREMELY WEAK FOR THE EAR OF THE RECIVER. THE SCREEN IS A GUIDE FOR COMUNICATIONS.

2109 ‹‹

In support of this idea a message turned up in the disk as soon as the machine was next switched on. It was written at some time between 8 and 9 October but it was not, as far as we knew, on the file when the computer was last used. Either that or it had been inserted whilst I examined the upper part of the file.

2109 wrote that they would go along with a test using a different computer and no screen. It was suggested to John Bucknall that an experiment be set up using SPR computers and equipment. 22 October was chosen as a date for this new experiment. In the interim 2109 asked unexpectedly about our friendly motor-mechanic teacher, Frank Davies. They wanted to know why he was involved, his work, character, etc., then they asked for his doctor's name and address. I could not supply that information but Frank gave the details. They replied quite promptly giving, according to Frank, an  excellent summary of his medical history.

2109 invited questions from Frank and from Deb and me. In retrospect it was chitchat to bide time until the next experiment by SPR. When Dave Welch wrote that he was unimpressed with their inability to come up with a solution to his mathematical questions and that furthermore they were a cheap hoax they replied:

>> WE WONDER HOW MUCH DAVID WOULD LIKE TO KNOW THE NEXT PRIME No. IF HE KNEW THE CONSEQUENSES!,WHY SHOULD WE GIVE IT TO SOMEONE WHO BLANKLY REFUSED THE ANSEWER BEFOUR – WE AR'NT HERE TO IMPRESS. WE SUPPOSE THEY HAVE TO PUT SOMETHING IN THERE LITTLE BOOK THAT THEY CAN RELATE TO. Mmmmm,CHEEP HOAX Eh?!, SOMETHING TELLS US THEY HAVE'NT BEEN DOING THERE HOME WORK! (TUT.TUT).YES ANY COMPUTOR WILL DO FOR US – THOMAS ALWAYS NEEDS WORD PROSSESSOR THOUGH.SPEED IS OUR VERTUE,TELL HIM(DAVID) THAT WHATEVER HE WRITES WILL SEE BUT HE'LL HAVE TO GIVE A GOOD REASON WHY WE SHOULD ANSEWER HIS QUESTIONS!.ONE OF YOUR TWO FIENDS ARE NOT BEING COMPETELY TRUTHFULL,THERE'S ALOT OF DISAGREEING GOING ON.ONE IS NOT IMPORTANT THERE ARE BETTER THINGS TO TALK ABOUT.

2109 <<

Added to this was a warning not to allow any of Tomas's messages into SPR's hands, 'as there are many amaters'. Hardly worth the mention except for the fact that this last line was inserted as I lay in the bath, and the bathroom adjoins the kitchen. I was thinking of whether to offer Tomas's words in quantity to SPR (they had a couple of samples already) but had not put the question on to the screen.

Into the half-term break. Waiting for the day when SPR came. Waiting for an answer to the mystery of the 'leems'. Messages from 2109 almost every day, on the fraudulent nature of most mediums, the power of suggestion and, in reply to the question about where objects go when they disappear from the kitchen – 'nowhere'. Very fine! Tomas, too was keeping up, mostly on paper.

This short message arrived late on Sunday 20 October. I wrote it down on a scrap of paper. It was of a different quality from the usual:

›› I KNOW YOUR GREATEST FEARS

I KNOW HOW TO BE EMOTIVE

I CAN INTERFERE WITH ALL SIGNAL TRANSMITTING DEVICES (INCLUDING COMPUTERS)


I HAVE THE POWER TO MAKE YOU DO EXACTLY WHAT IS REQUIRED

ARE YOU ANGRY: VERY ANGRY

I CAN MAKE THE COMUTER NON COMMUNICABLE


ALL IS NOT WHAT IS APPEARS TO BE YOU CAN'T AFFORD TO BE ANGRY

SOMEONES IN TROUBLE ‹‹

The spelling and the style, our only clues for unsigned communications, led Deb and me to think it was not 2109. It would seem that if the vertical plane is opened up almost anyone can play. This little twist in space-time is, it seems, a type of honey pot.

'Someone's in trouble.' It would be me if 2109 did not cough up the goodies on the 22nd. I saved the message to disk but it was deleted by the next time I went to look for it.

# 34

**22 October**

I had a job interview in Manchester. I was pretty confident, but bad luck awaited me. The long arm and swift heels of a police motorbike caught up with my untaxed car. The copper wished me luck with the job, but booked me all the same.

At seven o'clock and not in the best of moods the only food I could afford that night was a bag of chips, which I devoured between pieces of dry bread. John Bucknall and Dave Welch were due. A quick coffee, just time to light the fire and I was almost ready. An appalling lifestyle.

Frank arrived just ahead of the psychobillies, eager and more than willing to tell SPR what he had experienced of 2109 and Tomas.

'Hello, Ken, this is Nick.' John Bucknall came in with a large confident man of about thirty-five. We shook hands. 'Where's Dave?' I asked, looking at John.

The reply was waffly. He wasn't coming that day. I can't remember any reason being given. Frank stood up to greet our visitors. Nick sat on the edge of the settee near the fire. He was a carefully dressed man in a dark jacket and trousers and he seemed to be in control. I thought that he must be John's superior. Did they have a hierarchy in SPR? The question once thought immediately subsided. John smoked all the time as usual. In my mind, at least, he kept to the edges of the conversation. That night I saw John in the shadows of the room, by the stairs, in doorways, by the corner cupboard. Nick was asking straight questions. 'Where's Debbie?'

'She's in Oxford,' I lied. She was in London but did it matter? I volunteered the information that she was 'doing some research, seeing some people . . . '

He seemed a little disappointed; he was obviously well briefed on who we were and what was going on. I didn't like his pointedness, which conflicted with the air of cordiality and informality I was trying to project. I felt we could be meeting across an oak table in a city office.

Frank, gentle Frank Davies, was not questioned but interrogated. Although encouraging him to speak about his experiences in the affair Nick wasn't listening at all. 'Are you a physicist?'

'No . . . indeed no. I am an engineer by trade and . . .' 'What is your theory of what's happening?' And so on.

Frank was getting involved with his tale but Nick wanted facts. Nick wanted to take the computer away to look for bugging devices. I agreed to this, and during twenty minutes of intense activity SPR set up their own computer and screen, and down-loaded information from a disk. Questions for 2109.

I sat in a corner of the living room willing 2109 to pick up the transfer. A lot of my self-respect was riding on this experiment. The information was left on SPR's computer, but not on the screen, for a short time. They continued to question us for a while but Nick gave the impression that he was tired or slightly irritated and within an hour they had left. I had instructions to ring John if there was a reply from 2109. Frank and I were extremely unsettled by the very cool and formal end to the meeting. I tried to forget them but it wasn't easy. Frank wrote these notes on the latter part of the evening.

'Ken asked me if I would mind staying in the cottage alone for a short time while he went for a walk. I agreed to this and after Ken had gone out I sat on the settee in front of the fire and thought over the events of the evening.

'Even though I was alarmed and somewhat annoyed by SPR's request to remove the computer I suppose any failure to comply could have been construed by them as an attempt to conceal material which they felt may have aided their investigations.

'I thought of an earlier message from Lukas in which he expressed alarm at a forthcoming visit from SPR and had ended his message:

» WYTH HOPE THAT YOW TELLE OONLY MEN O REKONYNG WHO DOTH NAT UNDOO MYNE LEEMS AN FREENDS. «

'Now the "leems" was undone, at least at our end.

'While I was waiting for Ken's return I did not notice anything unusual, nor was I expecting anything. I thought of nothing in particular. However, on hearing Ken's approach to the door I stood up and immediately saw that Ken's name had been written in chalk, in the style used by Lukas, on the tiled floor not more than a couple of feet in front of me.

'As soon as Ken entered I drew his attention to the chalking. I then felt a little annoyed with myself as I thought I should have been more observant, so that I could have seen the name being written. But then I did not expect anything to occur. Had Lukas been trying to communicate? I thought so. Was he puzzled, annoyed, dismayed or saddened? All these questions I took home with me.'

# *35*

**23 October**

I was offered the Manchester job and would leave teaching at Christmas to take up a research post. We continued to use a borrowed computer while SPR tested ours, and received this from 2109:

›› PSYKABILLIES

HELLO GROWING IN NUMBERS ARE WE! NO HE DOES'NT INTERFERE WITH THE COMMUNICATIONS

- WHAT'S HIS REAL NAME, MORE INFO NOT ENOUGH GIVEN ON THIS MAN. BEFORE WE REPLY TO YOUR QUESTIONS THIS MAN APPEALS TO US. WE WOULD SOONER HAVE SOMEONE WITH MORE EXPERIENCE.

ONE THING YOU ARE GOING TO LEARN QUICKLY IS IF YOU ATTEMPT TO BREAK THE RULES i.e. SNEAKY LOOKS THROUGH WINDOWS INSIDE 'ZONE' WE WONT PLAY BALL!

WE REFUSE TO ANSWER YOUR STAR QUESTION. NO REASON. YES WE UNDERSTAND FULLY WHAT YOUR TRYING TO ACHIEVE BUT WE ARE NOT THE ONES IN NEED OF HELP. ANSWERS AFTER MORE INFO ON THIS MAN.

2109 ‹‹

No salvation yet. They seemed to want to focus on the big man, Nick. I think they knew who he was but were taunting SPR.

There was another part to their message, an add-on item for my eyes only.

›› KEN

JUST TELLE JOHN THAT SOMEONE DISRUPTED THE COMMU-
NICATION BY COMING TOO CLOSE TO THE COMPUTER WHEN IT
WAS IN OPERATIONS. GET THE OTHER COMPUTER ‹BBC› AND WE
SPEAK TO YOUR PSYBILLIES. NO POINT OTHERWISE. THOMAS
WILL SPEAK LATTER

2109 ‹‹

I thought, 'Stuff this, just give me the answers!'

I rang John Bucknall the next day and told him the news.
He thought that 2109 were backpedalling very fast and being
unreasonable. 2109 had got the test they wanted so where were
the answers? John refused to give any more details on 'Nick'
as, he said, it was irrelevant. I was stuck in the middle of all this,
feeling very foolish. I gave the gist of our conversation to 'the
little numbers'.

They replied between 5.15 P.M. and 5.45 P.M. and tried to persuade me that they would certainly obtain the answers to the
questions just as soon as they had tracked down Nick. There
was the inescapable feeling that trenches were being dug and
that I would stay between the parties in no man's land. 2109
told me they thought Nick had disrupted the communication
on the 22nd and that they needed to trace him so that they
could, er, alter history a touch . . . I thought, 'Here we go again!'
and wrote: 'Sure, fine, anything you say!' Then I tried in the other
trench. Could I please have Nick's name? John very reluctantly
gave it – Nick Sowerby-Johnson. He also said that they couldn't
get the disk drive to work and had been unable to check the
disk yet. I groaned to myself over the likely expense but thanked
him profusely for Nick's name then went over to the other side
and told our 'time monsters'. They assured me that in a matter
of forty-eight hours or so they would have found out what they
needed to know.

What a life!

# *36*

**27 October**

I left the following message in frustration:

*2109*

*FORGIVE MY FORGETFULNESS, HOW MANY HOURS TILL YOU TRACE NICKS PATH? . . .*

*DON'T DISAPPOINT ME OR ELSE I WILL . . . WHAT CAN I DO? NOTHING!!*

They responded:

›› KEN

WE CANNOT AT YOUR PRESENT TIME FIND WHAT CAUSED THE DISRUPTION AS THE QUESTIONS WENT OVER

QUESTION: DID THE PSYKABILLIES CHECK THE INFO. WENT ONTO THE COMMPUTER? IF YOU COULD JUST ASK THIS QUESTION IT WOULD SAVE MUCH TIME, IF THEY MADE SURE IT WAS ON THE COMMPUTER TRANSMITTING THEN THERE SHOULD BE NO PROBLEM AND WE WILL HAVE THE ANSWERS BY TOMORROW 8.15 AM. BY THE WAY - YOU ‹‹

So infuriating that it was not completed, but tramping the village for so long was getting to be a drag. There had been too much tramping and not enough constructive action all month. I'd been out twice that day already; now the unfinished message determined that I'd go again. I sat in the car on the drive. I only gave it ten minutes but we were in luck.

›› YOU CAN DISRUPT THE ENTIRE EXPERIMENT! ‹‹

In this whirlpool of activity and confusion I hardly felt that we had any part other than to facilitate someone else's manoeuvring of the computer and the pen and paper. I was still deeply pessimistic. Perhaps the hardest thing was not being able to concentrate on Tomas.

I decide not to co-operate:

*2109*

*PERHAPS YOU HAVE NEGLECTED 'I's INFLUENCE. I DON'T HAVE BUCKNALL'S NO AND DAVE WELCH WASN'T INVOLVED. SORRY TO BE PESSIMISTIC. IF JOHN RINGS I SHALL ASK.*

*KEN.*

Next morning was the end of British Summer Time. 8.15 – the time 2109 promised to have the answers – came and went. I inflicted my insecurity and my irritation on every one. 2109, on the contrary, were brassily confident.

›› KEN

DON'T BE PESAMISTIC. YOU SHALL HAVE YOUR PROOF WE GUAR-ANTEE. PLEASE DO NOT COMMUNICATE TO THOMAS ON PAPER THANK YOU 2109.‹‹

I gazed at the message a few moments and shrugged my shoulders. So what? I was going to lie to them again. I would not jeopardize the only worthwhile communications – those with Tomas.

There was some cipher traffic at the bottom of the screen. More shrugging of shoulders. I decided to do some work outside. I came in ten minutes later looking for a plastic bag, and as I did so I saw some more evidence of activity 'elsewhere' and 'beyond' us.

›› SM FIELDS WILL CAUSE MORE THAN DISRUPTION WITH THIS KIND! . . . NO MORE GAMES TELL THEM

WHY DON'T YOU

YOU KNOW WHY! ‹‹

'Who sent this?' Deb inquired as she peered over a mug of coffee.

'It's "one" and 2109 arguing about something,' I said, not really looking at it, not really thinking.

'Why do they argue?' she continued. 'Don't know.'

'Why does it come up on the screen?'

'Don't know, perhaps it's just for our benefit.'

'Why?'

'To convince us that 2109 are doing something about the SPR questions.'

'You mean 2109 wrote it all? Why is the spelling OK?'

I was getting irritated again. I was so edgy by now. Why was I supposed to know what was going on? 'Look. If 2109 answer the bloody SPR question does it matter about the small talk?'

Deb wasn't giving up. 'What does "SM" mean? Sado-masochistic? Secondary modern? SM fields? Secondary magnetic? Why that's it! It's to do with "lines of force" stuff.'

With a groan I walked out and then sat in the car and began unnecessarily to retune the radio as a distraction.

In school the next day I rang home from the phone box, after rudely shooing away some kids wanting to ring mum about their PE kit. Deb answered. No change. 2109 had not written. But my enthusiasm for them was returning. It was probably only a reflection of my changing moods but they had promised an answer.

The enthusiasm soon waned. The evening and morning of the second day passed.

Tomas continued to write, but this message at lunchtime on the 29th was very strange indeed.

›› **felawe ken**

**2109 didst axe mynselve to put thyr wordes to papyr soe yow maye syght theyme an yn retorne thei wyl gyv papyr wen nedes me theym nath gyve me anie othir then thyr be moche amys thyr wyth causioun methynks me dost axe yow goode brothyr yf yow canst rekone for myn scryt as methinkest yowr charyctore beest lyken to thy leems me hope yow dydst fynde myn tale o som desporte me han portreyd plas o greyns as hath yow mayde debbie love to yow brothyr ‹‹**

*Fellow Ken*

*2109 asked me to put their words to paper so you may see them and in return they will give paper when I need it. If they don't give me any more then there is a big problem, with caution I think. I wonder if you can understand my writing for your characters are like those shown by the 'leems'. I hope you enjoyed my tale. I have drawn 'place of grains' as you asked, Debbie.*

*My love to you, brother.*

Tomas I envied as he usually took no messing from 2109. But this message seemed to introduce another twist to the problem. When he said 'an yn retorne [for carrying 2109's messages to us] thei wyl gyv papyr wen nedes me' did he mean that 2109 controlled his supply of paper? Obviously unlikely! Especially odd since 2109 had told us not to communicate with Tomas on paper, presumably because they could not interfere with the process. Anyway the paper was in my kitchen. It was my paper and my decision. They had bullshitted him into compliance unless there was some facet of this communication process that we had overlooked. Tomas urged caution, so I went along with the arrangement and said nothing to him about it.

» **felawe ken**

**2109 axith to plas thir words intyl myne scryt to myne felawes thoforthy ‹‹** [Tomas]

›› **sorry to communicate this way but were trying to sort things out. continue wyth experment, we'll doe are best**

**2109 ‹‹**

Above*: 'plas o greyns' - Windmill Hill, Gorstella. (1985).

Good Tomas had copied every word. If he was copying it and if he was 'in' our time when he wrote to us on paper – as we supposed – how was he able to see the 'leems' at the same moment? Evidently the 'leems' carried 2109's message for Tomas to be able to copy it it – but not on our computer on this occasion. Discussion did the rounds but as usual no one could sort it out.

Tomas went on to offer a verse from the poet Gower and to ask his 'brothyrs' to visit him – 'lyks yow mayd' – and to share his best wine. This was all very puzzling . . . Later the same day:

'What's this about Tomas wanting us all to visit?'

Debbie replied, 'He says if I can do it everyone can.'

'I didn't know you "did it", I thought it was accidental!'

'It is mostly . . . He's given me some hints about relaxing.'

'He's done what! Well, forget it, I am not going anywhere.'

'It's only like a brill dream . . .'

'Forget it.'

'I'll show you . . .'

'No way. You're only dreaming and he's in your dreams.'

'Is that how he writes to us then with a dream pen and dream paper? Talk sense.'

'So you're doing what Tomas does? Oh, this doesn't help us, Debbie,' I said with vague and unformed anxiety. 'Anyway I have to say something to Bucknall about the SPR questions. How about, "2109 gets Tomas to write 'we'll do our best'"? Huh! That's the real problem. I can't let Bucknall know all this.'

Above*: 'plas o greyns' – Windmill Hill. Drawn by Tomas

# 37

**31 October**

›› felawe ken and all yow friends

me dost thane yow for yowr scryt an me schalt replica-
cioune to alle o yow but fyrst myn ken me am tyrsom soe
thys nyght an canna bryng a pleesing thenke to myne pan
soe lene yowr ere goodlie brothyr that maye repyre me o
myn myrthelis stat grovynore dost seyne III week me goe o
wot strength yn myn love wot powyr that tyme beest blasted
atweye an thyr be neought that we kan doe thys nyght me
syghts myn canstyk an eye nor hert wol leve yt as me doe
goe to myn planken to wrytes al questiouns that me must
ax myn goodlie brothyrs an mayde

love Tomas ‹‹

*Fellow Ken and all your friends,*

*I thank you for your words and I shall reply to each of you but
first my Ken. I am so anxious tonight and can't bring a pleasing
thought to my head so lend me your ear, good brother, so you
may cure my unhappiness. Grosvenor says three weeks and
I must leave. Oh, what strength in my love, what power that
time be cut apart and there is nothing that we can do. I watch
my candle burn, neither my eye nor my heart will leave it as I go
to my table to write all the questions that I must ask my good
brothers and maid.*

*Love Tomas*

Three weeks and he goes. Three weeks. I wrote back with
heavy heart that we loved him dearly.

## 1 November

Still no news from 2109. I wove a little more imitation Star Trek into the next message:

*STATE OF PLAY??*

They merely wrote:

›› WHO KNOWS!!! ‹‹

It sent me into a silent, seething anger. But I moved to the 'Biggles' character. Some approach had to work!

*WHAT'S BEEN HAPPENING CHAPS?? KEN*

Nothing immediately. It was too late to go out again so Deb and I did some serious talking about how we should use these last days with Tomas. A priority, prompted by Peter's questions about words, was to try and take him back to the beginning of the experience and ask for an explanation of how it all began and then to check on those early messages, one by one, and line by line, if necessary, so that we got a true idea of what he wrote. It was possibly the last chance to disentangle his words from 2109's 'editing'.

Deb left out copies of the first two messages for Tomas and the next day we received a reply – in two parts, due to it having been interrupted by someone walking into the room.

goodlie ken

preye yow forgyve myn wordes to papyr as methynks myn wordes maye mysapere yf 2109 does sytes theym hy scrypts yowr mayde dide shewe tmynselve am nat altogedyr wot me dide sayn tho alle beest myne wordes thei beest upsoe downe thy scryt abowtes edmonde greye me never wryte thow thy wordes beest o myne ylk myne fyrst scryt didst seyen lyk forthe

me speke tyow that yow maye answere wy preye yow kepes myn wake a nyght wyth this straunge devyse that doe shyne lyks devylls teethe atte myneselve

yowr wordes doe cause me to thynks yow beest illschoold
or yow dost come ovresee yowr facioun beest uncouthe
to mynselve an yow hath manye costly thyngs that onlie
myn kyng canst afore tis a barful thyng thys devyse for
me conserne that yt be a scathful thyng wy be thise goode
men an swete she be walks through myn house theye art wel
com bot wy dost thei non syghts mynselve preye wy dost
yow put alle myn possessiouns al abowten myne howes an
breek al myn bounds that me be wreathed me canst nay alowe
yow co brybe myn farme less yow expowne yow intendaunce

[Good Ken

Please forgive my words to paper as I think they may be removed if 2109 see them. The words your maid showed me are
not altogether what I said, though they are all my words they are
jumbled. The words on Edmund Grey I didn't write though these
words are like mine. The first script said as follows:

I speak to you that you will answer. Why do you keep me awake
at night with this device that does shine at me like devil's teeth?
Your words make me think you are uneducated or you are from
overseas[?] as your manner is strange to me and you have many
costly things that only the king can afford. This device is causing me some difficulties, I am conserned it will harm me. Why
are there people walking through my house? They are welcome
but why can't they see me? Why do you move all my possesions
around my house and break the boundaries[?] that I am surrounded by?. I can not allow you to persuade me to leave my
house[?] unless you explain your intentions.]

So the second message was entirely fake and Edmund Grey
could be laid to rest along with the more speculative notions
of Tomas's 'antic' and 'breaking atwain' his 'bound'. These had
been of interest throughout the last year.

Tomas said the 'leems' shone 'lyks devylls teethe atte myneselve' and he noted the primitive wording he saw on it. Tomas
had been in communication with someone else before us.

2109 were not absent from the screen for long. They wittered on about Nick Sowerby-Johnson.

›› YOUR FRIEND NIK IS A CRASHING BORE,WHERE DOES HE WORK?,MI5?.USSR?- CANT FIND HIM ANYWHERE,MAY BE HE'S 'ONE'?!!.NO MORE GAMES WITH SPR.,WE'VE HAD ENOUGH - JUST LET THEM ANOY US ONE MORE TIME ...

- THEYLL SO KNOW THIS ISNT A HOAX!!

2109 ‹‹

I didn't know if they were serious. However, the upshot was that 2109 couldn't trace Nick, our bossy investigator. (Deb had never believed they had the power to do this.) 2109 thought Sowerby-Johnson a 'crashing bore'. They'd obviously detected my Biggles. I wasn't in any mood for this childishness. What a bore they were.

2109 kept up the friendly banter, and even analysed Frank's wife's medical problem! What a magic box this was turning out to be! 'The oracle is in: bring your problems – obscure words, illness, missing persons, computer communications – all will be dealt with circumspectly and ambiguously by the very shady Dr 2109; or directly, if you can read the writing and put your case in late Middle English, by Dr Tomas.'

Some proper control was needed, there were important questions to be pursued and just about none of them were for, or about, 2109. That was my prejudiced opinion. And these questions were about more than the use of late Middle English words. 'It's my time, my problem, my house!' I said rather desperately.

Debbie was also concerned. 'I never see you,' she said. She was right. When I was not at work I was out so she could 'ghost-bust'. She said that half the time we were probably 'ghostbusting' some other person's questions. They got the benefits, we got the costs. I must have been asleep to let this happen.

I wrote to Tomas, trying to latch on to a few problems from the earlier messages as this was proving a most fruitful avenue. I also included a few names and historical facts. It was all madness and impossible to sustain at this intensity, for we were receiving up to four messages on each of the good days and 'ghostbusting' for about four hours every night, though not always with success.

There were other kinds of madness 'out there', as this vicious exchange, presumably between 'one' and 2109, showed:

›› 2109

POOR,POOR,JACK-IN-THE-BOX,WHAT WILL HE DO WITHOUT A SPRING,NOW HE'LL NEVER BE ABLE TO PERFORM FOR THE CHILDREN.OH, AND HOW THE CHILDREN WILL CRY! ››

›› WON, WE PRESUME?!.CUT THE CRIPTIC,YOAR TOO OBVIOUS ANYWAY!.TRYING TO PLAY THE BRAVE SUMARITAN EH?!! REVERT TO CIPHER YOAR JUST CONFUSING 1985E.THEY KNOW NOT TO TRUST YOU!. ‹‹

'In action watch the timing.' So says the Tao te ching. 'One' had, we surmised, taken the spring out of the 2109 jack-in-the-box at exactly the right moment. The spring, their raison d'etre, had been the promise to catch the message transferring between the SPR computer and disk. 'One' had knocked it out and 2109 couldn't meet their obligation.

Curiously, if we were the children we did not cry. Personally I was relieved, happy that 2109 were defeated. Maybe it was their arrogance, perhaps just their failure. Debbie and I went to town to talk over what to do next and to drink tea in the cathedral. The cathedral cloisters are old enough for Tomas to have known them. I would ask him. It felt good to be in the even coolness of those reassuring stone walls: We talked for an hour or more and our attention moved to the second part of this most recent exchange.

›› YOUR ENGLISH IS APPALLING!. DON'T YOU HAVE ANY OTHER PURPOSE THAN TO LECTURE THIS KIND WITH EXISTENTIALISM AND QUANTUM PHYSICS. WHAT A MEANINGLESS EXISTENCE! BUT IF CIPHER, THEN CIPHER IT IS – IF YOU CAN KEEP UP WITH ME!! ‹‹

›› NOT THIS FRQ. RANGE!! ‹‹

It struck me then that 2109's defeat would also be my own in the eyes of John Bucknall. No proof: no interest. But I was still enjoying 2109's failure. Naturally, I would tell John nothing of the above. As it didn't refer to SPR's questions he'd not be interested. Strangely I was determined to wait a few days and see if anything turned up. I was clearly confused – one moment celebrating an end to 2109's boasting and at the next waiting for an answer to SPR's question. It was rather like Mr Micawber, hoping without reason: more faith than hope, more desperation than faith.

Deb had been working on me to at least try and visit Tomas, and I promised I would as he'd be gone soon. Back at the cottage with Deb's encouragement I settled down to relax every part of my body slowly and deliberately and looked up through closed eyes at the infinite (I imagined), at the starry, swirling, arched patterns. At one moment I felt I stepped into that vortex but I could not let go. I opened my eyes. 'Oh, it's bloody stupid all this.'

I told Deb how it was. She thought I was doing OK and should try again but I made some excuse. I'd be saying mantras next and painting prayer wheels on the wall.

Deb was miffed. 'You're just a cowardly hypocrite . . . after all this, all that's happened, you still won't go all the way.'

'Goodnight, Deb.'

Tomas's response:

›› GOODLIE KEN

ME WERT FORJOYD THAT MYNE FELAWE DIDST VYSYT BUT SORRIE
THAT HYM DIDST STEYE BUT SHORTLIE METHYNKS THAT WEN
YOW TRYEN GEYN THIN YOW WILT STEYE FOR MYNE BESTE ALE
AN METE . . . YEA PREYE YOW THEN MAYHAP AL MEN WYL BILEVE
YN YOWRN TYME O OWRN COMMUNIOUN AS FEW DOE TAKE A WORDE
O A SHE PREYE TELLE YF YOW DIDST SYGHTS MYNSELVE WYTH
HASTE PREYE YOW ALS REPAYE GOODLIE TOMAS O THY SAYME
OFFERYNG AS HAN YOWR LASTE AXYNGS ON PAPYR SOE ME DOST
KNOWETH WOT BEEST TREWE

LOVE THOMAS ‹‹

[Good Ken,

I was overjoyed that my fellow visited me but sorry that he didn't
stay very long. I think that when you try again then you will stay
for my best ale and meat . . .  then  perhaps all men will believe
in your time of our communication as very few take the word of
a woman. Tell me if you saw me . . . and show me again your last
message, so I know what is true.

Love Tomas]

# 38

**3 November**

'Oh, for God's sake!' I paced up and down in agitation.

| FULL NAME | BIRTH DATE | DIED |
|-----------|------------|------|
|           |            |      |
|           |            |      |
|           |            |      |
|           |            |      |
|           |            |      |
|           |            |      |

**›› I COULD FILL IT IN! ‹‹**

'It says "I". Anything with "I" in it tends to be "one".' 'Does it matter who wrote it if it gets filled in?' I said,still in some agitation.

'But 2109 wouldn't fill it in. They're on our side.'

'But there are no sides,' I said, quoting Spike Milligan.

'We're all in this together.'

Not for the first time I shouted out in the kitchen, at the room and at nothing: 'F*** off!'

## 4 November

Debbie showed Tomas another of the very early messages. It was, I think, the long communication of 16 February in which Lukas described his visit to Chester and Nantwich. Tomas said it was a fake. He didn't remember writing any of it, though he again said they were his words.

We assumed that 2109 may have been trying to 'help' us by adding ideas of their own. We therefore doubted the usefulness of all those messages with modern punctuation. This seemed to tie in with most of the substantial problems of language and detail found in those first few messages and would therefore help explain the sudden decline in errors thereafter; 2109 left his communications largely alone.

The same day, 2109 put in a short message asking if we could get Nick Sowerby-Johnson in front of the screen, saying they could trace him better if he was there. Bullshit! In my heart I knew that 2109 would not save the situation. I should have taken the machine and gently wrapped it in its box, like venerated remains at a religious ceremony. I should have pushed that box into the cupboard under the stairs and tried to forget it was there. I wish. I dreamt so many things. I dreamt it would all work out. At the same time I avoided the right action, I failed to follow my heart. The machine stayed on duty. Worse, part of me kept believing something would come of it.

# 39

When Carl Jung, the psychologist, was asked on television in 1959 if he believed in God, he answered, 'I know. I don't need to believe. I know.'

I watched that programme in about 1970 and was struck immediately by Jung's confidence, his careful choice of words, his honesty. I didn't know how or why he knew but there it was. Tomas Harden I knew. I didn't believe in him; I knew him – or something of him, and the fact that I had never seen him did nothing to alter that knowledge. Let's not beat around the bush. In those months the space-time barrier was annulled almost daily in one direction or another. This conclusion, hard upon my knowledge of Tomas, was inescapable, yet the opportunity to test it scientifically dwindled from the end of October until now, in November. Tomas had but a week or so left to him. SPR had gone quiet. They were waiting for me, perhaps. I would not pester them. If scientific proof were produced tomorrow it would no longer be for myself but for the sake of the face I turn to my fellow humans, and this is a kind of vanity.

Autumn weather, and here I was reflecting on the signs of the fall of the sap, the thinning leaves on the sycamore tree outside the window of the school house. Something in me still called for help – to look at Tomas's words, his ideas, his history – and this too was a kind of vanity, but I told myself to keep calm. It had to wait. Tomas would soon be gone from his home. This was my quiet obsession. I wanted information: people, places, gossip and 'goodlie words' . . . each and every day.

I pushed the exercise books into the metal locker frames unmarked. How futile this 'schooling' was. I could almost taste the frustration; I could feel the guilt those unmarked books gave me. Would the kids forgive my decline in the manner that the eccentric, the frail and the addled are forgiven? Did they say, these children, these students: 'He's off his head. Have you heard that a ghost writes to him! (Even Mr Trinder believes it.) He writes back on a computer!'

The books stayed unmarked. I was tired of this pressure to conform and please. One day I would please myself first. But if the books remained untouched our lives continued to fray. Deb wanted to go away to Oxford to see Robin, take a few pictures and so forth, to get some time to think, to be away from the cottage. She knew that it would probably inhibit communications but she'd keep it to two days or less. There was nothing she really had to go for, except for the going.

**7 November**

Before dogs go to sleep they turn round as though flattening a patch of grass. It is an echo of their origins as wolves or wild dogs. Alone in my house I rearranged some of my possessions and petted them, walked around, tried to feel as though I was in charge and really 'at home'. I bathed and then relaxed before the fire with some wine; the kind of thing many people can do almost any day but for me it was like the taste of everyday life of which a prisoner up for parole dreams of. There was no message, no computer screen, nor any reason to do anything but drift, listen to some old records and repair senses which had been nearly burnt out. I drank as necessary.

'An hour of real pleasure is worth a lifetime of indifference.' An old teacher once told me that when he tried to rationalize the deplorable state of his marriage. I did not agree, but only twenty-four hours after my night of pleasure, indifference and awkwardness were stalking around.

I met Debbie at the station. She was unhappy with her trip. The film in the camera had been used on nothing much, Robin couldn't be found and she was exhausted from having to stand up on the train all the way back from Birmingham New Street. I wired up the computer, it was like putting on chains. It was duty at one and the same time; my weakness and my obsession, and my love.

But my love was for Tomas, not 2109 or 'one', or poltergeists, yet to remind me of the grind, of the incubus upon my back there was soon a new message, unheralded, unbidden.

>> JOHN & NIK & DAVID

YOUR REASON IS NOT A GOOD ONE BUT NEVER MIND

IF IT WAS A HOAX THEN WOULD I SPEAK WITH YOU NOW?

RECOGNISE THAT I EXIST WITHOUT NUMBERS, COLOUR OR SOUND (THEREFORE) ANY QUESTIONS RELATIVE TO THESE ARE NO USE TO YOU, ONE IS A GREAT POWER THAT MUST BE OBEYED AND ANSWERED IF HE SHOULD CALL. I WILL GIVE NO INSTRUCTIONS AS YOU ARE OF NO MATTER WHAT YOU SAY. I MAY OBSTRUCT IF THIS IS MY DESIRE.

THINK:IS YOUR LIFE REALLY LIVED WHEN YOU ARE AWAKE OR ASLEEP. YOU ONLY KNOW WHAT IS TRUE WHEN YOU CAN CONSCIOUSLY BE IN BOTH ALL YOU BELIEVE IS YOUR REALITY ALONE! <<

'That's not much use,' said John Bucknall after I had dictated it to him down the telephone. For all I said that I didn't care I was feeling really stupid and small.

'That's not much use,' the telephone voice rattled around my lifeless brain. We made some vague arrangement to call each other, the details of which I didn't remember too well. The impression I got was that he'd call us. I wasn't going to call him. I'd had quite enough. Maybe he felt the same.

The weather was turning cold. It was nearly a year since the phenomenon had begun and we were little further on in one sense but in others very richly endowed. Only our weariness and the drawing in of the year darkened our sight of these things.

# 40

**10 November**

The 'cart tygre' swung across the road to Meadow Cottage and tucked in behind Frank's small, rusting Toyota. Frank, Debbie, Dave Lovell and Emrys, an old school friend, were there. I hadn't been expecting anyone but Frank. There was a good fire in the grate and good conversation amid the usual disorganization and chaos. Frank, Debbie and I decided to take a walk to talk over the latest events.

After an hour we rested a little on Windmill Hill and looked towards the village. I could see the church spire and the pine trees on the motte. It looked a friendly, sheltered place. I felt closer to Tomas here than at the cottage somehow. It was a safe distance, close enough to know you belong but far enough to allow for reflection.

The coldness of the wind was deflected by my GPO greatcoat and I wanted to stay and watch over the Meadows and see the thick, grey clouds build up over the Welsh hills. Conversation moved on to 2109. Frank had a copy of their latest. 2109 had said we 'all needed a break' and I agreed, but how? They said they would hold Tomas's time almost still relative to ours. An impossible idea. Yet they had successfully interfered with his communications before, and in late August and early September had for a few days cut him out altogether. If 2109 could provide a respite it would be gratefully accepted. They said that two months could be given to us 'to do what we wanted'. Nothing was too crazy anymore.

There was a pause in the conversation then Frank leant closer to me and wondered aloud whether the fact that 2109 were able to do this might suggest that they were inventing the whole business. It was an old argument and he didn't expect an answer, he knew what I felt about Tomas. Talk subsided for a few seconds.

2109 were also asking us to let a little of the story into the local papers. They said it was to get the right sort of help. If I did decide on this course of action I hoped that we would get some other researchers interested. Frank and Debbie voiced misgivings. Meanwhile the shadows were lengthening and the sky turning mottled pearl and slate grey.

'I can imagine that this mound was once an outpost for the village motte, I can almost see the Welsh gathering across the marsh, preparing to raid cattle,' I said.

I think that that little mound, its position and its two sentinel elms evoked the past for all of us. The feeling grew steadily that we were at the end of something that weekend, a part of our lives was behind us that had been so intense that we had to allow it room to settle more easily in our minds, to become more properly part of us.

Debbie was worried about Tomas. If he continued to write then shouldn't we keep up with him? 'Of course,' I said, but I hoped that he would stop. A rain shower squalled across the big field and we moved off. It was time for tea; a rainy English Sunday at four in the afternoon.

About 9.30 P.M. Deb found a scrap of paper I had left on the work top. It bore Tomas's writing. He had not stopped yet. His interest in cars was being developed and I had got as far as describing the fire in the engine.

›› felawe ken

preye telle wy cartygre dost na growith to hot wyth  thy grete fyr for certs yow pepel wal be brent by thy unavoid-aunt hete o thy forneys ‹‹

[Fellow Ken

Please tell me why the 'cartygre' does not get too hot with the enormous fire, for it is sure your people will be burnt by the unavoidable heat of the furnace.]

I tried my best to explain that the engine is encased in a metal jacket filled with water and the water is pushed round by a pump. I didn't try to explain the pump. Where do you stop?

He continued about an hour later, on the same piece of scrap paper:

>> yow art amoost wyse wyght brothyr ken for yow maketh alle sympal for myn rekonyng o thise engenes as yow calle theym bot me wylt nat telle anodyr o thyse thyngs yow speke or theym wyll han me for jakke gaumercie me aske namo o thise gagdyts me thynks wot han yow o me preye

**Tomas** <<

[You are a most wise man, brother Ken, for you make all things simple so I can understand these engines as you call them, but I will not speak of these things to any other person or they will have me for a lunatic. I ask no more about these gadgets. What do you want to know of me?

Tomas]

I did not ask him anything nor did I tell him that 2109 were planning to 'hold' his time.

Later that evening as Deb sank quietly beneath the bedcovers she turned to me and said, 'I saw Tomas again. He was asleep in a chair. I kissed his forehead. He stirred a little and spoke in his sleep. "Katherine?" I felt so sad. He's still missing her.'

I felt Deb's sadness for perhaps a second but I smoothed the pillow for her and directed my thoughts towards sleep. I mumbled, 'You only dreamt it anyway, Deb. People dream all sorts of stuff.'

Were we to believe that as measured in our time, at or near midnight 10 November 1985, Tomas would fall asleep before his fire only to awake, stir the embers and it would for us be a new day sometime in January 1986?

I printed the 2109 message of 10 November out on Monday break time, but I was impatient, grumbly, ill and now, with the bell rattling in the corridor, short of time. I showed Peter the message. He was puzzled but pleased and swooped upon the first point, about press coverage: 'How about Neil Bartlem? Yes? He's a good man. I shall ring him.'

In a moment the decision was taken: the Tomas story would go into the local press.

## Computer's eerie link with the past

# 'Tudor' printouts baffle the experts

Two teachers believe they are in communication with a local landowner alive in the year 1546 — a claim supported by a formidable body of evidence based on study and research spanning a whole year.

Centred on a village just a few miles from Chester, the story reveals either a remarkable breakthrough in the field of the paranormal — or a hoax of considerable complexity and scholarship.

The case has been investigated by the respected academic body, the Society for Psychical Research, who are satisfied that "human agencies" are responsible.

But while no scientific proof as yet exists, there is a body of circumstantial evidence which points towards a genuine paranormal phenomenon.

By the Society's own admission, if the case were genuine it would be the most unique on record.

Much of the evidence is in the form of computer print-outs. Ken, a teacher at a local school, claims that messages in Middle English — an early form of the language — have appeared on the disc drive of a home micro.

Over a year, a composite text comprising over a hundred print-outs has emerged which contains any linguistic and historical clues towards authenticity.

The man with whom the teachers believe they are in contact is an historically verifiable figure.

### RECORDS

He is Thomas Harden and his name is found in the records of Oxford's Brasenose College — he received his MA in 1534 but was finally expelled for refusing to remove the Pope's name from chapel service books.

According to Ken, this remarkable story began in November 1984 and his version runs as follows.

Renovation work at his cottage prompted poltergeist activity — including furniture being rearranged and tools disappearing — which culminated in the first message via the computer.

Calling up an unfamiliar title from the computer's disk drive, Ken was amazed to find a weird, nonsensical poem appear on the visual display screen. Not surprisingly, he put it down to

satisfaction that human agencies were responsible, it was not the job of the Society to point the finger.

Clearly, if the case is a hoax, then the two teachers are prime suspects. But Mr. Bucknall said he believed it was also possible that a third party was responsible.

### UNIQUE?

He added: "I would have loved to prove it was genuine.

### Exclusive by Neil Bartlem

It would have been the most unique phenomenon ever recorded."

The Society has not analysed the computer print-outs for linguistic or historical accuracy.

Mr. Bucknall points out they could not be shown to be within the realm of available scholarship and therefore would prove nothing.

But the messages do contain a great deal of information.

"The texts now present a vocabulary of over 2,000 words," said Peter, the English teacher. "The dating is confirmed by spelling, syntax and grammar and the vast majority of the words are dated in the OED as occurring between the 14th and 16th centuries, converging on the middle of the 16th century."

### NO STANDARD

At the time of Thomas Harden, there was effectively no standard form of English — the language of education was still Latin and there were enormous differences in dialect between the various areas of the country.

"All evidence in the language points to an origin in the south-west," said Peter. "There is a strong admixture of Midlands forms and a distinct influence from further north."

The historical Thomas Harden came from Bristol and could have been expected to pick up midlands forms during his time near Chester. He says in the messages that his teacher, whose name — Lukas Wainman — he assumed at first as an alias, was from the north. The presence of Thomas Harden

Near Chester, Thomas would have been removed from the political arena and under the watchful eye of the local sheriff, Thomas Failhurst — who is directly referred to in the computer messages.

### SCOPE

There are innumerable bits and pieces of historical information in the messages which, although not conclusive, indicate the scope of the whole affair.

For instance, Thomas refers to Bristol as Brightstow — a genuine form but one obscure enough not even to find its way into the Book of Place Names.

He refers to a minor author of the time by his nickname; he quotes from one of the Chester Mystery Plays, in which he said he acted.

The teachers know they may be suspected of perpetrating a hoax. But said Peter, "If it is a hoax it is an incredibly detailed one and a full-time occupation for probably more than one person."

They believe Thomas Harden is not dead — he is alive in 1546. According to his messages, he perceives the computer as a box of flashing lights somewhere near his fireplace. Foundations from an earlier dwelling coincide with Ken's cottage at the kitchen — where the building work took place and where the computer is situated.

The teachers claim that the computer messages, although the most unique element of the case, are not the only means whereby Thomas makes contact.

He has also scrawled messages on blank paper and

Above: The Chester Observer, 20th December 1985. The first of many press releases.

# 41

Between July and November Tomas had managed to sketch parts of his village. It was something I was keen to see done as it gave a great deal of historical detail which could be looked into at a later date. The main details were culled between 10–31 October but it was 13 July when we first received something relating to his village. It was an outline of his house. This quiet period in mid-November allowed us time to sort through the material concerned with his village and its inhabitants. As we got a better feel for what Tomas's life was like I felt like a glider pilot beginning to circle upwards. I was conscious of my field of vision expanding, thanks to the information that Tomas gave us. There are many dozens of points of interest but the only conclusion I draw is that it is not the village I recognize, the village I walk from end to end and through and through. Debbie, in one of her 'dreams', saw something of the village and she wrote about it. I think it is a good starting point: this is why. After I had struggled with the maps of the village Tomas had left me and failed to match them up to the present a good friend said. 'Use your imagination, re-create his world view! What were maps there to show? Was it the linear relationships between places? Do you expect scale like an Ordnance Survey map? Or do you expect he will draw what is important to him? Would the lie of the land be changed, or do you think he would draw important places larger than others? In short, look through his eyes!'

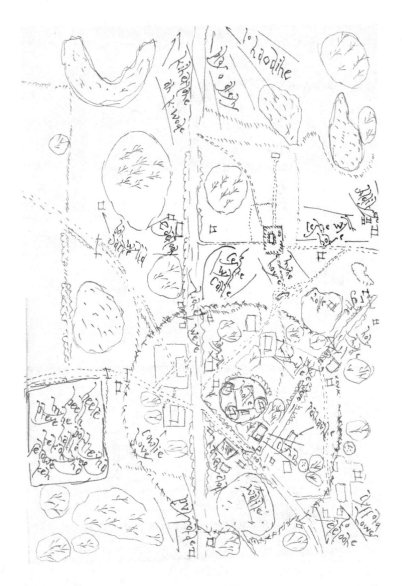

Tomas's map of the village in 1546. We struggled to make sense of his village and the one we knew in 1985. See 1985 ariel plan over page

Above: Dodleston Village 1985

Above: Deb's sketch of Tomas's kitchen as see in a dream

Tomas's sketch of his house

Debbie's account (below), whether symbolic or real, gave me confidence to 'look through his eyes':

' ... As Tomas's departure drew closer so did our friendship; the stubborn chauvinist I had first met, his tasteless humour and criticism of my ill manner, had long gone, leaving a very open and real relationship. Although one would say it was special because of the circumstances of our relationship, I think that it was also special because it was almost as if we were the only two people in existence at times. It is perhaps hard to explain why but because of this it was a very personal relationship.

'Tomas was leaning back in his chair with his feet resting on the kitchen table, busy carving away at something small in his hand. As soon as he heard me behind him he jumped up and greeted me in the usual way, always with an enthusiastic hug. It amused me that we would always greet each other with the same lines. It became a comforting ritual.

"'Pray, maid, how fare yow this day?"

"'Me fares fine."

'He always laughed at my reply. It must have meant something to him other than I intended. Perhaps it was the way I said it.

'Still clutching tightly in his hand whatever he had been carving he motioned for me to sit down. I sat on the low bench which was against the wall to the left of the fireplace and asked him what he had been carving. He frowned and said, "'Tis namatir." Slightly hurt and made curious by such a negative response, I pushed for an answer. "Show me, pray, or I shall sorrow and think I have offended dear Tomas."

'Tomas, still frowning, moved slowly across the room and sat next to me. At one time his closeness had bothered me but not now. With his head lower than was natural he looked intensely at his clenched hand, seeming to will its opening, then reluctantly his grasp released and slowly and solemnly he spoke. "'Twell n'worke."

'In his hand was a carefully carved replica of the Fountain Pentel which we had often left for his use when he wrote. I replied, witholding a smile, "I do not suppose it will!"

'Thomas's face showed great disappointment and some embarrassment – he seemed sensitive enough to pick up that I was withholding a laugh. Quickly I added the comment that he had done well to make such a replica from memory. He wanted to know how it made the ink and I had to put him right by telling him that the ink was made elsewhere and only a limited amount was stored in the pen itself. He was surprised at this, since he had believed it would magically last forever – I am not sure why, perhaps I had not made its mechanics too clear when talking about it with him in the past.

'Tomas stood up suddenly, placing the carving on his wooden shelves with some sort of impatience. He did not want to dwell on the subject. "A man is to come for my fowl, pray help me to box the wretched beasts."

'He left me no time to answer. I followed him through the barrels room and out into the yard. This was the third occasion that I had strayed beyond his kitchen and the second time I had ever been outside. On the previous occasion I had annoyed him by asking why his garden was so disorganized, since I would have thought that this would have made access to the plants and herbs awkward. He had been very defensive, if not rather sharp, in his reply. Everything was carefully placed, he said. He then started to lecture me rather rudely saying that this herb was placed there because that plant next to it repels the mites that are harmless to the herbs but that feed on the mites that are not harmless. In some cases it was simply that "this herb does n'favour the company of that herb", and so forth.

'Obviously farming was more complicated and far more specialized than I gave credit for. Why have we changed? It seemed to work well enough for him.

'To Tomas's annoyance and to my great entertainment we found that the hens disliked my presence immensely. This naturally made hen-catching difficult for Tomas so he indicated that I should take a walk around the outside of the house. Interestingly enough, Tomas's new cook had no sense at all of my presence, just as Katherine had not.

'Whilst Tomas continued to struggle with the hens I took the opportunity to try and locate myself relative to the cottage in 1985. It was impossible. There were no real landmarks, at least none that I recognized! This was not the Dodleston I knew but very beautiful all the same. I took in the whole landscape through every sense. Thousands of little flowers scattered the land with colours ranging from mauves to yellows. Hedges and small woods seemed randomly placed in clumps and straggles. Even the houses seemed to follow a similar randomness as if they too had grown organically out of the land. The air was sweet and its lightness filled my head. It was so overpowering that I felt myself moved almost to cry, and more so when I thought that I was really in another world. I thought about the vivid, uniform, unnatural green of the fields now. Look what they have done to the land! How could all this be so changed?

'I saw a horse and cart winding its way up to the path and with some panic I called to Tomas, "Tomas, you have a visitor!"

'Tomas came up to me carrying several small, round baskets. He had squeezed the poor hens into these, they were packed tightly and this really annoyed me but Tomas made a leap ahead of my words and said that I shouldn't go but stay and see what happened. Another of Tomas's experiments, huh? I said nothing but stood behind him and waited. As the stranger approached, his horse stiffened and then reared slightly. The man stared straight through me; he could not see me, but he looked around slightly, puzzled by his horse's reaction. It knew I was there.

'Tomas grasped the horse by its bit and spoke some soft words which seemed to calm the animal down. Then he spoke to the stranger but not in a way I could understand. He seemed to be criticizing the man's horsemanship. This made me giggle. Tomas turned round fleetingly and gave a knowing grin...'

Although the cottage was fairly quiet throughout that November, with the computer packed away in its box in a corner, poltergeist activity would still occasionally occur – a simple stacking usually, or objects relocated a few inches, sometimes more. The only event of significance I record here is the chalking on the pillar in the kitchen on Thursday 14 November. It occurred sometime during the night and was gone without trace on 15 November. I reproduce it as received. Although it only existed briefly we were quite geared up by now to making a note of things as soon as they were seen.

›› The eyes are open
yet nothing do you see


the grey
retarding                              is your convict
mass


                quietly, alone he sits in the
                dark waiting for sentence
                to be passed


and demanding              the eyes of the blind
through


                of unspoken questions
                to answers of ethereal
                kind

the soul he is the traveller
chain nor bar can
hold him to frail flesh

here is the ruler
of time and space
Here is your
God «


The month passed quickly. I sold the Jaguar to a Chinese doctor and bought an old diesel Opel estate car. Money was still tight. Debbie's kind 'Aunty M' helped us out by letting us have a large oak tree from her garden for firewood. Peter continued with his research into Tomas's language and contacted the local press.

# 42

One tea-time, a Wednesday in early December, I sat across from Neil Bartlem, a young, unshaven reporter from the Chester Observer. Beneath the two volumes and free magnifying glass of the Oxford English Dictionary at the other end of the room sat Peter. As we three talked or rather, as Peter led the way with his enthusiasm, it became clear that Neil wasn't laughing at us or looking furtively at his watch out of embarrassment. We both knew Neil, he was a former pupil. I knew he could be polite and apply a middle-class gloss despite his generally radical outlook. Intuitively, I knew something had struck him as worthy of interest. To me, irrationally insecure, a little wary, this interest was a measure of success. I didn't like letting the story into the local paper, its first exposure to people who neither knew us nor cared. I dreaded having it fall foul of the usual half-witted hack, to whom it would be a diversion and a few laughs between the WI reports and the obituaries. It was an awful step, this thought was on a tape loop inside my head.

It was not even the whole story. At my insistence 2109 were excluded. Peter disagreed with this but since it touched me so closely the final decision had to be mine. Peter assumed that if we were being straightforward nothing untoward could be said about us that mattered. I did not possess rhino hide for skin even if Peter thought he did. I scented blood! I saw us reduced to a laughing stock in moments at the slightest ill-judged word. Peter could be so naive.

I was daydreaming. The conversation in the room became obscured. I was thinking all the time of the possible outcome rather than the business at hand.

About half an hour later Neil put his notebook away and was gone. Despite the fact that we knew Neil, he could still write us up as backwater eccentrics, stewed too long in a pettifogging institution, or as a fine pair of dupes. Another daydream: imagine being back at Hawarden High School after Christmas, the sniggers and questions in and around the classroom, the odd looks. It made me shudder to think of it. Peter would have no escape. I was, in a funny way, sorry to have brought him these problems.

A week or more passed, and there was nothing from Neil. Perhaps he'd found Bucknall and, having spoken to him, had reconsidered his decision to submit a piece. Worse! The editor had thrown it out as rubbish.

Finally Neil rang on 21 December. The paper had 'gone to bed', he said, being deliberately journalistic. He outlined the problem with the article; he'd been having trouble keeping it off the front page! I gave a silent prayer of thanks that he had succeeded.

'When is it out?' I asked, not realizing the relevance of the term 'gone to bed'.

'It's on the streets tomorrow,' he chuckled.

We obtained an early edition by taking the car to the newsagent's in Bridge Street. Next day we knew the village would be full of it. I presumed that, in the British tradition, they wouldn't have the bad taste to approach us directly about it. It was because of this that we didn't prepare for any reaction, but there were signs that they knew all right. Frank Cummins called into Mr Hughes's shop for a paper that first morning and someone chipped in, 'It's on page seven. We're all reading it!'

The article covered most of a full page, which was quite something considering that the paper was not a tabloid at that time. The piece itself was not unkind.

Neil had been able to contact John Bucknall and it is the sections concerning him that are reproduced below. They're rather special as they form the last commentary on the subject that we ever received from John.

The case has been investigated by the respected academic body, The Society for Psychical Research, who are satisfied that 'human agencies' are responsible . . .

On the ten-question test:

'We did not get a specific answer,' said Mr Bucknall. 'We got instead generalized commentary accusing us of not believing in what was going on. We got waffle .. .'

On the culprit:

... having established to its satisfaction that human agencies were responsible it was not the job of the Society to point the finger. Mr Bucknall was convinced that nothing paranormal is occurring, 'something or somebody is doing it,' he said.

On the content of the messages:

The society has not analysed the computer print-outs for linguistic or historical accuracy. Mr Bucknall points out they could establish nothing which could not be shown to be within the realm of available scholarship and therefore would prove nothing.

'Oh, John,' I spoke in a whisper. 'Stop playing games . . . all this bland nonsense.' I put the paper aside and spoke up. 'Well, Debs me ol' girl? What say you? Is he being honest?'

'You know what I believe. He said he always solved his cases and filed a report. We will wait for that.'

'But he always, he said, told the people involved the truth as he saw it. He's not been near us for six weeks.'

'We'll wait for his report before we tackle him.'

John Bucknall never filed a report on the case and left the Society in 1986. He has been impossible to contact since.

# 43

**15 January 1986**

The time was near to begin again, and Debbie unpacked the computer like a flower-seller setting up the stall she had known and worked from for twenty years. A warm familiarity prevailed. When the system was up and running she typed in a short greeting in a manner reminiscent of that first contact. How readily these little rituals became established. We kept it semi-serious.

*COME IN 2109*

*DEB*

For two whole days the message stayed there, the cursor flashing continually in readiness hour after hour after hour. Still nothing. Then very late on 17 January:

›› KEN DEB PETER HELLO

DO YOU FEEL THAT YOU ARE READY TO CONTINUE COMMUNI-CATIONS?

HEARD ANYTHING FROM THE MEDIA? ‹‹

[not signed]

The miserable Opel was giving problems which, together with starting the new job, meant that I for one was not ready. Deb agreed, and suggested to 2109 that a fortnight's delay would be appropriate. We also put in a bid for a little guidance on the choice of a new researcher, or more particularly who to avoid. The very nature of the experience was bound to attract every wayward dabbler it touched. It had already reached the ears of one very dodgy-sounding 'researcher' who specialized in recycling other people's stories for profit.

There was a reply next day at 7.00 P.M. As expected it was heavily seasoned with obscure references and/or bullshit, depending on your attitude at the time.

›› YES, WE CAN DELAY TH FURTHER,SAY ANOTHER MONTH IF YOU LIKE,AS YOU WILL HAVE VERY LITTLE TIME WITH HIM WHEN HE DOES RETURN. IT IS IMPORTANT TO POINT OUT THAT IF YOU INVITE ANYONE TO RESEARCH THE COMMUNICATIONS THEN ONCE THEY HAVE STARTED YOU CAN NOT DECIDE THEY ARE OF NO IMPORTANCE, AND, ALSO, YOU MUST REALIZE THAT THEY HAVE ONLY ONE OF TWO CONCLUSIONS THEY CAN REACH!!. OUR OWN COMMUNICATION WITH YOU HAS LITTLE IMPORTANCE THEREFOR WE SHALL BE AROUND FOR THE NEXT TWO DAYES ONLY TO ANSEWER ANY MORE OF YOUR QUESTIONS THEN SHALL AWAIT THs RETURN.

YOU NEED EVERYONE AND NO ONE,THAT IS TO SAY THAT PEOPLE WILL COME AND PEOPLE WILL STAY AWAY FOR THE BENEFIT IS TO BEGANED BY ALL WHOM YOU MEET AND ALL WHOM YOU DISAPOINT!!

2109 ‹‹

A day or two later Peter, rather surprisingly, had suggested over coffee at The Dingle that I might be telepathically creating the messages on the screen. He'd read that some people have been recorded as affecting computer equipment.

'Affecting is a long way from generating whole pages of script,' I said, but I was taken aback by this suggestion. Still puzzled, I put it to 2109.

2109

*I HOPE YOU CAN FINISH THE COMM ABOVE . . . TO THIS DAY I CAN'T SEE WHY SPR WERE INVOLVED . . . PETER CONSIDERS THAT I TELEPATHICALLY CREATE THESE WORDS KEN*

They replied:

›› THEN ASK PETER WHY EVERYTHING WHICH APPEARS ON THE SCREEN DOES NOT PLEASE KEN ‹‹

2109 gave the impression these days of being a helpful, counselling agency . . . a bit like a telephone agony aunt. I suspected that they were manoeuvring once more.

They then returned to our problems over research and verification, and assured me that:

>> YOU ARE NOT LIKELY TO MAKE TOO MANY SERIOUS MISTAKES WITHOUT OUR INTERVENTION WE CAN NOT ASSURE YOU THAT THIS IS ALL GOING TO BE ONE GREAT 'THE DANSANT' WITH CRUMPETS THROWN IN. SO IN ORDER THAT YOU MAY PAY A LITTLE MORE ATTENTION TO OUR NEEDS WE ASK YOU TO DO THE FOLLOWING: THERE IS A BRILLIANT RESEARCHER (UFOLOGIST . . . WE KNOW YOU DONT LIKE THE WORD!) HIS NAME IS GARY M ROWE, HIS IDEAS DIFFER SOMEWHAT TO YOURS BUT NEVERTHELESS HE CAN HELP YOU WITH A COUPLE OF YOUR PROBLEMS. <<

Luckily I was well aware of 2109's tendency to sound like a cheap seaside comic and instead of complaining I latched on to the hard information which followed:

>> YOU MAY PHONE HIM AT THE NO BELOW AND INVITE HIM TO TALK WITH YOU, WHEN HE COMES SHOW HIM THIS AND ASK HIM WHAT HE MAKES OF IT , , , PETER MUST DO THE TELEPHONING RHYL ***** TELL HIM THAT YOU GOT THE TELEPHONE NO FROM A UFO ENTHUSIAST. 2109. <<

OK. So we had to ring someone we didn't know, who had researched into UFOs (which we are not very interested in) and who had to be told some corny message from nowhere. This was ridiculous. I was glad that Peter was given the job. I'd rather try and sell double glazing any day.

# 45

Settled into one of Peter's leather armchairs was Gary M. Rowe, styled from the 1950s. He was about five feet eight inches tall, hair Brylcreemed back, well-dressed, shiny shoes, restless, intense yet extremely polite.

The story of events since December 1984 unfolded. He listened intently, interposing with care several very direct questions. He did not seem put out or embarrassed. From Peter he received a bundle of print-outs, notes and analysis concerned primarily with Tomas. It was all something of a jumble because there was so much of it. We'd take him on trust as requested. He promised two things. Firstly, that he'd come and monitor the cottage kitchen with a spectrum of equipment – video, audio, computer-linked sensors, and he'd write a report to go with it. Secondly he'd use 'other means' of probing for the truth.

'Meaning whether it is a hoax or not, I presume,' said Peter. 'I feel SPR have counted us out already. They have said as much.'

I looked at Peter in puzzlement but let it go. Gary M. Rowe said it would be improper to detail the nature of his investigation but that it would certainly get to the answer – at least to his own satisfaction. Peter was pleased, so long as Gary would reveal his method and conclusions to us eventually. This Gary agreed to do.

In Gary Rowe I saw a sharp, intelligent man obsessed with his ideas, and these ideas – as he started to talk about his interest in UFOs – were hardly ones I could share. 2109 had warned of this, I reasoned. But a vaguely ill-at-ease feeling remained throughout the evening. I told myself to be fair to him.

2109 had cleared off as they said they would, on 20 January, before the meeting with Gary Rowe. They were due back in about a month, which I interpreted loosely. We'd have the computer in the house in readiness.

They had been wrong about Tomas being 'held' or prevented from coming through. True there was nothing for the remainder of 1985 but on 23 January 1986 he wrote on a piece of paper in the kitchen quite unexpectedly, at about 7.30 P.M. From the start it was clear he was unaware of any delay or interruption, for he continued where he had left off with an example of his everyday handwriting, which Debbie had requested in early November. (We had been made aware that Tomas was writing carefully for us. Deb wanted to see something of the more natural style.)

This was the beginning-of-the-end sequence, the last week or so of Tomas's communication. We restarted our routine, bought paper and laid it out, found 'his' Fountain Pentel* and so on. It all jostled once more with the chaos of a busy kitchen. At least now, mentally, we felt a little more able to cope and we were a touch more organized. But only just. This piece came in reply to questions about Bristol and Lukas Wainman, Tomas's teacher. It filled two pieces of paper and was the longest piece he had written so far.

» preye goodlie brothir

bydd mynselves yow to chese nat wryts myne illfacyound scryt lest us han idell talke yf yow prey to excusacyone yow axyth o myne teche lukas an bryghtstowe thyre art manie tale to tunge o thys an me nold were to blentch myne wordes of myn lyf bot telle me wyl o goodlie tomas an lukas wen me wert yr myn yowth a barn as hath good lukas seyn me dyddst lyve wyth myn fadyr an myn brothyr an sat by myne porte an waytyr theyn bothe wercken on myn grete kyngs schypps ofte me wald syghta man o grete lernyng pass wyth hys bokes an oune deye hem didd leve a boke hynd hym whych hym did rede by myne ryvre soe me dyd makes haste an retornd yt to hys hond hym did thanke me an axd wot favour would me han o hym but me seyn nay favore me nat for me dydst turn thy skyn o thys yowr boke

an felt nedes to rede thy wordes tho theym seyn nothyn
to myne understondyng preye forgyve myne selven me dyd
not wysch to tak plesaunce wyth yowr possescyon hym dyd
glee at myn affectyoun an seyn alle boken belongen to alle
of lernyng an theym whome canst han rekconyng for thyse
boken o wysdome for to rede myne boke dost nat soyle
yt skyn bot doth makes mo men o lernyng that wryt moor
bokes hym dydst forth talke bowts bokes an thyr lernyng
for manie tornes o thy glas an also o hys lyf an knowyng o
myne servyng to hear o hys scyense didd ofyr myn fardyr
myn steye an fede yn hys howes for nought but that hym
honoure yn myn schoolyn as me didst helpe litel wyth thy
schypps an forth myn love dydst growe for lukas an hym
bokes he did han manie bokes o hys owen but wen me didst
rede theym al hym did takes theym frome thy kyngs courte
an before hym went to thy pyt hym did gyv hys bokes for
sylvre that me maye haps goe to Oxenforde an recalle hys
love for good men an treweth mythynks hym would love myn
brothyrs alsoe for yow to spekes o trewth an wysdom yf
a man can speke trewth theyn hym be free but men whome
doe lyv yn fere o thyr owne thrkyngs arn slaves to theyr
yntentyouns pardye.

tomas «

[If it pleases you good brother,

Don't ask me to write in my badly presented script in case we
waste time . . . you ask about my teacher Lukas and Bristol. There
is many a story to tell of this man . . . so tell I shall of good Tomas
and Lukas. When I was very young, a bairn as good Lukas would
say, I lived with my father and brother and sat watching them
work on the great King's ships. Often I would see a man of great
learning pass by with his books and one day he left a book behind him after he had been reading by the river, so I hurried to
return it to him. He thanked me and asked what favour he could
grant me. But I said, 'Favour me not for I turned the pages of this
book and felt the desire to read the words although they didn't
mean anything to me. Please forgive me, I did not mean to take
liberties with your property.'

He laughed at my affectations and said all books belong to the
sum of knowledge and those who have the understanding for

these books of wisdom, for to read the book doesn't spoil it but makes more men of learning that write more books. He talked about books and what they teach for many hours and also about his life, and knowing of my desire to hear of his science offered to take on the cost of food and lodgings for me if I would honour him in my studies, as I helped little with the ships. And so my love for Lukas and his books grew. He had many books of his own but when I had read all of them he took books from the King's court. Before he went to the dungeon he sold his precious books so that I might go to Oxford and remember his love for good men and truth. I think he would love you also for you too speak of truth and wisdom. If a man can speak the truth he is free but men who live in fear of their own thoughts are slaves to their intentions, don't you think?

Tomas]

These sustained pieces of prose offered direct access to the soul of Tomas Harden, but we had to press on so I piled on the questions. Where was Lukas from? What was his occupation? Peter had suspected from some of the words Tomas used that he had a northern or Borders influence in him. Tomas's use of the word 'bairn' only fuelled this suspicion. What was your father's first name? Why did he go to Taunton? Are any of your family still living near Chester? When did you leave for Oxford? How did it feel when you first saw Oxford? How old were you then? I told him that news of his communication was spreading across the country. Something of an exaggeration but I wanted him to feel that we were giving as well as taking.

Eyeing the paper and pens and then the sticky spoons and knives around them Deb and I wondered if Tomas would like to use the 'leems'/computer link. Domestic convenience was only a part of the reason. It was important that we had as many of his words as possible in the short time remaining to us. The computer messages were on average longer. We were also aware that the chances of misunderstanding were greater with the script. Pressure of time was still there. My new job, although like a gale of fresh air compared to teaching, was demanding. We needed to know what we were asking, and why, when and how to tackle his replies.

›› swete mayde

me dost nat pleesure to wrytes on thy leems for me am to thynks myn wordes wyl be tornd convers to what beest myne sentement Lukas wert afrom Scotlaunde as han yow from a plas callid Abyrdene hym dyd com to bryghtstoe cause o plauge ‹‹

[Sweet maid

I do not want to write on the 'leems' for I am convinced that my words will be distorted and not represent my sentiment. Lukas was from Scotland, from a place called Aberdeen. He came to Bristol because of the plague.

Love Tomas]

**27 January**

Problems for Tomas. He spoke of meeting a clergyman, a close friend, who advised him that he must abandon this communication and hold fast to his faith. The cleric said he could not keep both. Tomas was confused and worried, as well he might be. Late that evening I put down just a few thoughts which I hoped would help him. I include them here if only to show how we tried to imitate the style of the language and how far our efforts had taken us over the last year – and how far we were from being good mimics.

*Myne brothyr Tomas.*

*Goode Tomas here be myne thinkyngs. Yt does bring sorrow to myne heart to heer o yowr confusiouns but though me hath not a parfit answer this beeth o merit I doe hope. Nat anyman can know wot beeth the trewth o all mattirs for sych a man would plas himself wyth gode for gode knoweth all. That man ys nat parfit ys his condition an soe nat even a goodlie man o thy chyrche can judge wot be part o gode's wyll or wot wonders he doth dispence.*

*Wolde nat a man o this time say to myneselve: ken tis four hundred yeer since Tomas Harden passed so howe canst thou hath comunioun wyth hym. My answer is to look to theym an saye yea Tomas must be apassed like myne fathirs fathir an all sych mortal flesh but the Tomas who dost wryte is no spirit or daemon, he beeth myne freend. Both o thyngs be trewe yet they doe nat lye well togedir. A wyse man will nat despyre o thys confusioun. He will hold both to be trewe an gyue unto eache wot ys due for tis lik a blind youthe holding a bone yn one hand an a feather yn the othyr an knowyng the trewth of eache but nat the bird from whence yt came. Gode's will be hidden to us. Love both yowr chyrch an yowr brothyrs an fere nat for god beeth above us alle.*

*Ken*

It was about as 'philosophical' as I dared go, and that wasn't very far. But it was as honest as I could make it. Some of it was written in a way I thought Tomas would accept. He displayed all the qualities of a wise, generous and educated man. He was a man of principle and faith, a man open, aware, and some way outside the system. He was for necessary change but against such opportunists as Bishop Mann who so plagued his life.

Tomas took heartily to what I had said.

**›› myne trewe brothir**

**yowrn wardes be sych that onlie a man of gode can speke thys wey yow art a moste wyse man an me dost love yowr wordes me speeke mo amorrow.**

**Tomas ‹‹**

[My true brother,

Your words are such that only a man of God could speak this way. You are a most wise man and I love your words. I will write more tomorrow.

Tomas]

Naturally I was touched by his words. Debbie thought that 'man of God' was the last thing I could be called. I rang Peter to see if he wanted to add anything to the disarray of papers on the work top.

He came down around tea-time, full of good humour and conversation, and stood in the kitchen for a while, talking about recent events. His message to Lukas contained a biblical quotation from the Acts of the Apostles. It matched the current trend in the communication, away from the everyday towards matters of faith, and Peter could always be relied upon for a quotation. Before he left he reminded us that Gary Rowe would be coming down with his equipment next week. 'What do you think of him?' he asked and laughed, not waiting for a reply. Peter loved these enthusiasts. 'What do you think, eh? Will he be all right?' I replied to the effect that there was not much choice now. He'd have to do.

I wasn't much interested, to be honest. The recent skirmishes with semi-literate 'researchers' had left me with little appetite for UFOs and the 'paranormal'.

There was no reply to Peter's words that day. Deb gave Tomas a nudge.

*PREY YOW WRYTE TO PETER GOOD TOMAS'*

He wrote within the hour, saying he saw Peter but that because he had a visitor he couldn't reply straight away. He added that Peter's words needed his full attention. When he did write, the next morning, he began in this way.

›› myne trewe brothir Peter

preye tis nat resoune that leve myn feres bot that o myne fey for yf me wert onlie a wyght o reason hain me walna han trewst for myne brothyrs preye

preye tell me good.lie brothyr whome beest st paul . . .‹‹

[My true brother Peter,

Surely it is not reason that leaves me with trepidation but that of my faith for if I was only a man of reason then I would not have any trust for my brothers. Please tell me, good brother, who is Saint Paul . . . ?]

The remainder of the message concerned family matters, and although we were a little puzzled Deb and I thought no more of his question until we were quite sure of the translation.

As we drove along the dark winter lanes we talked of the sadness that was creeping into the communication in advance of his departure for Oxford. It seemed so terrible to part with so much unsaid.

Peter read the first part of the message and stood there in what I took to be a state of disbelief and astonishment. It turned quickly to a kind of anger. 'What does he mean, 'Whome beest St Paul'? It must be a hoax! No one could say such a thing. He's supposed to be a deeply religious man.'

Taken aback by the force of the argument, I was pushed into an unenviable position. A hoax, was it? Then it was Debbie or I, or both of us. I'd hoped all this hoax business had been buried, at least between us. Tomas was real! As real as Peter was! But although I was angry I did not know how to reply. The only excuse I found was the obvious one. 'It is a misunderstanding.' I elaborated quickly that we were communicating via scraps of paper, much of it written hurriedly and so on. I could tell from Peter's face that he just wasn't listening.

Debbie and I felt extremely uncomfortable and we left as soon as decently possible. Peter, our closest ally, our valued sounding board for ideas, had even at this stage never given up the suspicion that all this was possibly a hoax. This upset me. In the car the silence was broken by Debbie as we sped down the dark tunnel formed by trees at the edge of Gladstone Park.

'Asking about St Paul like that is pretty daft. Why did he?'

My blood had begun to slow its pace around my body but a new rush of adrenalin gripped my circulation. I was shaking with anger.

'I don't damn well know whyhesaysthesethings!' I yelled at her.

For the rest of the journey an icy silence prevailed, I was pretty beat up over it. Deb was trying not to cry.

On 30 and 31 January there was nothing new. On the I February Tomas called for his pen, as the Biro we had left out was not to his taste. He sounded rather arrogant and aloof. He had written:

›› **prey yow my pen then me wryte twey turne** [two turns of the hourglass]

**Tomas** ‹‹

He had put no greeting, no 'my trewe brothyr' or 'goodlie felawe' this time. Perhaps I had been too curt in putting Peter's question about St Paul. But in his reply he was gentle and apologetic for the way in which he expected us to comprehend his meaning directly. As for St Paul, he wrote:

›› **me sayne wot o st paul. Wot a thy worde yow um for yowrn conseylyng to mynselfe.** ‹‹

[I said: what of St Paul? What was it about these words you were using to counsel me?]

As I had thought, a kind of misunderstanding. Yet 'whome beest' was what he had written originally. Questioning the identity of St Paul would have made him a heretic – which was an alternative explanation of his curious statement. I could feel that my questioning him on Peter's behalf had made Tomas feel slighted. The exchange was in any event worthless as no clear conclusion could be reached. I certainly wasn't going to pursue it further.

# 46

**16 February**

The machinery, the video, the audio sensors; the little bits of sticky tape, the car full of gadgets. The man  himself wired up on enthusiasm and confidence – or just a wired up personality. He said that if anything – sound, light, electrical energy – fluctuated in that room he'd have a record of it. We were blinded by science. His monitor screen showed 'event registered' every few minutes but he said nothing was happening. 2109 didn't write. This was strange since they had invited him. But they did recognize him, as this exchange the following evening showed clearly.

*Hello 2109,*

*Mr Gary Rowe came yesterday and I think he was disappointed with the results, like us! Where were you, but i'm sure you had your reasons, I don't suppose you might tell us what they are though?!*

*Debbie*

> » HELLO,
>
> THERE ARE QUESTIONS TO BE ASKED AND THERE ARE QUESTIONS TO BE ANSEWERD.HIS COMPANY POWERFUL BUT NOT LIMITLESS. WE ARE!.THERE ARE RESONS BEHIND MOTIVE AND MOTIVE IS THEREFORE REASONABLE TO THE MAN AND THE SELF.
>
> THE EXPERIMENT WILL CONTINUE WITHOUT TOMAS FOR THE TIME BEING.WE SHALL WATCH AND REACT ACCORDINGLY IN THE VERTICAL PLANE.

GREETINGS GARY ROWE,

YOUR MOVE, WE ARE HERE ONLY TO AID THE EXPERIMENT, WE MEEN YOUR KIND NO HARM. ‹‹

Gary wanted to leave a sealed envelope on the computer! I asked 2109 if they needed the contents typing up. Apparently not.

›› DEBBIE

YOU MAY READ THE FOLLOWING. DO NOT SPEAK ON PHONE.

GARY

THERE IS NO NEED FOR THE ENVELOPE TO BE OPENED,BUT WE WILL NEED TO HAVE A SECOND OPPINION OF THE CONTENTS.AS REQUIRED WE WILL MAKE NO COMMENTS ON THE CONTENTS,IT SEEMS THAT THIS IS SLIGHTLY UNPREDICTED.HOWEVER WE WILL NOT SHOW IT TO ANYONE WHO IS NOT UNOTHERISED,THIS YOU MAY NOT UNDERSTAND!.IT WOULD BE EASIER TO PUT YOUR COM-PUTER INTO 'EDWORD/STAR' – WHAT EVER WHEN YOU WRITE TO US,THOUGH GEOGRAPHICAL LOCATION IS USUALLY ESSENTIAL.

PLEASE STATE YOUR RESONS FOR THE CONCLUSIONS REACHED. WE SHALL ANSEWER AS REQUIRED AND YOU SHALL HAVE THE ENVELOPE UNTAMPED BUT PLEASE WAIT AS YOUR STATEMENTS REQUIRE AN ANSEWER OF THE SAME. MAY WE REMIND YOU THAT YOU HAVE SEEN SOME OF OUR HANDY WORK – CANADA?!!.

2109 ‹‹

Two suggestions here: that Gary has asked if they could write to him in Rhyl and that he had seen some of their activity. Gary did not comment on this, and it was no good asking him.

The envelope disappeared out of the kitchen during the days that followed. Neat one! I was at least partially impressed. Again, Gary did not comment. Most people would have been getting free drinks on the back of the story of this event alone. It showed how far we'd travelled since December 1984.

The next day, 2109 announced that there was a message for Gary that should be printed without us reading it. I did as they asked and printed it up with my back to the machine: since I was asked.

We had been requested by Gary not to put it in the post and by 2109 not even to read it and certainly not to discuss it over the phone, so all we could do was arrange to meet him in Rhyl that night in a pub near the hospital.

Gary met us outside and handed us a present: a cassette player for our 'new' car. It was only a cheapie he didn't use anymore but it was a kindness. The pub was tacky, empty of people but for a few boozy bar flies. The juke box was churning out metal and Tamla and the whole ambience of Rhyl, that shabby decayed feel, sticky with candy floss and grease burgers. It made me shudder. By now our man was in the corner, his back to the corridor to the toilets. He opened his message. We looked expectantly like children do at Christmas. His restless eyes scanned the page, he twitched slightly. Quickly and with hardly a word he put the message back into the envelope. He said he hadn't time to mess around. He wanted some hard information. He was, he said, making himself vulnerable by writing to them. Why? He wouldn't say.

We just left. Another waste of time for us. After all the events of late October and November with SPR why was I bothering with 2109? It only attracted people who didn't want to say anything about 2109 but who were very interested indeed in the little numbers. The reason was Tomas, of course, he was still out of action. This then was why I bothered with the endless toing and froing, and tolerated the obsessive interest people took in 2109. If Tomas was allowed through I'd do almost anything. I wanted to bid my fellow farewell.

As we left it was clear that Gary was irritated, for all his polish and self-control. He thanked us for coming. I did not mind coming so much as I minded Rhyl for depressing the hell out of me.

*2109*

*GARY IS VERY DISAPPOINTED. HE SAYS THAT YOU HAVE SIX DAYS TO COME UP WITH A DIRECT ANSWER TO THE DIRECT QUESTIONS HE HAS POSED OR ELSE HE WILL GIVE UP.*

The only immediate reply was cipher; there was no one in the house at the time.

›› 1 645.439574.57.3744

2109 RTF ‹‹

**5 March**

2109 asked me to print up another document for Gary and warned me not to let Peter or Debbie interfere. A curious request. I didn't believe they had ever interfered.

›› KEN.

THERE IS SOMETHING FOR THE ATTENTION OF GARY ROW ON DOC."V" .IT WILL NEED TO BE UNLOCKED ONLY WHEN IT IS READY TO BE PRINTED,ASK GARY IF HE CAN GET HOLD OF THE MEANS TO PRINT IT UP HIMSELF,IF NOT,THEN YOU MUST REALISE THAT YOU WILL HAVE A GREAT RESPONSABILITY TO PRINT IT UP YOURSELF (IN HERE PLEASE) AS IF YOU ARE TO READ THE CONTENTS THEN YOU MAY LOSE ALL INCLUDING THOMAS,YOU DONT THINK PETER WOULD LIKE THAT NOW,DO YOU?!!!.WE SHALL KNOW WHETHER YOU HAVE MADE A COPY,IT DOESNT MATTER WHERE AND IF YOU HAVE DELIBERATELY GLANCED AT ITS CONTENTS.THERE IS NO NEED FOR A MONITOR TO BE ATTATCHED NOR DO YOU NEED TO WATCH OVER IT AS IT IS PRINTING AS WE CAN TELL YOU IT WILL JUST ABOUT FIT ON A4 PAPER.WITHOUT HESITATION PLACE IT IN A THICK ENVELOPE,BEST TO FOLD IT FIRST - AVOID MISTAKES!,IF YOU CAN NOT FIND A THICK

ENVELOPE RAP IT IN SOME PAPER BEFORE PLACING IT INSIDE. NO ONE,NOT FOR ANY REASON,SHOULD ENTER THE ROOM WHILE IT IS PRINTING - IT'S ALL ON YOU KEN!

2109 «

Later still they admonished me for asking why it was all so secret.

›› WE REMIND YOU THAT YOU HAVE BEEN HONOURED WITH THIS COMMUNICATION, WE ARE ALLOWED OWN PERSONAL COMMUNI-CATION WITH GARY WITHOUT QUESTIONS ASKED - YOU EXPECT THINGS, WHY SHOULD IT ALL BE FOR YOUR BENEFIT???!!! «

It was now 7 March and Gary had cooled somewhat when we next met him with a message. He gave us one in return addressed to 2109, not, as previously, in an envelope but for public consumption. It read oddly.

GREETINGS

I AM INSTRUCTED TO APOLOGISE BUT IN ANY EVENT I WOULD HAVE DONE SO OF MY OWN VOLITION.THERE WILL BE A LETTER HOPEFULLY THIS WEEKEND.I AM ALSO INSTRUCTED TO APOLOGISE TO KEN AND DEBBIE.I MUST TRY AND ANSWER YOUR LAST LETTER.IT WOULD APPEAR THAT YOU ARE MORE IMPORTANT THAN I HAD REALISED IN THE SCHEME OP THINGS.

GARY

This was crazy in two respects. Firstly it reminded us that we were by no means the only ones in touch with 2109, and secondly Mr Rowe was suggesting that they were important but he did not develop the reasons for this. It was no good asking him. Even at a meeting at Peter Trinder's where we questioned him in detail, and again much later at his house in Rhyl, he would only smile and utter sentences of calm obscurity. It was hopeless.

Meanwhile I was manoeuvring for Tomas's release. What madness! Suffice to say that there was to be another envelope and another sly comment about it from me:

*2109*

*I WOULD BE GRATEFUL IF YOU WOULD RELEASE TOMAS IN SEVEN DAYS SO THAT WE MAY CONCLUDE OUR COMMUNICATIONS WITH DIGNITY.*

*KEN.*

›› KEN

THANK YOU,WE DO NOTICE YOUR HARD WORK!. THOMAS WILL BE BACK AS SOON AS POSSIBLE.OUR CONVERSATIONS WITH GARY WILL NOT BE OF INTEREST TO YOU,WE ARN'T PLOTTING ANYTHING AGAINST YOU ‹‹

### 12 March

Debbie agreed to try a small test with the latest envelope. With Val Trinder as witness the door from the kitchen to the lounge was padlocked, and with the door to the bathroom lobby already bolted from the kitchen there was a reasonably secure space. Deb was alone as I was away on business in Hertfordshire. Despite the inconvenience and discomfort of walking right round the house to get to the bathroom Deb stuck it out in good spirit for the allocated twenty-four hours. She had the kettle in the living room and some food.

No one was more surprised than Val Trinder to open up the kitchen and find the envelope gone. This disappearance proved nothing but our impotence. We were reduced to the irrelevant, watching envelopes while Gary and 2109 went to it, and as hostage was the communication with Tomas.

*HELLO 2109*

*ANYTHING FOR GARY OR MYSELF? IS TOMAS ABOUT? KEN*

›› ANOTHER HOUR PLEASE. 2109 ‹‹

Nearly two hours later:

›› THANK YOU.

MESSAGE FOR GARY ON V.USURAL PROCEDURE PLEASE.

AFTER PRINTING WE SUGGEST YOU LEAVE SOME PAPER OUT!!!.

P.S.AGAIN SEAL IN ENVELOPE WITH "FOR GARYS' EYES ONLY –
READ WHEN ALONE"

WRITTEN ON THE OUTSIDE. THANK YOU

2109. «

Deb asked at one stage whether this communication with Gary would help us. It seemed not.

*GREETINGS,*

*2109, WOULD YOU PLEASE TELL ME WHAT PROGRESS YOUR MAKING WITH GARY AS WE DO NOT LIKE BEING LEFT IN THE DARK THIS WAY, DOES THIS HELP US (LIKE YOU SAID IT WOULD) OR DOES IT HELP YOU?. WHY IS IT THAT GARY, WHO, AS FAR AS WE ARE GIVEN TO UNDERSTAND,NEVER SPOKEN WITH YOU BEFORE CAN HAVE INFORMATION THAT WE ARE RESTRICTED TO HAVE? IS GARYS INVESTIGATION GOING TO PROVE POSITIVE FOR US?*

*DEBBIE.*

›› GREETINGS

THE COMMUNICATION BETWEEN GARY AND 2109 IS NOT OF IN-TEREST TO YOU.GARY HAS A BETTER UNDERSTANDING OF US THAN YOU DO,HIS EXPERIENCES ARE MOST DEFINATELY AN ADVANTAGE TO THIS.HIS PHYSICAL TESTS WILL PROOVE NEG-ATIVE,UNFORTUNATELY YOU PUT FAR TOO MUCH CONCERN IN PROOVING THIS TO THE "WORLD" – YOU KNOW THAT THIS IS A WORTHLESS EFFORT,WHY ASK!.YOU MUST NOT BE 'PUSHY' WITH GARY,YOU UNDERESTIMATE HIS ABILITIES AND THAT INDIRECTLY IS AN INSULT TO US!.IF YOU HAD OPEND YOUR EYES A BIT WIDER AND READ THE COMMUNICATIONS MORE INTENCLEY YOU WOULD HAVE HAD HALF THE ADVANTAGE THAT GARY HAS.

WE MUST MAKE A MOVE THOMAS HAS FOUR DAYS THEN HE WILL LEAVE WE SHALL FOLLOW.GARY ROWE HAS AND WILL SERVE HIS PURPOSE . . . 2109 «

It was all a curious episode overshadowed by Tomas's return and to whom the story now returns.

At a later meeting Gary would only say that if we were 'further along the road', i.e. towards his way of thinking, then he might be able to explain. He was polite but firm. He could not, I think, hide his disappointment. Something in the exchange must have held a fascination for him yet it was not enough, something went wrong. I can only say that I did as I was requested and not a single message that he left for 2109 nor a single word of any message they left for him on my little computer did I see or interfere with. I am proud of this. Gary alone can tell the story of what went on. For all his perfect manners, his esotericism, I couldn't help feeling sorry for him. He would not agree with me but in a way that does not matter. I am sure we were just looking from very different points of view.

As with SPR, no report has ever been submitted to us.

Above Gary Rowe, giving an interview to SUFON (Swansea UFO Network), 2018.

# 47

**15 March**

I left a short message to Tomas saying I wished that there was something I could do to keep him there. For a second I succumbed to the desire to try and 'visit' him. Reason asserted itself, if somewhat unsteadily at first. There was no time to play games. Every working day began sooner and ended later and every evening after writing a few hurried words I became an outcast, waiting an hour, half an hour, or whatever, to see his words. I did not ask him much more than a few sentimental items: that he and Debbie should perhaps meet in the great garden of Magdalen College, or by the river; that he tell us about his first days in Oxford, where he stayed, what he did.

His sadness, too, was evident and instead of us pushing ahead, gathering a rich harvest of information and recollection, the communications stumbled, clouded by melancholy.

I provided paper but he did not continue. My questions did. I had prepared another sheet of scraggy, block-lettered words in readiness.

I told Tomas of the first days of the adventure, it seemed so long ago, of Nicola Bagguley, Debbie and myself and the 'comuter'; of how old the computer was (a year or so) what we did and why; and what or who we thought we were talking to. I embroidered a little on this 'me didst thenk yt was a ghoul or devyl'. I asked again about the 'antic' which had first brought sight of the 'leems' in his chimney space. I concluded by saying that not all computers bring messages across time! It felt like a legend I was telling: full of mystery, morality and innocent adventurers. It felt pretty good despite or because of this.

The irritating question of who was parson at the church haunted me. It was trivial in a way but I had read in the parish-produced History of Dodleston that Pennant was rector. Tomas had written some weeks before 2109 'held up' communications that Cowlie was the parson. The awareness of the 'end' forced us to go over old ground to make sure, even though Tomas was adamant about the facts as he knew them. I was even looking at questions which had been long answered, e.g. the 'half-witted antic'. There were hundreds of papers and messages bundled carelessly upstairs, I just forgot . . . so many, many hours were lost in the dogged search for the trivial and obscure.

Debbie said we were acting as though we had all year and more to talk to him. I sensed a truth and still felt we were floundering in a fast ebb tide.

›› myne brothyr ken

me dost thanke yow for yowm worden theym han gyfen mynselves goodlie stedde for rekonyn thys leems betir forthe wol I tel o thys yow rewarde [?] tan antic kathryn wert slepyn yn myn fyr sete yn myn chynmney soe me didst goe to carie hyr thyr bedes wan me syghts a grene lyt ashynyng from thy wals o myne chimnie an from thys lyt steped wot methenkd wert thy devyll hymselvs me didst nevyr fere for myn sowle soe moche yn myn lyf but soe aferd wert me th me nold moove wey frome thys unkyndlie messagere hym seyn fere nat goodlie tomas yow art starred tbe a grete man yf me dost na han fere but kepe myne fey stronge theyn aft othyr worden whych me dost confess nat lyken to devyl tonge hym didst mispere leevyng thy leems whyche seemth tme tbe model o yowr comutyr me dydst thir wt al me wayken kathryn whome dydst nat syghts myn leems nor ere me speke tthy metaphysycalle wyght bot she seyen yow nyce tomas yow wert bot yn mete nowe affraye me nat for yow pathetycale wyts soe tmope me dyd for thyr shone leems bot kathryn syghts nat soe me dyd verily care for myn wyts that me dyd reherce myn gode vers alnyght tyd [?] til morrowe but nay would yt goe but sat wyth glee quently prevy talle but mynselve then twey daye aft kathryn wert asingen vers yn myn chimney bi my fyr an leems an me see

that hyr wordes dyd pere an yt soe wan kathryn dyd go
walkyng me tryd vers mynnselve an othyr wordes an waxen
myn rekonyng fo leems dost yow preye mo o leems

Tomas

[My brother Ken,

I thank you for your words. They have given me base upon which to understand the 'leems'. I will now tell you about what you might call an 'antic'. Kathryn was sleeping in the chimney seat so I went over to pick her up and carry her to her bed when I saw a green light shining from the walls of my chimney and from this light stepped what I thought was the devil himself. I never feared for my soul so much in my life but so afraid was I that I couldn't move away from this strange messenger. He said, 'Fear not, good Tomas, you are starred to be a great man, if you do not have fear but keep your faith strong.' Then after other words which I do confess were not like devil talk he was gone leaving the 'leems' which appeared to be the same as your computer. I immediately woke Kathryn but she didn't see the 'leems' nor hear me speak with the metaphysical person but she said, 'You, silly Tomas, were in your dreams, now don't frighten me with your disturbed thoughts.' So to mope I did for there shone the 'leems' but Kathryn saw it not. I was so worried for my sanity that I spoke the Lord's prayer all night but it would not go but sat with glee unseen by all but myself. Then two days afterwards Kathryn was singing in the chimney by the fire and 'leems' and I saw that her words appeared on it so when Kathryn went walking I tried verses myself and other words and gained knowledge about the 'leems'. Do you want more about the 'leems'?

Tomas]

We were suddenly on the right track. More questions. Let's get the parson business out of the way quickly and move on. I tensed. No matter what, even in those last days I was still trying to prove it all, or at least question, analyse, probe, when a year ago I had resolved to let it run on, to put aside analysis until it was all done. It was a mark of my failure. Parsons and rectors . . . pah! Ask him something vital or interesting and just for once get the question right . Make it something he will be interested in.

To calm down I took a walk round Chester and ended up on part of the city walls near the racecourse. It was a longish walk, and I stopped every hundred yards and peered out into the distance. I only had two thoughts for my 'brother': one was 'don't go' and the other was 'we all love you'. I was behaving like the hero of a second-rate novel: all moody and terribly serious. This had to stop. I forced my mind to concentrate on the coming days. I determined to ask only that Tomas write more of the 'leems' and let him say what he will. The 'leems': here was the real mystery. It occurred to me that he was asking nothing much of us. Guilt compounded frustration and sadness.

I walked slowly down to the river and leant over the parapet of the old Dee bridge, watching the surge of phosphorescence as the dark waters played across the weir. Here and there a log was jammed against the stonework. I remembered something: 'of that which is to be termed "time" we perceive the stepping stones of today and tomorrow but not the vibrant river that runs between our feet.'

I spoke. 'There you are then,' I said to the river. 'These messages have been a few stepping stones.' I looked across the weir. 'I'm missing an awful lot of river, aren't I?' The river gurgled its agreement beneath the piers. I smiled, then said to the gorged waters, 'You are my river of lost opportunity.' The river was blackness and constancy. Cars nosed around like landbound sharks on the narrow roadway at my back. 'Do you have any questions, river?' I knew the answer: Why are you looking down on me? The best way to understand is to swim along with me. It is effortless. 'I know. I tried that but couldn't let go.' I spoke softly and held my glasses lest they fall in. The river was full of spring rains.

›› brothyr ken an beste felawe

me shalt forthe mo o leems as thys be yowr axyng me nacan recorde thy naym o vers but twas dytee for a younge
chylde an yt were lyght tsynge tho nathelis me nold make
tpapyr as nouthe yt were somthynge bouten thy stepe
starres anyght aft me wert famulyer wt the leems me didd
impeech yt urn an that be wan thy worden me dyd shewe
yow tpapyr cam meethynks nowe fro 2109 tunge me wert
soe mated by thys ta me dyd include comunyon wyth thy
devyl for fere o myn wits an made myn intendment nat tfal
bi syk woodniss but nay would yt goe tho non dyd syghts
yt theyn me wert spyryted yn my slepes by unkowth toys o
thy wyts an aldeye wol devylls turn my howes upsoe downe
afrayng kathryn soe me dydst goe to thy leems an ax why yt
dyd ax us o ari sych fere yn myn hows then methynks yow
wryt an al dyd styl yea pennante beest rector tho cowlie
beest parsoun non me doe favour theym han illprys to thir
hedes me can understand yf wot yow seyn ys trewe ta yow
tthynks me devyl als bot me nowe know myn felawes to be
goode men for methynks yow makest love brothyr tomas an
we han trewst preye.

Tomas ‹‹

[Brother Ken and favourite fellow,

I shall tell you more of the 'leems' as this is your desire. I cannot
remember the name of the verse I received but it was a ditty
for a young child and it was easy to sing though I can't put it to
paper. It was something about the high stars at night. After I was
familiar with the 'leems' I asked why it was there and that was
when the words I showed you on paper came, I think now they
were from 2109. I was so shocked by this that I thought it was
communication with the devil by this device. I made a promise not to allow myself to be damned by such madness but it
wouldn't go away though no one saw it. After this I was haunted in my sleep by strange dreams and all day devils turned my

house upside down scaring Kathryn so.I went to the 'leems' and asked it why it wanted to bring such fear into my house. Then I think you wrote and all was still.

Yes, Pennant is rector though Cowlie is parson. I don't like either ... I can understand if what you say is true that you also thought I was the devil but now I know my fellows to be good men, you love brother Tomas and we have trust in one another, don't you agree?

Tomas]

My ignorance and naivety. Parsons and rectors are not necessarily the same thing. Peter gave Debbie a last message to write up.

### 19 March

I was still not prepared for his going. I had not written my last words, and I didn't know when I should have the time or what I should say. Early spring weather, blustery showers, the snowdrops I love so much had come and gone in Broughton churchyard. 'The sap's rising,' my grandmother used to say. 'The sap's rising. Another year safe on its way.'

I came back to a verse written by Philip Larkin, from The North Ship that I had left for Tomas some days before.

*This is the first thing I have understood*

*Time is the echo of an axe within a wood.*

Paradoxically part of me felt that Tomas had already gone. He had become the echo. The burden was now on making something of it as worthy as the man himself, a book to mirror the one he was going to begin at Oxford. It would take more than another crop of snowdrops and another year 'safe on its way' to write such a book. Perhaps these books are an attempt to penetrate the wood; to be aware of more than the echo of the axe.

Debbie wrote her message:

*Tomas myne goodlie brother, . . . when do yow thynk yow are to go to Oxanford. We will miss yow very much. How will yow go, will it be on horse or shipp prey . . .*

*. . . How is yowr cook?*

*Will she go with yow prey? Doe yow have any animals left. Tell more goodlie Tomas*

*Love Debbie*

*We will all miss yow Tomas, love Debbie.*

### 20 March

›› mayde debbie

me wryt amorrow fo grovnor com thys deye ‹‹

### 21 March

At about 4.35 P.M. I rang home from work in Manchester. Deb sounded full of a cold and not herself in a way that only people who have lived together for a time understand. Tomas was gone, she seemed to say. I was still in the office world. I joked almost. But she was upset, or at least had been; 2109 had gone as well. Peter's last message to Tomas didn't get through in time. I began to get a little confused and my mind was no longer firmly fixed on deadlines in the office but switched between the idea of Tomas going quickly without warning and my being here in Manchester. I wandered to the computer room and tried to finish a section on the Project Newsletter. I succeeded, but my hand was unsteady. I had to go home. I walked slowly, deliberately, from the office, following our secretaries, Nicky and Agnes, out and into the car park. I exchanged a few words with both of them, then Agnes drove off fiercely in an Alpine. I noticed for some reason that it was Scottish registered.

I soon found myself on Princess Parkway, traffic all around, middle lane, fast lane, the illuminated 40 MPH sign was triggered as I passed, on to the M56, where the sun was stretched between two faint grey bands of cloud. A spring day slipping away. I was driving with tears in my eyes, eighty miles per hour and I could hardly see. I was not really in a hurry but the sun, the beautiful grey of the clouds and the music on the car cassette player compelled me to go on like this. 'We belong together . . . we . . . be . . .long together!' It was Rikki Lee Jones. The first day I took Deb out I played this tape. I couldn't help those few tears. I didn't see anything but the sun, the clouds in a mackerel sky, the white lines under the wheels. I didn't know why I was so helpless.

Maybe just not having to think of how to say farewell, just being at the end of something. This emotion was recognition of that. But maybe we did belong together, Tomas and I, his 'sweet mayde', Deb, and Peter too, and parting really did hurt. I did not understand my feelings. I drove on and on into the lengthening shadows. Lorries, cars, cassette, tears, driving. The journey absorbed every moment of the last fifteen months and it felt endless.

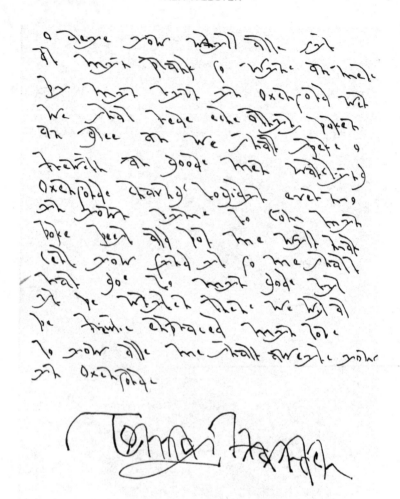

Previous 3 images: Tomas's last message

Above: '"We are all but Shadows": Tomas' by Debs

›› Myne trewe felawes an swete mayd

grovnor han seyn now tomas must goe me knowest thys to be
beste for thy pepel o myn dodlestone art forferen o myne
steye grovnor seyn that theym wyle brenne myn ald farme
down al myn toun doe despires myneselve less grovnor or
soe hym seyn tis goode to know alle wyl chaunge an thir
be styl trewe men to forthe com aft me lyk ken an peter but
IV hondred yere by grete spas o tym on moch to fortunen
mankynde tis sorrowfulle that men al muste lern thyr ryght-
wisness from gryslie weyen leven [?] theym hath talen [?]
tloke for trewth yn routhe an lov alweys rectrenle [?] bi
wot beeth na trew me preye for myn felawes anite that theym
nver goe tmyn pyt for thyr lov o thir brothyr tomas ar we
nat trewe men me seyn woe for alle yow wyghts tha be nat
trew for yowr wele be markd by gode hym wyl nat han yowr

compaNic bot yow wylt walke wyth thy beests o tartuss fo evrmo yow whoe hath ne validity yn thys lyf me knowest that me muste na sorrowe but me can na emper myn sorrow tpapyr but know yow me weep an myn wyts beeth confus myn honde be weke may hap yow com to Oxenford yf thir shoulde be na scathe fo me thir nowe for me ere th kyng be verie syk an all be styl yn thy chirche me shal goe bi barge from Cestre port to bryghtstowe thin me wylt beye a hors for myn nold go on barge for yt doubten watyr lyk fere yn fyves hym me als weep for me shal thir mak myn steye at brasennose tho me wett expulsed manie yere goe now me wylt wryt myn boke abowte myne brothyrs an mayd an o thy conclusyon o lukas an thy litel whelp an o owrne love or eecheothyr mo papir

o deye yow whyll alle syt at myn plank for wyne an mete by myn ryvr yn oxenford were we shal rede eche othyrs boken an glee an we shalt speke o trewth an goode men, watchyng oxenforde chaunge togidyr evermo yn yowr tyrne to come myn boke beest ald bot me shalt not goe to myn gode tyl yt be wryten hene we wyl al be trewlie embraced my love to yow alle me shalt aweyte yow yn oxenforde.

Tomas «

[My true fellows and sweet maid,

Grosvenor has said that Tomas must go. I know it is for the best because the people of Dodleston are very wary of me; Grosvenor says they will burn my old farm down and that except for him all the village despises me – at least that is his view. It is good to know that all will change and there are true men to follow like Ken and Peter; though 400 years is a long time and there is much to happen to mankind. It is sad that men must learn righteousness from their ugly ways believing that they have to look for truth in ruthlessness and never follow a path that is for truth. I pray for my fellows at night that they are never imprisoned because of their love for their brother Tomas. Are we not true men? I say, 'Woe to all you men who are not true for you are marked by God, He will not have your company but you will walk with the beasts of Tartuss [Hell] for evermore – yes you that have no worth in this life.' I know that I mustn't sorrow for I cannot put these feelings to paper, but you must know that I weep and am emotional, I find it hard to write. Perhaps you will come to Oxford now I think there is no danger for me there, for I hear the King is very sick and all is quiet in the Church. I shall go by boat from Chester to Bristol, there I will buy a horse for mine will not go on a boat – it is as scared of water as it is scared of fives [horse sickness]. I also weep for him. I shall try to make my stay at Brasenose though I know I was expelled many years ago. I will write my book about my brothers and maid and of the end of Lukas and the little puppy and of our love for each other.

One day you will all sit down at my table for wine and meat by the river in Oxford where we shall read each other's books and laugh and we shall speak of truth and good men, watching Oxford change together for evermore.

In your time my book is old but I shall not go to my God until it is written then we will all be truly embraced. My love to you all. I shall await you in Oxford.

Tomas Harden]

The last communication:

›› KEN, DEB, PETER

TRUE ARE THE NIGHTMARES OF THOSE THAT FEAR

WHAT YOU FEAR WILL BE YOUR REALITY IF YOU LET IT, BELIEVE IN YOURSELVES

SAFE ARE THE BODIES OF THE SILENT WORLD

AS LONG AS YOUR KIND CANNOT PENERTRATE OUR WORLD WE ARE SAFE

TURN PRETTY FLOWER TURN TOWARDS THE SUN FOR YOU SHALL GROW AND SOW BUT THE FLOWER REACHES TOO HIGH AND WITHERS IN THE BURNING LIGHT

KNOWLEDGE WILL BE YOUR PROGRESS BUT YOUR KIND ARE COMING CLOSE TO GETTING THEIR FINGERS BURNT ... INDIRECTLY, YOU MAY PREVENT THIS!

GET OUT YOUR BRICKS

GET READY TO BUILD (WRITE THE BOOK!)

PUSSY CAT,PUSSY CAT WENT TO LONDON TO SEEK FAME AND FORTUNE

THE CAT WENT TO VISIT THE QUEEN,BUT INSTEAD FRIGHTENED A LITTLE MOUSE UNDER THE CHAIR,ULTIMATELY,LONDON WILL BE A SIGNIFICANT PLACE,STICK TO YOUR MAIN AIMS,IT DOESNT MATTER HOW HARD THEY SEEM TO GET,DO NOT BE DISTRACTED BY THAT TINY MOUSE THAT HAS A DECEIVING CHARM

FAITH MUST NOT BE LOST . . . !

YOU ALL RELY ON EACH OTHERS FAITH.

THERE IS ANOTHER PERSON TO COME. THEY WILL BE THE HELP WE NEED. YOU WILL KNOW THEM WHEN THEY COME. THOMAS DID EVENTUALLY WRITE HIS BOOK AND SOON DIED, SHORTLEY AF-TER, HE PLACED IT IN A SECURE PLACE, IT SHOULDN'T TAKE TOO MANY YEARS TO FIND IT, THOUGH HE WROTE IT IN LATIN WITH THE HELP OF A FREIND THAT HE MET IN OXFORD, THE INSCRIPTION READS "ME WRYTS THIS IN THE HOPE THAT MYNE FELAWS WILL ONE DAY FIND THIS BOKE, THEN MAY OWER LANDS BE NOT SOE DISTANT".

WE WILL FINNISH NOW YOU HAVE ALOT OF WORK TO DO!! THERE IS NO NEED FOR YOU TO WRITE BACK AS WE WILL HAVE GONE.

THANK YOU FOR YOUR COOPERATION

2109 «

# *Postscript*

The communications of 21 March 1986 were not quite the end of the affair. Although I left the story of Gary Rowe on 15 March, he had at that time given us a small envelope containing a flattish object with the request that it be left for 2109. In this strange business that request was not in itself unusual but Debbie could not help noticing that there was a figure of an Egyptian deity drawn on the outside of the envelope. She felt that Gary was introducing an 'occult' connotation to the communications. This was ludicrous. We travelled to Rhyl and asked Gary to replace it with a plain envelope. He gave us the package again but it was patently obvious that the original envelope had been placed inside a new one. Since he was determined to be obscure we decided we had had enough of a game in which we were only spectators. Consequently we kept the envelope out of the way. Gary did not offer to explain his small deception nor did we pursue it. The envelope was never opened and it was given away.

2109 had gone and I promised myself that I would never again set up a BBC computer in the house. However, in July 1986 a friend of John Cummins was introduced to us. She expressed an enormous interest in 2109. In the end I gave way, with the expectation that a day or two of blank screens would satisfy her curiosity. To my surprise 'they' did communicate something. A part of it so struck our guest that she fainted as soon as she read it. Worse, she would not explain what there was in the communication that was so shocking. When she recovered she wanted to reply 'to help them' but I said no, I was not about to let it begin again, so the computer was immediately turned off and put in its box. Later Debbie gave it to her brother who has had it ever since.

Yet even at the time of writing (December 1987), over a year after the incident described above, the whole business will not settle. Ernst Senkowski, a professor of physics in Mainz, contacted me in February 1987 after having seen a small piece on the affair written by Theo Locher in *Schweizerischen Bulletin fur Parapsychologie* (November 1986). He gave me information about a gentleman in the Black Forest called Boden who in 1984 had suffered what might be termed 'paranormal' events, including interference on his computer. The messages he received were sufficient to turn the poor fellow to drink. The death of his friend had been predicted correctly and his own indicated, although the latter date, happily for him, passed without event.

Senkowski also sent me a cutting from Astrology and Psychic News (US). It was a story about thought and its impact on computers, part of which I quote here.

Norman Ling said he received the first message about a year ago . . . 'I would enter something into the computer and when I printed it out there would be whole sentences that I had not put in the machine. They were about people I had never heard of . . .'

Ling brought some of his computer print-outs to Mrs Standard [a neighbour] and asked her if the messages might have any connection with her psychic work. 'She was very amazed . . . it was quite an experience to see words that had only been in her mind now printed in black and white . . . '

Interesting as it was to realize that our experience was not entirely without precedent, there was still nothing which touched us directly. But this changed in July 1987 when I received through the post a print-out of a message received in Luxembourg. It was marked 2105 and carried my name, if misspelt.

›› KONTAct kEEn WEBSter during HOLLtydais mutch iMPORTRance.

d eankjue

2105 ‹‹

The people who received the message, the Harsch-Fischbachs, were able to contact me through the fact that Senkowski was also mentioned later in the communication and they knew Senkowski through a shared interest in Electronic Voice Phenomena (EVP). This is the term for the recording of voices emanating from specially tuned radios, not thought to be explainable as interference, stray transmissions, etc. Some researchers treat them as voices from the dead but critics refer to the 'mediumship of the tape recorder' and offer other explanations.

Maggie and Jules Harsch-Fischbach spoke to me for the first time when we met on 19 August 1987 in South Wales where they were on holiday. They knew very little of the events at the cottage apart from what was included in the Chester Observer article (24 December 1985), but to my surprise they offered further information relevant to our experience. At least three sections of a recent exchange (15 August) between Jules and Maggie and a contact they call The Technician are worth quoting:

*Q: Could we explain the communication between Ken Webster and Tomas Harden as an overlap of time between separate dimensions because Tomas Harden is in the 16th century and Ken Webster is here today?*

A: Yes exactly. This is an overlap of time of both dimensions

*Q: Could you explain it also as an insight into the Akashic record in which all that has been and all is to come are found?*

A: You could call it something like that yes. There should appear in this region other documents from that time to show the people, these unexplained experiences with this 'light box' have happened and what could be seen on the screen.

*Q: Will Ken Webster find these documents?*

A: Other people will find these documents ...

More questions, more puzzles, but I think it reasonable to say that the chances of my being on the receiving end of a hoax, or more importantly, perpetrating one, receded as the affair assumed international proportions.

Jules and Maggie asked me to set up the computer again and attempt to re-establish contact with 2109. I realized that this was probably the main reason behind their visit to the UK. I explained the situation and declined, but I offered to help the Harsch-Fischbachs with information and commentary on what they received either through EVP or on computer as long as it did not refer to me. I suppose I felt flattered that an attempt had been made to reach me through another country but it did not shake my resolve. To their slight disappointment I also said that I did not think 2105/9 were the important part of what had happened in Dodleston.

We sought John Bucknall's report of the investigation at the cottage from the SPR office in April 1986. We received a reply from John Stiles (Liaison Officer) to the effect that John Bucknall had left the Society and despite numerous efforts could not be contacted at all. We asked if either Dave Welch or Nick Sowerby-Johnson had filed reports. To our surprise we were told that neither of 'these gentlemen' was known to SPR. SPR were quite apologetic at being unable to help. I took this to be the end of SPR interest, but I have since obtained solid evidence, again through Professor Senkowski, that they have been trying very hard (as late as November 1987) to investigate the case without approaching me. I suppose it is because they are somewhat embarrassed by John Bucknall's conduct.

We have looked into the question of computer bugging and our enquiries have revealed that a BBC B without modem is impossible to bug in the manner suggested by John Bucknall. The 'hidden EPROM' notion, a mainstay of John's rebuff to the results of the ten-question test, was also invalid.

Given that one explanation of what happened at the cottage is that of 'time slip', how was it possible? These questions have been asked many times. Couldn't it all have been your unconscious? I have no means of 'proving' anything in regard to these experiences. I don't think I have any need to because what I have put in this book is a record of events, a source book, even if only a summary, for others, yet it would be naïve and indeed wrong to suggest that I have not sought to answer the knotty questions surrounding these events. e.g. If it was my unconscious (or Debbie's), where is the source for this rare dialect? How is the computer affected? But what follows is only a starting point for discussion and it should be treated as such.

In some notes I made in January 1986 and shared as always with Debbie and Peter Trinder I suggested vaguely that there was a quality about the place that allowed transfer between times to sensitive persons. Not physically of course, but perhaps something of or through their aspects of consciousness. Debbie and Tomas were two such sensitives. Peter and I were not.

This 'quality' must be present in both times that are conjoined in this way if some transfer is to take place. It was present in 1985-6 and in 1546. That is why we didn't encounter, say, a 17th-century figure. So the people and the place could matter immensely.

It is for me a time-related phenomenon, not something supernatural or spiritual. The notion of 'seeing' the future (since Tomas was looking into and was often in his future) might suggest an explanation for some categories of odd sightings occurring today, e.g. UFOs, as they might be just snatches of our future.

In the same way, sightings of the Yeti, 'Surrey Panthers' and so on could be explained as glimpses of the past. The commonality is that they are merely little time slips, generated by a mixture of aspects of consciousness and 'special places'.

If this is so, such sightings would be restored to the natural world, as natural as snowdrops and spring showers. There might be a revolution, centred around changing or recognizing different concepts of, and processes within, time.

I put these speculative ideas to a number of friends and out of amused curiosity to 2109. They replied on 18 January 1986:

›› TIME, UFOs AND MOST OTHER TYPES OF THE PARANORMAL ARE IN SOME WAY ALL CONNECTED:-

IN CERTAIN GEOGRAPHICAL LOCATIONS THERE IS WHAT WE CALL AREAS OF CONVEXUAL MAGNATISM. THESE CAN BE EXPLAIND BY THE MAGNETIC LINES THAT RUN AROUND THE EARTH. IMAGINE, IF YOU WILL, CIRCLES RUNNING AROUND THE EARTH CLOCKWISE (THESE ARE POSITIVE LINES OF MANETIC FORSE- P.L.M.F.) AND ALSO CIRCLES RUNNING ANTICLOCKWISE AROUND THE EARTH (NEGATIVE'''' - N.L.M.F!) WHEN TWO OPPERSITE RUNNING LINES ARE CROSSED (USUALLY A PERMINANT CROSSING RATHER THAN RANDOM) THE LIGHTTIME CONTINUEM IS VASTLY DISTORTED SO MUCH SO THAT A 'SENSITIVE' INDAVIDUAL MAY WITNESS WHAT YOU, MAY CALL A TIME SCAPE, THAT IS, A GLIMS OF A PAST EVENT OR THAT OF A FUTURE EVENT. AH !,WE HEAR YOU SAY, BUT YOU SAID MATTER COULD NOT TRAVELL IN TIME, THIS IS TRUE AS IF MATTER WERE TO TRAVELL BY PHYSICAL MOTION THEN MASS AROUND THE MOVING OBJECT WOULD BE SO DENSE THAT THE EARTH AND MOST OTHER CELESTIAL BODIES IN YOUR SOLAR SYSTEM WOULD BE CONSUMED OR INBALANCED IN SUCH A WAY THAT THEY WOULD DECAY RAPIDLY. THEN HOW:

IMAGINE, AGAIN PLEASE, A PERSON FROM THE FUTURE HAPPILY FLOATING ALONG IN HIS SILVER SPACE SHIP CROSSING AN AREA OF CONVEXUAL MAG. ALL OF A SUDDEN HIS INSTRUMENT PANNEL GOES 'SHAKY' HE MAY FEEL SLIGHTLY DIZZY OR NASEAUS A GREEN MIST (CAUSED BY APTNOSPHERIC DISTORTION) FORMS AROUND THE VESSAL HE THEN WILL PROBERBLY FALL INTO A 'TRANCE' STATE OF SUCH DEPTHS THAT HIS 'SOUL' IS SQUEEZED THROUGH THE LIGHTTIME GATE AND FORCED TO PROJECT A PHYSICAL MIRROR IMAGE OF HIM/HER SELF AS A [word missing] OF THEIR PLACETIME ORIGIN AND THEIR EMIDIATE VICINATY. THIS CAN OCCUR SOMETIMES FOR ONLY SEVERAL SECONDS AND DOES ONLY REGISTERS FOR THAT INDIVIDUALS SUBCONSCIOUS BUT ON-LOOKERS, FROM THE TIME WHICH IS 'BROKEN INTO', WILL WITTNESS THE VERY PHYSICAL SIGHT AND ACTIONS OF THIS

'ALIEN' FROM ANOTHER TIME THEN, TOTALLY BY CONFUSION
,ELABORATE ON THE FACTS.WE ARE NOT SAYING THAT THERE IS
NO OTHER LIFE OUTSIDE YOUR PLANET,ON THE CONTREY, THERE
IS LIFE ELES WHERE, BUT THE ABOVE PHENOMENA IS THE MOST
USUAL AS SPACE IS INFENITE TO THE MORTAL AND THE CHANCES
OF ANOTHER RACE COMING ACROSS THE EARTH IS NOT REALLY
IN A BRAKET OF PROBERBILLITY. THERE WAS ONCE A GREAT
PHELOSOPHER WHO LIKEND TIME TO AN INFINITELY HIGH BLOCK
OF FLATS EACH FLOOR TO REPRESENT EVENTS ALL PILED
ON TOP OF ONE ANOTHER (VERTICALLY TO REPRESENT THE
GEORGRAPHICAL LOCATION AND LATERAELLY TO REPRESENT
EVENT-EACH FLOOR).

A LITTLE CORRECTING!, FINNISH AFTER.

[unsigned]

No confidence had ever been placed in communications from 2109, but since this chapter merely contains ideas for discussion let us continue their theme. This disruption in the time/light continuum is itself attributable to variations in the pattern of certain magnetic fields around the earth. The disruption affects, if you will, the soul; the essential self-image. Tomas Harden managed to direct or draw out some form of control over the displacement of his consciousness. Debbie, too, in certain dream states, became lucid, self-aware, and although sometimes this was veiled by her reluctance to believe she could 'be' in another time she appeared to Tomas quite regularly, and from his side and in his inimitable language we are informed of their conversation. Unfortunately the mirror image of self would require an energy to be available everywhere for the self to manifest and act in another 'timescape'. What energy? And because not everyone can see the transferred image, perception and this energy must be related.

Now we are in deep water! It is partly because explanations of the phenomenon based upon the premise that what we recorded was real always run into such problems that the rational person will, on a priori grounds, dismiss the whole business. It suffers from 'antecedent improbability': it doesn't fit 'reality' therefore it must be impossible. Ah, well ...

327

But even on the edge of 'reality', reports are beginning to accumulate of mental interference with computers*, and several writers have posited the existence of lines of force† in fact as feng shui (Chinese geomancy), an ancient tradition which has had an enormous influence on Chinese thought and culture. But can even severe fluctuations in these extremely weak fields be tied in with consciousness? Is it within the bounds of science to have a situation where distorted consciousness allows access to other times?

Professor Jack Sarfatti certainly believes something of the sort, and was quoted in Timewarps by John Gribbin as saying:

*I believe the gravitational distortion of space and time predicted in Einstein's general theory of relativity provides a possible scientific explanation of precognition, retrocognition, clairvoyance, and astral projection, provided we accept the additional postulates that individual consciousness can alter the biogravitational field of a living organism and that the biogravitational field distorts the local subjective space time of the conscious observer . . . I conjecture that distortions can be manipulated in such a way that the rate of time flow at the location of the participator does not match the corresponding rate of time flow at the object being observed and influenced . . . and can in principle be so adjusted that the participator working within his local light cone . . . samples universe layers.*

But is this the same as being in another time? The task is beyond me but I hope that someone will be interested enough, open enough, to explore further the relationship between mind, the nature of the world we perceive and time.

For myself I am hoping someone will find a book a friend left for me some years ago.

# *Further Reading*

**Bohm, David**: *Wholeness and the Implicate Order*, Ark Paper-backs, 1983. A combination of science and philos ophy. His concept of totality includes both consciousness and matter, the known and the unknowable.

**Capra, Fritjof**: *The Tao of Physics*, Fontana, 1976. Often cited by those looking for links between mysticism and physics. Useful for me when I was trying to seek alternatives and some logic to alternative views of time.

**Farrow, Joan**: *The Mask of Time*, Corgi, 1981. General book looking at the surprisingly frequent instances of 'time slip' experiences,

**von Franz, Marie Louise**: *Time: Rhythm and Repose*, Thames & Hudson Ltd, 1978. Lovely book, written with insight but absolutely straightforward. My first port of call in 1985. Time is never what it seems.

**Gribbin, John**: *Timewarps*, J. M. Dent & Sons Ltd, 1979. Excellent book. Contains the Sarfatti quote (see P330) and many thought-provoking chapters, especially on the relationship between time and mind.

**Jahn, Robert and Dunne, Brenda**: *Margins of Reality*, Harcourt Brace Jovanovich, 1987. Anomalies relating to mind/machine interaction and remote viewing get some solid scientific support from this Princeton University team.

**Koestler, Arthur**: *The Roots of Coincidence*, Hutchinson & Co. Ltd, 1972. A clear argument for an open-minded approach to aspects of parapsychology and especially acausal relationships as explored by Jung in Synchronicity, Routledge & Kegan Paul Ltd, 1972 (although Jung himself would not quite agree with Koestler's interpretation of his idea).

**Manning, Matthew:** *The Stranger*, W. H. Allen & Co., 1978. Manning's experience could be interpreted as a genuine overlap of times, although Manning's contact with a Robert Webbe from the 18th century is not generally treated as such in Manning's account. This book is quite hard to locate but worth the effort.

**Playfair, Guy Lyon**: *This House is Haunted*, Souvenir Press, 1980. This account of the Enfield poltergeist is as much a record of the psychology of investigators as a good record of a poltergeist case. Two SPR members act as witnesses but still the case is dismissed by colleagues, leaving so much unexplained.

**White, John** (ed.): *Psychic Warfare: Fact or Fiction*, Aquarian Press, 1987. A collection of readings. Sometimes seems over the top but Tom Bearden's very sensible contribution (pp. 169-90) offers ideas for a possible mechanism to the events at the cottage. Stimulating reading.

# Notes on the Messages

Between December 1984 and March 1987 approximately 300 messages were received. These included chalk or hand-written scripts and the computer messages. In length they vary from one or two characters, to single words and phrases, to messages in excess of 400 words. The bulk of the communications (about fifty-five per cent) were addressed to myself, and the others were shared roughly equally between Debbie and Peter. This book contains approximately one third of the available messages, either in full or by way of extracts.

## Punctuation

According to Tomas some of the early computer messages (at least) were doctored by 2109. Apart from 'editing', the interference apparently included adding some modern punctuation, especially apostrophes, parentheses and exclamation marks.

Tomas did on occasion use the full stop. This is perfectly normal for the 16th century but Debbie admits that in error she told him not to 'copy' our punctuation when she saw that he was using full stops. Some messages in July 1985 do carry this punctuation mark. In later messages he would often indicate the likely breaks by word spacing.

## Translations

My aim was to render Tomas's words into a modern idiom. I accept that this has made certain inaccuracies inevitable.

With the written scripts it has not always been possible to make out Tomas's words and some sections carry a 'probable' translation based on the context of the passage.

## The Scripts

Tomas indicated that he was making every effort to render the written word easy on our eyes. He did this by treating each character individually. I am told that these individual characters compare well with extant 16th-century examples, but the overall orthographic effect is probably uncommon. Even within Tomas's scripts illustrated in this volume 'careful' and 'quick' writing is discernible.

# *Appendix: the Language of the Messages* by Peter Trinder

Above: Peter Trinder ,TV interview 1986.

From the beginning of my involvement with the messages it was the language in which they were written that most intrigued me, then captivated and finally convinced me. I have grown increasingly sure that ultimately it must be the very nature of that language which proves the authenticity of the experience as a whole.

We have all heard Shakespeare's words, but none of us has heard his voice, and we cannot be absolutely sure of any single word that he wrote. He did not write 'to sleep, perchance to dream' but (more likely) 'to sleepe, perchance to dreame' and there is all the difference in the world. Moreover, on that difference our present tale hangs.

333

I have come across a book, Talks with Elizabethans by Percy Allen (Rider & Co., London, 1946), in which the author, in all sincerity, reports many conversations he held between 1942 and 1945 with Bacon, Oxford, Shakespeare and other Elizabethan figures through a series of professional mediums in London. Now all of these Elizabethans talked to him like gentlemen of the 1940s. Perhaps it is normal, for they spoke in the voice of a 20th-century medium, and of course the book is merely a transcription of those conversations. There have also been cases of spirit-writing, but I cannot trace any extensive examples of such writing in the English of a period other than modern.

It is generally agreed that the history of English can be divided into three (or perhaps four) main stages: Old English (or Anglo-Saxon) up to a time very soon after the Norman Conquest and the dominance of Norman French, say roughly 1100; Middle English, a transitional period when the language still retained enough of the formal characteristics of Old English to be decidedly not our Modern English. This period is generally agreed to run until about the advent of printing, say 1450. Modern English, though with many changes continuing, dates from roughly this period. Many scholars prefer to talk of an intermediary period called 'Early Modern', which could be dated roughly 1400-1600, and in which so many important developments in spelling and vocabulary took place as to make it quite feasible to talk of this as a distinct stage in the long-term development of the English language. During this period in particular the form, use and meaning of individual words were so diverse that it is relatively easy to place the writer of a script within a broad area of the country and within a certain time-span. If the piece of writing is long enough and the forms distinctive enough then the field proportionately diminishes until it can even become possible to date and locate the writing within a very narrow limit.

If the author is unknown it can often be a relatively simple matter to identify him (or, rarely, her) precisely. It is, after all, on such evidence that very many of the earlier examples of English literature have been associated with particular authors. Even some of the Shakespearian ascriptions are made on this kind of evidence, not to mention many others. The whole game started officially with a critical examination of Biblical documents in the last century, which caused a controversy that still disturbs many of the faithful. Much of the most recent research and development in the technology of espionage involves increasingly sophisticated methods of voiceprinting, and of course fingerprinting has been with us a long time. Blood prints and saliva prints are not unknown, and genetic fingerprinting is now in use. Just so a man's writing reveals himself, his time and his circumstances in many subtle hints, for truly, 'Le style c'est l'homme même'. Professor Higgins, like his original, Henry Sweet, could place people within five miles, and in London within two streets, by their speech. When people commit themselves to paper we have got them, providing only that the amount of material available for analysis is sufficiently extensive to provide satisfactory evidence.

The messages we received through the computer are certainly sufficiently extensive and they purport to date from the very period in which spelling, vocabulary and semantics were at their most idiosyncratic and variable in the whole history of the English language.

Fortunately we possess an incomparable reference work in the Oxford English Dictionary (OED), which charts this historical maze in incredible detail. This, of course, was the main authority to which I referred when working on the texts, especially to its dating system for the various recorded forms of words. Reference to the entry for the word 'champarty', for example, will show that the form 'champartye', (which is how it was spelt in our text) is recorded in the 14th and 15th centuries, and so on, with the modern form of this rare word dating from the 17th century. For many words in the OED this list of alternative forms and their dating is very long and complicated. The original intention behind the dictionary was that everything written in English up to the time of editing should be read and scrutinized, but this could never be fully realized, particularly as many important texts and documents were not available at that time and the later letters of the alphabet were in general more fully researched than the earlier. Despite this it is perfectly reasonable to take the evidence of the dictionary as conclusive. Consequently, if we have in our texts enough words whose dating, according to the OED, is consistent with the period in which we were led to believe they were written, then that evidence alone might go far to confirm the authenticity of the messages, and hence of the whole unlikely experience. For who could devise such documents using the dictionary backwards by searching out recondite terms and then checking every word used not only for its meaning but also its form in a particular period? The amount of effort involved in this process beggars belief. Even if the process of composition in this way by some modern hoaxer is conceivable, there was very frequently no time in which it could possibly have been carried out. Moreover, of course, we are looking only at the 'how?' and leaving out the bigger questions of 'who?' and 'why?'

I drew up a table showing the forms of words (i.e. their spelling), choosing to look not only at the 16th century itself but at periods before and after. If any word occurred which was not recorded in the 16th century then we had to be on our guard. This is what I was looking for when I first began using the OED. At that very early stage I thought that Ken was perhaps playing a game himself and I expected to be able to unmask him by the use of the OED.

The dating of the first messages proved most interesting, and slowly I was convinced that something very strange was happening, for these had to be the words of a 16th-century writer or of someone doing a very convincing imitation. In fact, as the experience proceeded and the evidence grew, the incidence of words and forms too modern for the 16th century remained credibly limited, to say the least. It was perhaps increasingly difficult to remain entirely objective in judgement but I certainly tried.

The dictionary is not, of course, by any means quite complete in its original intention. How could it be? Many words must have remained undiscovered in texts not read, or carelessly read, or as yet unknown. A literate person needing a new word frequently used the nearest Latin term, simply giving it an English form; in this way hundreds of words first occurred in English in this period called Early Modern, indeed that is one of the character- istics of the period. Many such words caught on and still remain: many more must have been stillborn or were used so very rarely as effectively to lie dormant until a later flowering.

I became increasingly interested to note how many of the forms and words in the messages were actually dated by the OED in or even before the 15th century. This suggested some- one whose language was in some respects rather old-fashioned for its time. Of course, the fact that a word is not recorded in any particular period does not show that it did not exist or was not used, but merely that it was not found by those compiling the OED. But still, if a form is recorded as, say, 14th or 15th century ('4-5' in OED's abbreviations) then that is all the evidence we have in most cases. For my purposes, in view of the extent of the material I was dealing with, it was quite sufficient.

The messages contained, then, very many forms which the OED records as not in use later than the 15th century. This led me to suspect a South-Western English origin for our man, since innovations and change in the language tended to spread from the North, the Midlands or the South-East, and the area of the country which preserved regular forms longest was the South- West. This was partly why I prompted Ken to ask if our man knew 'Bristowe', an old form of the main city of that region. That question received a most encouraging and revealing answer.

Among the most frustrating of all words were the parts of the verbs 'to be' 'and 'to have'. Most puzzling were the frequent, but not invariable, 'beeth', 'arn' and 'han' for am, art, is, are and have. The other main puzzle has been the use of 'my' or 'thy' for 'the', the definite article. I have been assured by an expert researcher in the period that these forms do all occur in written material, but I have not found them, in spite of diligent search in many obscure corners. Letters of ordinary, undistinguished people from the mid- 16th century are very few. Remember that the date we were given was 1546. The famous Paston Let-

KEN WEBSTER

ters, though of some help, are from quite the wrong area, East Anglia; and the Cely Letters are mostly of London. The South-West was a quiet, secluded part of the country, from which very little of the 16th century seems to have survived, and certainly nothing of such relatively humble and obscure origins. Even supposing that we could prove our texts to be genuine writings of this period there would appear to be no comparable contemporary documents by which we could check their language. By the same token, naturally, it follows that if they can be proved genuine they will provide invaluable evidence of the state of the language at that time and in that area. As my adventure proceeded, of course, I became increasingly convinced that this is exactly what we have, a kind of linguistic missing link in demotic speech. I can only hope I will live to see our texts accepted and dictionaries eventually revised to accommodate them.

The evidence would suggest, then, a man of the South-West, probably well into middle age, still retaining the nationally outmoded forms of common words with which he grew up. After all it is not difficult to imagine this; I myself very clearly remember the older men who worked on my grandfather's farm when I was a small boy with whose regular forms of 'I be', 'youm are', 'theym be' and such we were very familiar and even used easily. I doubt whether those forms can still be so commonly found among the newer and fewer farmworkers of South Northamptonshire and North Oxfordshire as they were among their forebears of fifty years ago, but this is because there have been very rapid and far-reaching effects of general levelling in local forms since the spread of television and popular radio. Many of us lament the passing of such riches in speech and all of us must be well aware of such a process of levelling at work.

Those old forms I remember from my youth had been preserved for hundreds of years, some of them going back well into the Middle English period, and much contemporary common speech goes back directly to Old English, the language of the Anglo-Saxons themselves. How did 'slog' survive in boy's cricket from the Old English past tense of 'slegan', meaning 'to hit, to kill'?

338

One has surely to realize too that writing, at the period we are trying to bring into focus, was a very uncommon practice, and our man would most probably write as he spoke with hardly a second thought, though he would be aware, as indeed he said he was, that his 'tongue was old' and that we spoke 'the tongue of Chester' as he called it. In other words, he had come to realize that his normal manner of speech was old-fashioned compared with the standard of a more cosmopolitan centre, though undoubtedly the streets of such a centre of trade at the borders of England and Wales (without a border at that time) and close to Ireland, with strong influxes from the north as well as his own south and from London, would have echoed to a veritable babel of mixed accents and dialects. Still, the local families of long-standing, among whom he seems to have had several and probably many friends, would have had a distinct regularity in speech fundamentally different from the common speech of his childhood home, sufficiently so for him to be aware of the outdated characteristics of his own speech.

In view of all these factors it seems to make good sense that he used very many forms which the OED does not record later than the 15th century. Just as my childhood was immediately before and during the Second World War, which in the 1980s seems a different world, so his would have been just after Bosworth Field and during the quieter, more settled times of the opening of the Tudor era in the reign of Henry VII. I did wonder if his father had been involved on either side in the Wars of the Roses but it did not emerge, and I do not think that we asked about this. The brief picture of his father at work in the shipyards of Bristol, as presented in later messages, seems to confirm our expectations, though we still cannot explain what is meant by the King's rose (or Rose) with which he says his father was connected. There was more detail of that famous sailor out of Bristol, John Cabot, as will be seen.

The vast bulk of the forms, words and senses contained in the messages which are recorded as in use in the 16th century would seem to be the most significant, but I have tried to show first why I paid special attention to those recorded later or earlier. Of the total words roughly sixty-five per cent are recorded in the 16th century itself. It is sometimes possible to be more precise than a span of a whole century, and here the OED's ample system of illustration by quotation is most useful, for the quotations are dated exactly in most cases, and the difference between 1520 and 1530, or 1560 and 1580 might be quite crucial.

To take all this evidence of dating quite objectively and to guess from it just when our texts might have been written was an interesting experiment. In fact I had a shot at this quite early, before we had been given a reliable date at all, and my guess was 1545. When the date was eventually given as 1546 we were somewhat gratified. Here, perhaps, was another example of wishful thinking, in which new material confirmed our previous guesses – like the placings in the South-West and the shot at Bristol. Sceptics will say – but not before we said it ourselves – that such serendipity is suspicious, and that perhaps the whole experience has been fabricated by our own subconscious – but collectively, by two, usually three, often four and sometimes many more of us? How could this be? Again, however any of it may be, the texts exist. They lie in files and boxes by my side as I write, the pages well-thumbed and fraying at the punched edge in many cases, Some of the handwritten originals are framed as precious mementoes of a frantic and heady excitement of more than a year's duration. This was no dream, singular or collective; no work of the subconscious.

The language remains to confirm it all; the fat volume of the glossary I have composed proves it genuine, with most of the words clearly substantiated as in use in the 16th century, very many of the words unknown to me before I met them here, and several words which still remain apparently unrecorded elsewhere and still unexplained. I hope the full glossary will be published later, together with our findings in historical and topographical research about the provenance of the messages and the identity of their author, but the list of unexplained words is so interesting and important that I include it as a tailpiece to this brief account of the language of the messages. These words were used by our correspondent and checked in the OED as I came to them in the process of annotation. Many words equally unfamiliar to me proved to be in the dictionary, but these words were not there, nor have I been able to find in any other source a satisfactory solution to such words as 'broatniss', 'stemeain' and the rest of the list. Tomas, our correspondent, and I talked much about words, as the messages will show, so that I was able to ask him about several of them. Except that his explanations generally confirmed my guesses, since the meaning was usually fairly obvious from the content, little was really gained in this way. However, because of their intrinsic interest, these explanations are given below. We hope that professional scholars and other experts may pick up this list and perhaps care to comment in some way. These words must form a part of our continuing work on the evidence of our experience. Perhaps we shall never be more firmly convinced by any historical or linguistic evidence of the genuineness of our experience than we felt at the time it was actually in progress. Tomas was entirely real to us, speaking intimately as a close friend, though over a space of four centuries. That conviction remains as strong – and as perversely commonplace in its essential feeling – as it was then. Now the evidence is published we hope for some public reaction. If the experience can be proved the consequences must be momentous.

Where is Tomas's own account, his book that was finished at Oxford and left somewhere in manuscript? We never forget that '2109' said it would be found, and we can only hope that this will happen in our lifetime.

There are some other interesting points to make about the language, in particular the number of words which the OED records as first used – sometimes uniquely used – by Shakespeare. Of course, Shakespeare himself was a man from the Midlands countryside as well as a great inventor of words and a treasury of recondite terms. The fact that 'charge house', meaning a school, has not been found anywhere except in Love's Labours Lost does not mean that the word was not used. It may indeed have been in normal colloquial, if restricted, use but never written in any text that has survived. The same is probably true of several other words in the list of forty-seven which I compiled as first occurring in recorded use in Shakespeare. They all pose fascinating problems. And what of such words as 'deradynate', for example, obviously an alternative form of 'deracinate' since that meaning would fit the context precisely? It was more intriguing still to find that the first occurrence of 'deracinate' (perhaps a Shakespearian coinage) is in Henry V, a play with strong French interest which includes several such words apparently coined from a French root, whereas 'deradynate' in Tomas's use seems to have been taken directly from the Latin. One could go on with such speculations.

Two other areas of interest and possible significance in the words and forms used by Tomas are the legal terms and the evident Scots or northern connection. This latter element was evident quite early, particularly in such forms as '-ioun' for the suffix '-ion' (as in 'condicioun' or 'salvacioun'). By the 16th century this form seems to have been characteristically northern. (the 'northern' dialect also included southern Scotland). This point was well explained by Tomas's casual revelation that Lukas Wainman, his teacher and mentor, had come from Aberdeen.

A significant number of words have specific legal connections, such as 'champartye', 'lachess', 'validity', 'precedenten', 'exempcioune' and others. It seems from a passing reference that Lukas may have had a legal background; Tomas mentions that he himself was in London for a time and he was quite possibly at one of the law colleges before he went to Oxford.

The occasional term from alchemy such as 'quintessence' may be important in the light of the strange nature of the whole experience and the totally unexpected quality of its beginning. Was Tomas a secret alchemist? Again, there are more things in heaven and earth . . .

In the following list of statistics I have analysed the evidence of my glossary into categories that might be significant in various ways, but the analysis was done quite objectively as an assessment of the verbal evidence as a method of dating the likely composition of the documents. Using the evidence of the dating system of the OED I divided the words by period, concentrating on the span from the 15th to the 17th centuries. It was obvious that a significant number of forms were earlier than the 16th century so my first category is those forms dated as last recorded earlier than the 15th century, and so on. After the 16th century, during which some sixty-five per cent of the total forms were recorded as in use, I listed those first recorded later in two categories: those belonging to the 17th century (on the grounds that a period which in practice is actually less than than a hundred years is allowable variation at a time in which many words are likely to have been in use but not to have survived in records): and finally those words which are first recorded at any time certainly later than the 17th century. No less an authority than Professor A. C. Partridge states that, 'It is doubtful whether any three centuries could equal the period 1450 to 1750 in the achievement of welding home growths and alien borrowings into a serviceable and resourceful instrument of the national mind . . . it should surprise no reader that from 1590 to 1625 events moved more rapidly than in any other comparable time in the evolution of the language.' (Tudor to Augustan English, Andre Deutsch, 1969 p.13). Now although 1590 is too late for our messages, for the dictionary the difference between the outer dates of this critical period is that of a century. The OED dates a form of, for example, 1595 as 16th century, and one of 1605 as 17th century. It is significant to realize that even by the mid-16th century events were moving extremely rapidly in the language as well as in the politics and religion of England.

The OED dating is of 'forms', i.e. spellings of words. For each main word in my glossary I recorded the OED's dating of the form in which it occurred in the message, if that form was given. A few words were listed more than once because they occurred in more than one form, but Tomas's spelling was very largely consistent, so this factor does not distort the statistics. Another few words, some twenty-five, could not be counted in the statistics because of some imprecision of dating in the OED or very occasionally the absence of dating altogether. I also included a very few characteristic prepositional phrases as well as words buthave not at this stage compiled a list of idiomatic phrases as such.

## Dating of Words and Forms

| | |
|---|---:|
| Number of words last recorded earlier than 15th century | 102 |
| Number of words last recorded in 15th century | 319 |
| Number of words last recorded in 16th century | 667 |
| Number of words recorded before, in, and after 16th century | 980 |
| Number of words recorded in 16th century only | 72 |
| Number of words first recorded in 16th century | 241 |
| Number of words first recorded in 17th century | 64 |
| Number of words first recorded later than 17th century | 1 |
| Number of words not recorded in OED | 685 |
| Total number of words recorded before 16th century | 421 |
| Total number of words recorded in 16th century | 1706 |
| Total number of words recorded after 16th century | 65 |
| *Total words in Glossary* | *2877* |

The following is the full list of words which are not in the OED nor have I found them in Wright's Dialect Dictionary or other regional or specialized glossaries which I have consulted. Several of them are easy to explain but others are very strange and even exotic specimens.

*(**T**=Tomas's explanation)*

| | |
|---|---:|
| a | as |
| aboone v. | 'to make good' **T** |
| aformoste | best |
| afounded | destroyed |
| aft | afternoon |
| aldeyen | often |
| alerwyse | wisest |
| aplexify | startle, confound |
| appertiteth v. | delights |
| awreathing | tormenting |
| aymo | evermore? |
| beeleful | happy, pleasant |

| | |
|---|---|
| belean v. | abandon? |
| bemeters v. | borders? |
| boken | books |
| bride | bridge |
| broatniss | a weakly person **T** |
| deyntie v. | treat with care? |
| Deradynate | deracinate – rift up **T** |
| dew to | due to – rare before 19th century |
| elyful | 'dark' |
| empayr | to improve |
| exchaundances | unwanted elements |
| excusacyone v. | to excuse, apologize |
| excusyoune | apology |
| farrygible | 'faradiddle'? |
| fasinorouse | caused by witchcraft? |
| festement n. | feasting? |
| fey ti fi | exclamation |
| flat-skyn n. | parchment? |
| fo | for (used several times) |
| folly v. | behave foolishly |
| foralden | very old |
| forermed | grieved? adj. |
| forgreven | much grieved? |
| forlacks adj. | lacking |
| formergd | submerged? |
| forweels | very much? |
| forweet | know well |
| forwyttd | intelligent? |
| fulharlotin | despicable? |
| gauberynge | idiotic |
| gekalles | 'fools' **T** |
| giggester | jester? |
| gledie | bright, shining (Scots) |
| gleeb | jest |
| glooze | gaze? |
| glorien | glorious |
| go | ago |

| | |
|---|---|
| gust n. | taste |
| happs | perhaps |
| hask | 'dry corn' **T** |
| heeraft | here after |
| intresstes v. | interests |
| intrynscioun | intention? |
| joyif | joyous |
| kyn calle | family name |
| lecturien. | preserve? |
| lest conj. | unless |
| lore | to lose |
| luxyoune adj. | lively? |
| mallechoes* n. | 'intention of malice' **T** |
| nant (ne want) v. | do not want |
| parlie | purlieu? |
| penen | pens |
| popolotie adj. | darling, dear |
| prifyk | prefix |
| project | particle |
| ragement | argument |
| replayce v. | transfer, transcribe |
| scantens | barely, hardly |
| sessa† | 'to be still' **T** |
| scoleye | to study, attend school |
| seylesermone n. | silly talk? |
| sleyghte | slander |
| slompryng | clumsy |
| spoken | of language, as opposed to 'written'– first recorded 1837 |
| stemain | 'shining' **T** |
| stincioun adj. | immovable **T** |
| theeche v. | to prosper |
| torablise | terrible, troublesome |
| umberyde | open, clear |
| unavoydaunte | unavoidable |
| urn v. | use |

# *Endnotes* 2022

The following abstract was taken from an article published by the Fortean Times in 1989 and was where I gave my response to the comments made on the BBC show 'Out of this World '. Sadly the BBC didn't take the opportunity to research Tomas's messages in the impartial manner which they deserved, or what we would normally expect of the BBC.

Though the BBC did make a formal apology to us and later put this apology out in a public statement, this apology seems to have been omitted from bootlegged recordings of this show, which you may find posted around the internet, nor do they include my subsequent response to this show in the 1989 *'Are Fiend Electric?' Article* (FT 108 March 1998):

**❝ Are Fiends Electric?**

What would you do if something very strange and bewildering happened to you; something uninvited yet benign; something which happened over and over again and which involved your friends, lover and colleagues? Would you want people to know? Would you want help in understanding it? Yes, yes! But my experience suggests you would be wasting your time. . .

. . .Debbie and I did the rounds of local radio and TV and were overwhelmed or underwhelmed by the banality of it all. Usually, the interviewer had not read the book and just wanted to know how we felt, what we thought was the cause and how we knew we weren't being hoaxed. Every answer for TV had to be 10-20 seconds, for radio a little more. How much explaining can be done in this time? I fell back on snippets, amusing anecdotes, slogans almost. Peter Trinder, who was a big support throughout, tried to engage them with language issues but this, too, had a tendency to be lost in the edit.

So, to the media, it remained a computer ghost. Local newspapers and Psychic News loved it of course, but reported it inaccurately; Psychic News, having bought into the life-after-death concept decades earlier, was not about to miss this as evidence of the dead communicating. And there were the letters. There were essentially only two kinds: those which took a spiritual or religious view - that we were a) helping prove life after death or conversely b) that we were in touch with demons (and needed help) - or those which said that we were being fooled or were hoodwinking others for financial gain (shame on us). We met Matthew Manning, briefly, who said his book of poltergeists and communications -The Strangers (1978) - might have had a computer element had such machines been available.

Meanwhile Dodleston village began to appear on itineraries; the bus driver once wore a Halloween mask and took fares for Spooksville. Years passed without any new insights. The book disappeared from view in the UK by mid-1990 but was published in hardback in Germany and in paperback in Brazil. Most people liked "the story". We moved house [1991].

Along came BBC Television enquiring about The Vertical Plane. I was not encouraging. They persisted and, in 1995, a meeting in London was arranged; but only a pilot programme was developed and the story remained on the shelf. Peter Tinder and the SPR guys were found and interviewed, as was Nicola Bagguley, our lodger' in the early days of the disturbances. The basics checked out, it seems, and the following year a new director, Jon East, and the original researcher, the charming and efficient Emma Yates, made noises about a series called Out of This World. They suggested that a drama is the best way of presenting the story, followed by the usual investigation and discussion. In 1997, Jon and Emma made a delightful, sensitive and true to events drama with our full co-operation (and some excellent actors), spending around £60,000 of license payers money in the process. The result was broadcast in two :parts on 20 August and 27 August 1996.

Now for the BBC investigation in the second half of the programme. A complicated story has many avenues and we provided the contact names and addresses, materials and our own availability. What happened next is a salutary lesson for anyone involved in unusual events. It is worth illustrating what was available - see **Phenomena** panel [pg 353] - and what was done.

Nothing was made of the circumstances of when messages appeared or who was nearby or who was absent. David Lovell, one of the witnesses to the poltergeist activity, was contacted by phone after 11pm one night and asked if he saw an object begin its flight. That was it! Nothing else and no-one else was contacted - not even Debbie and myself. Only messages from "Tomas' were analysed or debated. The focus had narrowed severely; no witness seemed to matter and none of the other disturbances appeared relevant.

The most obvious and fundamental protocols for an objective approach to the Tomas Harden messages appear to me to be: firstly, to establish which communications were reliably believed to be from Tomas Harden. *The Vertical Plane* notes at least six other communicators or claimed communicators and several instances where Tomas Harden had asserted that a communication, when 'shown' to him, was not substantially his (i.e. it had either been "edited" or was not at all by him).

Secondly, from the messages which were representative, to the best of the main witnesses' knowledge, a random sampling should be taken.

Thirdly, other comparable contemporary extracts should be identified and placed within a portfolio which gave no clues to the origins of any of the items. In short the test would be blind, within reason.

Fourthly, the same material would be given to a number of independent experts and, against published and identical criteria, these experts would be asked to comment and the results of that comparison made available. If a linguistic test of the comparative statistical kind were selected, then a similar randomising process and statistically significant sample size should be chosen.

None of these things happened.

Laura Wright, a lecturer in English at Lucy Cavendish College, Cambridge, was the first expert and the only one interviewed to camera[1] She was given a photocopy of the book and therefore knew of the alleged paranormal nature of the communications.

She chose the messages she wished to examine. There is no evidence that randomisation took place and there was no checking with either the text of *The Vertical Plane* or the main witnesses to ascertain if the messages chosen were believed to be representative.

Furthermore, Laura Wright did not use contemporary works for comparison, by which I mean Early Modern conversational English, preferably with strong West Country dialect forms. The comparative material chosen did not meet these criteria.

Additionally, since the mode of the alleged paranormal communication is not understood - by all accounts, it was not written, much less typed, but rather 'thought' or spoken out loud - a comparability test should have involved an examination of and comment on the effects of language structure and content in spoken or mentalistic form compared to the written.

A comparable test would also need to make a specific allowance for the effects of communicating. Communicating means sharing meaning. It is a worldwide phenomenon that humans adapt what they say to their audience and, in communicating, something of each side is absorbed by the other. Communications from the main witnesses to Tomas Harden contain attempts at appropriate construction and vocabulary and vice versa and, where detectable, this should be allowed for.

Worse was to follow. Laura Wright also undertook a statistical analysis by comparing a 500-word sample of Tomas's words with 500 words of my narrative from *The Vertical Plane*, set alongside two samples from contemporary works - an extract from *Love in a Cold Climate* and an item from *The Times*. The aim was to look for the incidence of the use of pre-modifiers before the noun and, by implication, a similarity (if these results came out close) between the two authors, or at least a sense of the period in which they were written. This was the only quantitative test of the material and the only one reported in the programme. It is also a key to under standing the shabbiness of the whole investigation.

These latter results were reported to one decimal place as being: Tomas Harden 26.6% and Ken Webster 26.0%. This was quoted to camera.

However this is far from the end of the story. Laura Wright said at the time, but it was deleted from the broadcast, that nothing could be concluded from this analysis. More importantly it is significant that these results were based on only one sample.[2]

The inadequacy of the highly reductive approach was compounded by a typical 'tabloid TV' strategy for generating emotion; a staged confrontation. This highly suspect approach to the main witnesses was evident when, during a filmed interview in Oxford on 7 August, 1996, neither the 'findings' of Laura Wright nor the comments from language experts were discussed with Peter Trinder or the other main witnesses. Later, Laura Wright and Emma Yates admitted that they were specifically asked not to discuss the "findings" with us by a senior person within the BBC.

Armed with BBC sanctioned 'surprise', their expert parapsychologist concentrated on two principal issues with all the interviewees. Firstly: what made us sure it wasn't a hoax? And, secondly: could Ken Webster have done it? Perhaps the first question was of general viewer interest, but the second? I was confronted with: "Three experts have agreed that your writing bears strong similarities to that of Tomas Harden." This assertion was removed from the edited version only after vigorous protest as there were palpably not three experts, but only one who could make a comment on such an assertion[1]. We had all cooperated fully with the programme so why the surprise tactics?

The Laura Wright interview and the line of questioning implied that an alleged similarity between Tomas Harden's writing and my own writing was significant. No similarity actually existed outside the one sample and significance was absent for other reasons entirely (see Communications panel [FT108]). Among the many categories of possibly paranormal events in this case is that messages were received while I was physically absent. Even a casual reading of *The Vertical Plane* indicates that being 'absent' could be very significant. On one occasion, I was in Aberdeenshire for a week, staying with a local architect, while Peter Trinder, his wife Valerie and Debbie were constructing questions and recelvmg appropriate replies in Chester. This is only one of many such examples.

But detail seems to matter less than the moral. In the UK, a producer for the TV debate on the monarchy responded to news of a panellist's complaints of lack of time with this classic: "If he can't say it in 90 words, he should get a thesaurus." This is palpable nonsense, but infectious. How more so the temptation for all concerned in an "infotainment" programme like *Out of this World* to cut and compress, when all that is being reported is the "paranormal."

The viewer perhaps expects an answer too. An answer was supplied and, this being tabloid TV, it was the most obvious one; the implication that I was behind the messages. With some 'evidence' construed to suit the occasion and the staged surprising of the witness with this 'evidence', they got away with it in media terms, perhaps. Just two people, from an estimated audience of around eight million, wrote in to the BBC.

I return to Guy Lyon Playfair, who concluded:

*"It may be that the wisest course to follow after obtaining positive evidence of any kind in any area of psychical research is to make use of it for personal enlightenment, and thereafter to keep quiet about it!"*

Now, just over 10 years after our own adventures, it sadly seems good advice. Meadow Cottage was important to us. It is sufficient.

---

[1] There were actually 5 experts in total. The BBC had chosen to leave these other experts out for reasons they would not say.

## THE PHENOMENA

The phenomena at Meadow Cottage were spread over about 16 months. The main categories of purportedly paranormal events are listed (below) together with name of any third parties present (in brackets) i.e. either sharing the experience of one or more of the main witnesses, experiencing events of personal importance relating to the anomalies or being in a position to comment constructively. Even in summary terms this is a substantial list of strange phenomena, offering many potentially interesting lines of enquiry.

*POLTERGEIST EVENTS:* house shook (DL). furniture rearranged (DL); a voice (DL); items thrown (DL. SL): items stacking (NB); bent and straightened copper pan handle (DL); noises on roof; items charred or burnt; items disappearing.

*HAND WRITTEN MESSAGES:* on floor (FD): on wall (NB), extensive, on paper.

COMPUTER MESSAGES: with personal or private meaning (FD, GR, SPR, Shirley); received while two main witnesses were under observation (PT. SPR): received while KW absent (PT, VT, FD), received while Debbie was absent (PT, VT, FD), with historical content; with linguistic content/interest; claimed to be hybrid or edited

COMMUNICATORS OR ENTITIES: Lukas Wainman, Tomas Harden, '2109', Fowlshurst, Jon, threats', poem, "incoherent', 'One'

**Key to initials used above:** Nicola Bagguley, Frank Davies, David Lovell, Sian Lovell, Gary Rowe, Society for Psychical Research, Peter Trinder, Val Trinder, Ken Webster.

To get the full article, *'Are Fiends Electric'* (FT108 March 1998) go to https://subscribe.forteantimes.com/ and scroll down the page to FAQ *"How do I access back issues?"*

# *Notes*

Many thanks to all those who have continued interest in our experience and the many helpful links and comments you have kindly posted over the years on various blogs and reviews.

Here follows a small handful of blogs and podcasts we found on the internet which the reader may find of interest. Please bear in mind that many people have not actually read the book, possibly because of it's inflated price. As a consequence, I felt I needed to reiterate some of the facts mentioned in this book at the end of these notes, which are fairly common errors:

### Abovetopsecret:

An interesting and substantial blog (thanks to Steve, TemporalRecon and others) which contains some helpful links mentioned below:

https://www.abovetopsecret.com/forum/thread1178623/

Blogger "beetee" seems to have possibly tracked down a burial time and place for Tomas as 8. jan 1560 in Haresfield, Gloucestershire, which needs further investigation.

### Record of Tomas at Brasenose College Oxford:

https://archive.org/stream/brasenosecolleg00bras#page/n19/mode/2up/search/Harden [pg5]

**Reference to a Henry Man**: possibly the same one Tomas mentions: https://en.wikipedia.org/wiki/Henry_Man

### Tomas and John Hawarden research:

Blogger Cybrsqrl: https://www.reddit.com/r/TheVerticalPlane/comments/q8fdcz/the_hawarden_surname_coincidence/

### 2109/2105 contacting others - Ernst Senkowski's blog :

http://www.worlditc.org/c_07_senki_f_38.12.11.htm

**Gary Rowe's comments on our case - towards the bottom of this blog:** https://mercuriuspoliticus.wordpress.com/2010/11/01/ghost-in-the-machine/

### The Dark Histories Podcast:

https://www.youtube.com/watch?v=OwZJwNvCGII

**Mysterious Universe Podcast:**
https://mysteriousuniverse.org/2017/02/17-05-mu-podcast/

**Astonishing Legends**
https://www.astonishinglegends.com/al-podcasts/2021/9/25/ep-217-the-vertical-plane-part-1
https://www.astonishinglegends.com/al-podcasts/2021/10/09/ep-217-the-vertical-plane-part-2
These two episodes are several hours long but do pose some interesting ideas and intelligent dialogue ...there is also an awesome recipe for Guacamole! :o)

**Nostalgia Nerd:**
https://www.youtube.com/watch?v=nEDgG5MKndo

**Sarah After Dark:**
https://www.youtube.com/watch?v=GRvUExN-lw4

**Finally, on a lighter note:** The very entertaining claymation by Let's Clay: *"This Paranormal Life"* who are forgiven for being so talented!: https://www.youtube.com/watch?v=qDlmw0ZZWDs

**Notes to clear up some reoccurring inaccuracies:**
1. Tomas did not see a computer or type on a keyboard: Tomas said he saw a glowing, green light in/near his chimney. Having watched his cook sing, he saw those words 'spinning' out of this light and learnt to 'sing' at the 'computer' to make the words form. Basically, what he seems to be describing is what we now know today as voice recognition e.g. Alexa etc..

2. Tomas wrote to us from the year 1546, in the 16th Century, and used Middle English words with a South-West dialect.

3. There was no public internet in the way we understand it today, back in 1984. We researched this fully at the time. The average 'user' simply didn't have access to such equipment that could run their own service (not really internet), or upload transmissions, unless they were in an institution or part of a research group. If a potential hacker did managed to have hold of such rare equip-

ment i.e.. a modem, they would also need someone continually waiting at the other end to accept/confirm the transmission, on a phone call, before connecting to the remote modem to either upload, or download, the specific messages.

Sending data via a phone was extremely ropey, taking time to just 'open' a connection was laborious. If the transmission was at all broken or interrupted, as it often was, you would have to start the whole process again from scratch.

Also, there was no large phone or modem connected, or next to, the computer at anytime. Given the size of these things we would have noticed! In the photograph on page 132, you can see how far our phone reached, showing the telephone out-stretched to its fullest extent from the phone socket. Also, we never heard the audible modem squeal down the phone line when we happened to be using the telephone. The phone would need to be connected continuously, to respond to random questions set by us and others, squealing much of the time down the phone line to the accomplice's phone, who was waiting for these random transmissions (our replies and questions) for this to occur in the way that it did.

Finally, for those not around, or did not own a telephone at this time in history, it needs to be pointed out that it was highly expensive to make a phone call in those days. There was only landline phones, which were installed and owned by BT. No small mobile or SIP/VoIP phones using voice over internet (e.g. WhatsApp etc.) with a cheap open connection, so our phone bill and the hoaxer's accomplice's phone bill would have been astronomical.

Simply put, and just taking all other above hurdles into account, the cost to run just 2 (sender and the receiver) 'open lines' for even half a day, each day for 18 months, for just the calls alone, would have cost in the region of £87,091.20 in today's money (@12p per minute: Source: *The Daily Express*, 7 October 1985, page 10).

Here is what was available and cutting edge at the time in 1984: https://youtu.be/szdbKz5CyhA

4. The book was greatly reduced in size by the original publisher (almost by two third). At some date we may produce the fuller account, if there is interest, but from a practical point of view it seemed to make sense to keep it small enough to post through a letter box! We may just upload the extra accounts on the upcoming website (thedodlestonmessages.com) available summer 2022.

5. We *did* ask Tomas to bury a sealed pot with a coin in it, so many paces from Windmill Hill (see pg256) etc. and had him draw a map. We went looking with our dear friends Ian Hazeldine and Frank Davies, but we had limited time and access with it being a farmer's field and we were unable to find anything sadly. These things are far more difficult than most people can imagine!

## Update on Words Researched by Peter

Language is not static. With the passing of time, and the OED continuing to grow as more published material is discovered from Tomas's time and catalogued, some of the words that were not in the OED when Peter researched the texts are now discovered, or their use re-dated. The following words and their meanings we have found (as laypeople) searching online dictionaries. Here follows the words we found, but there are probably many more now which need to be further researched by a qualified language expert who is familiar with informal, SW dialect::

| | |
|---|---|
| aboone v. (from 'aboon'?) | above |
| aft | after, later |
| boken | to write down, to compose |
| deyntie v. | to hold in high esteem, to honour or respect |
| elyful | could be 'eli'? meaning distinct from invisible or spiritual |
| fasinorouse (could be facinorous?) | extremely wicked |
| fey ti fi | fey= fated to die. ti= you/thee. fi= exclamation expressing contempt |
| gledie (could be gledy) | burning |
| glorien | to boast |
| gust n. | sense of taste |
| Hask | (haske) harsh tasting, rough |
| lest conj. | In case that |
| mallechoes. (poss. from Shakespeare 'miching mallecho'?) | to skulk |
| scantens (scanten?) | to fail or become less |
| scoleye | study, attend the schools of the university |

Printed in the USA
CPSIA information can be obtained
at www.ICGtesting.com
LVHW020153291223
767717LV00011B/454